Chief Men
Among the Brethren

Chief Men Among the Brethren

Compiled by

Henry Pickering

LOIZEAUX
Neptune, New Jersey

First Printing, 1918
First U.S. Printing, March 1986

Published with the permission of
the British publishers
MARSHALL PICKERING

First edition
Powerscourt Classic Library
1996

A publication of
LOIZEAUX BROTHERS, Inc.
*A Nonprofit Organization Devoted to the Lord's Work
and to the Spread of His Truth*

Library of Congress Cataloging-in-Publication Data

Pickering, Hy.
Chief men among the Brethren / compiled by Henry Pickering.
— 1st Powerscourt ed.
Previously published: 1986.
ISBN 0-87213-798-8
1. Plymouth Brethren—Great Britain—Biography. I. Title.
[BX8808.P53 1996]
289.9—dc20   96-13526

Printed in the United States of America

10 9 8 7 6 5 4 3 2 1

CONTENTS

Anderson, Peter Greenhill   11
Anderson, Sir Robert   13
Anderson-Berry, Dr. David   17
Arnot, Frederick Stanley   21

Baedeker, Dr. Frederick, W.   27
Bellett, John Gifford   31
Bennet William Henry   35
Bewley Henry   39
Bland, F. C.   41
Brealey, George   45

Caldwell, John R.   51
Carrick, The Earl of   57
Cavan, The Earl of   61
Cecil, Lord Adalbert   65
Chapman, Robert Cleaver   69
Code, John Marsden   75
Collingwood, William   77
Congleton, Lord   81
Craik, Henry   85
Crawford, Dan   89
Cronin, Dr. Edward   93
Crosbie, William Talbot   95

Darby, John Nelson   99
Deck, James George   105
Dennett, Edward   111
Denny, Sir Edward, Bart.   113

Dickie, John   117
Dorman, William Henry   121
Dyer, Henry   123

Farnham, Lord   127
Fegan, James W. C.   129
Fenn, Albert R.   135
Forlong, Gordon   139
Francis Samuel Trevor   143
Frowde Henry, M.A.   147

Grant, F. W.   151
Groves, Anthony Norris   155
Groves, Henry   159
Guicciardini, Count   163

Hall, Captain Percy Francis   167
Halliday, General John S.   171
Hambleton, John   173
Harris, James L.   177
Hawkins, James E.   181
Heath, Henry   185
Henry, T. Shuldham   189
Hill, Richard   193
Hinman, Charles H.   195
Holiday, Alfred J.   199
Howard, John Eliot   203
Hull, Captain Thomas Hillman   205
Hutchinson, Francis   207

Jones, Theodore B.   211

Kelly, William   215
Kingscote, Captain R. F.   219

Lincoln, William   221

M'Killiam, Dr. Robert   227

M'Vicker, John G.   231
Mackintosh, Charles Henry   235
Maclean, Dr. J. L.   239
Mahony, Richard J.   245
Marshall, Alexander   249
Midlane, Albert   253
Miller, Andrew   259
Miller, T. B.   263
Moorhouse, Henry   267
Morley, John   273
Muller, George   277

Neatby, Dr. Thomas   283
Newberry, Thomas   287

Ord, Harrison   291
Owens, Richard W.   295

Penstone, John Jewell   299

Rhind, Captain William Graeme   303
Ritchie, John   307
Rossetti, Teodoro P.   311
Ross, Donald   317
Ryan, Thomas   321

Schofield, Dr. Alfred T.   325
Scobell, John N.   329
Scott, Maj.-Gen. Sir Charles   331
Smith, Joseph Denham   335
Snell, Hugh Henry   339
Soltau, Henry William   341
Stancomb, Joseph   347
Stanley, Charles   351
Stewart, Alexander   355
Stokes, William James   359
Stoney, James Butler   363

Strong, Leonard   367
Stuart, Clarence Esme   371

Taylor, Herbert Wilbraham   375
Trench, George Frederick   377
Trotter, William   381

Victor, John   383

Wellesley, Captain Hon. William H. G.   387
Wigram, George V.   391
Wolston, Dr. Walter T. P.   395
Wright, James   399

Yapp, William   403

PREFACE

———∞∞∞———

Numerous lives of well-known Christians who have done yeoman service for the Master being in print, it was thought wise to attempt a few brief records of chief men in what has become known as the Brethren Movement.

The Scriptural phrase "chief men among the brethren" (Acts 15:22) seemed so appropriate that we have ventured to use it without in any way claiming it as a party or exclusive title.

It indicated brethren known and beloved in the first century who sought to be guided by the Scriptures; it may rightly indicate the leaders in a movement in the 19th and 20th centuries.

Any arrangement as to celebrity, ability, or position has been avoided. Much more could have been told concerning each individual but space had ever to be considered. Other names might have been added but the aim has been to select the most representative and the best known.

As far as possible those who actually knew the individual or had first-hand information have supplied the record. This will explain the variety of style, and a little repetition of facts. Initials are given unless in the case of composite records, or where the writer desired to remain anonymous.

HENRY PICKERING

Peter Greenhill Anderson
1811-1907

P. G. ANDERSON

PETER GREENHILL ANDERSON, who was born January 29th, 1811, was a native of Scotland, his father possessing a freehold farm near Perth. After several changes of residence, he removed from Liverpool to Birmingham, establishing himself there as a schoolmaster. Some of his pupils became eminent in their native city and brought honor to him in after life. He was an earnest God-taught man, studying his Bible not only in the English version, but in the original tongues. As a preacher of the gospel of the grace of God, it pleased God to give His servant the power to bring convincingly before men's minds the eternal realities of the world to come, and to make them feel the responsibility of accepting or rejecting the message he delivered.

In season and out of season Mr. Anderson was indefatigable in visiting the poor and sick, in looking after the stray sheep, and in seeking to restore the backslider or to convince the objector.

He was seldom absent from the Leominster Conferences, and one of his last addresses was given there on 1 Corinthians 15, when he set forth the evidences of the resurrection of the Lord Jesus in a manner which will not soon be forgotten.

Wm. Trotter, writing in 1843, mentions that "P. G. Anderson had been visiting the newly formed assemblies and greatly strengthening them." He was a great friend of R. C. Chapman.

Thus throughout a life prolonged to an unusual period, our friend was ever assiduous to do the Lord's work, whether as an evangelist, as a pastor, or as a pattern to the flock; and all who knew him loved him for the likeness he bore to the divine Master. When the sister who cared for him bade him "good night" for the last time, he replied, "We can rest in the love of Jesus," and these were his last words.

He died April 6th, 1907. His body sleeps in Witton Cemetery, after a pilgrimage of ninety-seven years.—W.A.

Sir Robert Anderson
1841-1918

SIR ROBERT ANDERSON

———◦◦◦———

SIR ROBERT ANDERSON, K. C. B., LL. D., though of Scottish descent, was born in Dublin on May 29, 1841. His father, Matthew Anderson, was Crown Solicitor in the Irish capital, and was descended from one of the "No Surrender" group of Derry defenders.

On leaving school he was given a good opening for a business career in a large brewery; but after eighteen months he turned away from this, and entered Trinity College, Dublin, where he graduated B.A. in 1862 with Moderatorship and medal, receiving the LL. D, of his Alma Mater in 1875.

After studying at Boulogne and Paris he entered Trinity College, Dublin, and in due course was called to the Irish Bar. In 1865 he assisted the Irish government in treason charges. His special knowledge of the ways of conspirators led to his appointment as Irish Agent at the Home Office, and to his becoming Chief of the Criminal Investigation Department, Scotland Yard at a time when London was in the midst of the "Jack-the-Ripper" scare. He directed this work till 1901, when he was made K.C.B. on his retiral. He was the colleague or friend of Lord Guthrie, Lord Salisbury, Lord Wolseley, Lord Blythswood, Sir Wm. Harcourt, Rt. Hon. W. E. Gladstone, and many celebrities of days gone by. His story told in "The Lighter Side of My Official Life," touching incidentally on most of his work during his thirty-five years of public service, forms interesting reading.

W. H. Smith, on the floor of the House of Commons, stated that Sir Robert "had discharged his duties with great ability and perfect faithfulness to the public." Raymond Blathwayt, in *Great Thoughts*, wrote: "Sir Robert Anderson is one of the men to whom the country, without knowing it, owes a great debt."

As an author his name will go down to generations yet unborn. His general books: "Criminals and Crime," "Sidelights on the Home Rule Movement," and "The Lighter Side of My Official Life," dealing mainly with "things present," may not survive, but his theological volumes, dealing with "things eternal," will remain.

Among his many books, "The Gospel and Its Ministry" is the best known; "Human Destiny," which C. H. Spurgeon describes as "the most valuable contribution on the subject I have seen;" "The Silence of God," the "book which astounded religious Europe" and helped many during the Great War; "The Coming Prince," which deals with the 70 weeks of Daniel; "In Defence," "Daniel in the Critics' Den," "The Hebrews Epistle," "The Honor of His Name," "The Bible and Modern Criticism," "Misunderstood Texts," and other volumes, indicate how prolific his pen and industrious his life. Almost his latest, and certainly his sweetest volume, "The Lord from Heaven," was highly commended by the Bishop of Durham, Dr. Griffith Thomas, Miss Catherine Marsh, and many others.

The two main points in Sir Robert Anderson's books which made them readable and profitable were the strength and certainty of his own beliefs and the clearness of their expression. "Amidst all the weakness and mystifying," said Sir Hugh Gilzean Reid, "it gives one hope to read your strong words." "Your writings are specially helpful to me," wrote a very old friend, Mrs. Pery-Knox-Gore, "there is always in every chapter that which you must either accept or reject. You must stop and think, and not pass on unheeding."

When in Dublin he attended Merrion Hall. For some time in London he assembled with believers in Camberwell and other parts. A few months before his death he explained to the writer that he would have been much more with "Brethren" in later years but for the question of ministry. The "open meeting," with its many abuses, did not naturally appeal to such an orderly mind. Yet his heart was ever there. His ministry at the Half-Yearly Meetings in Glasgow was greatly appreciated.

In 1873 he married Lady Agnes Moore, sister of the Earl of Drogheda, a true helpmeet in every good work, and a leader in many branches of women's work in London.

Now, what was the secret spring of this mighty man of valor? Here it is as given by himself not long before his Home-call:

He had been brought up in a Christian home, and had led what is known as a religious life, with occasional transient fits of penitence and anxiety; but in 1860 the conversion of one of his sisters through services held in Dublin by J. Denham Smith awakened new spiritual longings. He was persuaded to accompany her to one of these meetings; but the light came the following Sunday evening through a sermon in his own church. The preacher was the Rev. John Hall (afterwards of New York), who "boldly proclaimed forgiveness of sins, and eternal life as God's gift in grace, unreserved and unconditional, to be received by us as we sat in the pews. His sermon thrilled me," Sir Robert said when describing the event, "and yet I deemed his doctrine to be unscriptural. So I waylaid him as he left the vestry, and on our homeward walk I tackled him about his heresies....At last he let go my arm, and, facing me as we stood upon the pavement, he repeated with great solemnity his gospel message and appeal: 'I tell you,' he said, 'as a minister of Christ, and in His name, that there is life for you here and now if you will accept Him. Will you accept Christ, or will you reject Him?' After a pause—how prolonged I know not—I exclaimed, 'In God's name I will accept Christ.' Not another word passed between us; but after another pause he wrung my hand and left me. And I turned homewards with the peace of God filling my heart."

After an attack of influenza, he in measure recovered, sat working till 10:30 on November 15th, 1918, in his seventy-seventh year, retired to rest, and at 11:00 quietly passed into the presence of the Master whom he loved.—HY.P.

Dr. David Anderson-Berry
1862-1926

DR. ANDERSON-BERRY

———⊰⊱———

D AVID ANDERSON-BERRY, M.D., LL.D., F.R.S. (Edin.), was born in Wick in 1862. His father being a Presbyterian minister, he was brought up under good religious influence. The particular truth that led to his conversion was the imminent return of the Lord Jesus Christ. He had heard of certain Christians to whom that blessed truth had become so real and precious that they had dispensed with all useless ornaments, such as bracelets, lockets, breast-pins, and to one so full of worldliness as he was, this devotion greatly impressed him. Further, to those people, the doctrine of the Lord's return afforded them joy, while to him it caused concern and sadness.

He had known the gospel from his youngest day; he firmly believed that if he was to be saved he must as a sinner accept by faith the Lord Jesus Christ as his personal Saviour, but his hope was that, as there is generally some little warning before death, he would enjoy the world, and at the end of life's brief day make the great decision before passing hence. This truth of the Lord's coming, however, upset all such theories. To think that at any moment the Lord would return to this earth, take His own people to Himself and leave the unconverted for judgment disturbed him greatly. Under the gracious influence of the Holy Spirit he yielded heart and will to the Saviour and gladly owned Him as his Lord and Master. Becoming a student of the Scriptures, he very soon learned the truth of the priesthood of all believers and the simple Scriptural principles of gathering. Having a great desire to work for his worthy Master, yet naturally diffident, it gave him considerable mental concern before he could speak to another about his soul or give away a gospel tract.

"Not many mighty are called;" "to the poor the gospel is preached," and when our Lord was here on earth it was the common people who heard Him gladly. It is the same to-day, for the Lord's people are generally found in the humbler walks of life. It took great courage on the part of Dr. Anderson-Berry to meet to worship with unlettered brethren, and indeed to profit by the ministry of such, but our brother has testified that the happiest moments in life for him were spent in the humblest surroundings.

He entered Glasgow University as a law student, but soon changed to medicine, studying in Edinburgh under Lord Kelvin and other professors. He obtained his degree when he was twenty-two. Prosecuting his studies, he entered the Sal-petriere Hospital in Paris, took lessons on mental diseases under the celebrated Dr. Charcot, whom he valued as a friend through life; then spent some time among professors in Germany, further developing his knowledge and gaining experience. As a young man he travelled much, going round the world, and spending some time in U.S.A.

Qualified, and with great expectations, he commenced practice in London, where he was for some time in fellowship in Overstone Hall, Hammersmith. After this he acted as a sort of pastor in Copse Road Chapel (connected with George Muller), Clevedon, then he moved to Boscombe in 1897. There being no Scriptural meeting as he understood it, the doctor found a building in Drummond Road which had been built as a Reformed Church of England. The congregation had dwindled, so Dr. Anderson-Berry rented the building, and set up a Table where true Christians, as such, would be welcomed.

After some three years in Boscombe he moved to Redhill, then to St. Leonards, where he spent some years, and where a good part of his literary work was done. From there he moved to Highgate, London, in the year 1910, and practised as a consulting physician.

An able minister of the Word of God, with a manner all his own, which made him unique, his services at conferences were sought after; and out of a busy life he gave considerable time to the study and ministry of the Scriptures. He helped acceptably in Cholmeley Hall for some years, and several times his helpful ministry was enjoyed at the Half-Yearly Conferences in Glasgow.

A strong fundamentalist, he stood foursquare on the Word of God and by lip and pen contended earnestly for the faith once for all delivered to the saints.

For years he contributed helpful articles to *The Witness*;, a series of papers on "The Acts of the Apostles" and "Seven Cries from the Cross" were reprinted in book form.

Several books and pamphlets have come from his pen confuting error and defending the fundamentals of the faith. Two of these issues, namely,

"After Death—What?" which clearly distinguishes between "spirit and soul and body," and "Seventh Day Adventism," which is the standard exposure of that peculiar system, have had a considerable sale.

For several years Dr. Anderson-Berry was in declining health, and he entered into his rest on 5th June 1926. All that was mortal of the beloved physician was laid to rest in the family burying ground, at Winchelsea, to await the great gathering shout which will waken the sleeping saints and change the living ones.—HY.P.

Frederick Stanley Arnot
1858-1914

FREDERICK STANLEY ARNOT

———◦∘◦———

IN THE YEAR 1864, in the town of Hamilton, there was a prize distribution at a school. The gentleman who was giving the prizes away was the intrepid pioneer-missionary-explorer, Dr. David Livingstone, then on what proved to be his last visit to his own country. He related many of his adventures in Africa to the boys, telling them too something about the terrible cruelty of the slave trade, and in burning words describing some of Africa's needs.

Among his hearers was a little boy, Frederick Stanley Arnot by name, whose mother had brought him to hear the great traveller and preacher of the gospel. Fred was born in Glasgow, on Sept. 12th, 1858, but the family soon removed to Hamilton. He was only six years old at the time, but he listened to the address, and from thence forward Africa drew him like a magnet. Friendship with the Livingstones, who also lived in Hamilton, deepened his interest. Boy-like, he determined that he must go out to help his hero, a resolution which colored all his studies and thoughts, and set his feet in a direction from which they never diverged.

Arnot's parents were Christians; he himself was converted when ten years old. It came about in this way. One day he and a companion, Jimmie, were appropriating and eating plums from a neighbour's garden, and Jimmie's older brother, from a window, called them thieves. Fred Arnot felt as though a pistol had gone off at his very head. "Thief! Thief!" rang in his ears all the time. Next day he had to pass Hamilton prison, and did so in a state of terror, fearing he might be taken off to prison. To his horror he saw a policeman leading a little boy to the very place, and in his other hand the policeman held a pair of new boots which the barefooted little boy had stolen. Fred felt that he was much more wicked than that small needy boy. He rushed off home and hid himself till bedtime. He said: "I dreaded to pass another night; I could not tell anyone what a wicked boy I was. I knew I ought to tell God about it, but I trembled to do so at my usual evening prayer, so I waited until all were in bed and the house quiet, then up I got. Now, I thought, I will ask God to forgive me, but words would not come, and, at last, I burst into a flood of tears. I felt I was too wicked even for God to forgive; yet a glimmer of light and hope came to me with this thought: 'That is why Jesus died on the cross for me, because I am so wicked.' Among many texts of Scripture that my parents had taught me was John 3:16. I repeated it to myself on my knees about two o'clock one morning, and that 'whosoever' took me in. I awoke next day with a light heart, the burden was gone."

His desire to help Africa increased tenfold. He realized, as never before, what her need was, and now he really had something which he could offer her—God's great salvation (the only foundation of real good to this perishing world). As the years went by his purpose deepened. At fifteen he felt that God had called him to a missionary life, and therefore with God-given wisdom he set to work from that time to learn and practice anything which would be of service in far Africa—joinery, blacksmith's work, watch repairs, all came in for his attention; he also accustomed himself to find his way in lonely and unfamiliar districts with the aid of the compass only; and preached frequently in the open air with his father, as well as helping in village work.

In 1881, on July 19th, at the age of twenty-three, his cherished hope was realized. He sailed for Africa on the "Dublin Castle," accompanied by Donald M'Lean, who intended to go into the interior with him. At Durban, where they arrived on August 20th, this friend was taken ill, and being told by the doctor that he was not fit for such a journey, he remained in Natal and Arnot, when his preparations were completed proceeded alone.

At that time the railway reached only as far as Pietermaritzburg; the rest of the journey had to be made by oxwagon. The difficulties, dangers, sickness, and privations which Arnot endured, served only to strengthen his faith in God. He realized, as he tells us in his diary, that God's promises were not mere words, written for the instruction of our minds or for repetition with our lips, but certainties to go by; and the assurance of one of these is better than an army.

On the 19th of November he left Maritzburg for the interior. Progress was slow at first on account of the long continued drought, but when rain fell they were able to cross the desert country beyond the Limpopo River, arriving at Shoshong, the Bamangwato capital, on March 11th, where King Khama, the Christian ruler, received him very kindly. He remained there three months. Then as he wished to visit the Barotse, King Khama offered his Christian headman, Tinka, as escort as far as the Mababi River, a charge which the good black guide performed most thoroughly. On December 19th, 1882, after tedious negotiations with various headmen and King Liwanika, conducted by a kind trader, he reached Lealui, the principal Barotse town. Arnot spent about eighteen months in that part making occasional brief voyages up the Zambezi and teaching some of the children. In July 1883, he went down to Panda-ma-tenka to hear if someone was going to join him in his work, and also to procure supplies, and during this interval he made visits to several outlying places, returning to Lealui by Oct. 22nd, when he received a very hearty welcome and a present of a nice, snug hut in the town from Liwanika himself.

Liwanika, who had many talks with Arnot, had been very urgent at first that he should not teach his people the Word of God, and especially such a thing as that a poor slave might be seated in the palace of God, and a king or chief shut out. Arnot begged the king not to be angry with him, for the words were God's words, not man's. As time went on, and especially after Arnot's return from Panda-matenka, Liwanika became quieter and gave permission to the missionary to preach more freely—and indeed, what else could such a missionary do than proclaim the whole counsel of God?

Often he used to hear the natives talking among themselves about the things he had told them. "Monare's words pierce the heart," one man said, and the poor slaves found it hard to believe that the Heavenly position could be theirs too. Many times some of the people would come to him after several days, to discuss questions weighing on their minds in respect of his solemn words.

In 1884, as civil war was threatening, Arnot was advised to leave Lealui and so, on May 1st, in company with a friendly Portuguese trader, Senhor Porto, he started for Benguella on the West Coast. After various hindrances and adventures, he arrived there in November 1884, having thus travelled clear across Africa from Durban on the East coast to Benguella on the West.

In June of 1885, after collecting stores and carriers, he started for Garenganze (now called Katanga), a journey of twelve thousand miles, the country ruled by Msidi, who was anxious to have white traders there. Arnot, on the strength of that wish, and having something better to offer than trading goods, accepted the invitation for himself, and reached Msidi's on February 14th, 1886.

He frankly showed the king, when breakfasting with him, that he had to speak some very terrible and unpalatable truths, as well as proclaiming God's love in sending His Son to die for fallen man. He feared if he did not fairly warn the king of his intentions that Msidi would think that he had intentionally deceived him.

After a residence of more than two years in Garenganze, during which time he had much encouragement, Arnot returned to England—his first visit in seven years. While there, he married Miss Harriet Jane Fisher, who returned to Africa with him in March 1889.

Between 1889 and 1908 he made several voyages to England, partly on account of ill health, which often compelled him to remain some years in his native land. He also established the long line of mission stations between Benguella and Garenganze during this period.

In 1908 he settled in Johannesburg with his family, using that town as a base for his many operations in the interior. He and Mrs. Arnot paid a visit to Liwanika. Here too Arnot saw Dick, his native servant, who had been baptized on confessing his faith in the Lord Jesus, February 13th, 1887, nearly thirty years earlier.

For six years Arnot continued his work, though often suffering severe bouts of illness, but in May 1914, his busy life on earth, in which he spent thirty-three years in or for Africa, traversed thirty thousand miles of its trodden and untrodden paths, came to an end at the age of fifty-five. Not a long life, but how full of labor for the Saviour whom he so early learnt to love.—E.E.E.

Dr. Frederick W. Baedeker
1823-1906

DR. F. W. BAEDEKER

FREDERICK W. BAEDEKER, though he was born in Germany, spent by far the greater part of his life away from it. After some years, as a young man, spent in professional pursuits in the Australasian Colonies (where he had gone as a hopeless consumptive, the French ship in which he sailed nearly wrecked, and he—the traveler of future years—landing in Australia literally on crutches), he returned to the northern hemisphere, his steps directed to England and Weston-super-Mare, which was destined to be the scene and base of his life and labors for the remainder of his days. For the first half of his earthly career, while strictly moral and outwardly correct, he lived without God and was, as he often expressed it, "a German infidel." But He who brings the blind by a way that they knew not and leads them in paths they have not known, was guiding the doctor towards a crisis in his life, which would bring untold blessing to himself and to countless others through him.

Earl Cavan, of fragrant memory, in the year 1866, invited Lord Radstock to take possession of The Lodge for two or three months, in order that he might devote himself to evangelistic work in Weston and neighborhood. Meetings were arranged in the Assembly Rooms, and were carried on almost nightly for the space of eight months, resulting in a work of grace for extent, depth, and as time has proved, permanency such as Weston had never experienced before.

All classes of the community were more or less affected by the movement but, on account of the high station of the chief actors in it, perhaps the converts were chiefly from the upper grades of society.

Through the importunity of a Christian military officer, of whom he had some acquaintance, Dr. Baedeker at length reluctantly consented to attend one meeting. Interest was awakened sufficient for his repeating his visit, but he was careful to make his exit before the noble preacher could reach him at the closing of the first service. Having attended several meetings, the doctor one evening lingered long enough, or got far enough in without the ability to get out faster than the crowd would admit of, for Lord Radstock to reach him. Putting his hand on his shoulder,

27

said he, "My man, God has a message through me for you tonight," urging him to enter the anteroom. In presence of the crowd he did so, and the two were soon on their knees. During those solemn moments a work was done in this suddenly convicted soul whereby the accumulated infidelity of years was dissipated for ever. God was believed, the Saviour trusted, and the joy of salvation filled his soul. The experience of that memorable night would be by himself thus tersely expressed: "I went in a proud German infidel, and came out a humble, believing disciple of the Lord Jesus Christ. Praise God!"

Soon the young convert was set to work to point other anxious souls to Christ, which he found to be a service for his new Master at once delightful and fruitful. As a coincidence, interesting and remarkable, Dr. Baedeker gave his first gospel address on the theme dear to his own heart in the village of Kewstoke, on the other side of the Worle Hill from Weston; and having expressed a desire to revisit the same village after a long absence, he accompanied a friend over the hill on Sunday evening, 30th September, and in the Iron Room there gave his last gospel address—1866-1906! He found the ruin of men the same as forty years ago, and he knew no remedy but the one old, unchanged, inspired Gospel.

Lord Radstock had opened to him in Russia "a wide door and effectual," large numbers high in rank being among the fruit of his labor there. Dr. Baedeker, having passed through ten years of preparation in the study of God's Word, and the exercise of his gift at home, felt drawn to go forth and carry the gospel to the regions beyond, and in 1876 started on his first evangelistic journey through continental lands. After some time in Berlin and other parts of Germany, having been commended to Russian friends by his spiritual father and predecessor in the field, the call to come over into Russia was responded to, there to further help in the work begun and carry the gospel still further afield. Deeply impressed by what he had seen of the condition of things in the great Russian empire with its teeming millions sitting in darkness and the shadow of death, needing the gospel which was eagerly heard as often as preached, in the following year 1877, Dr. Baedeker, having let his house for three years, again went forth, this time accompanied by his wife and their adopted daughter, and devoted almost the whole of this period to labor for the Lord among the peoples of that vast empire.

As years went by, annual visits were paid to Russia and other European countries, his purpose ever the same, until he would be much more abroad than at home. Thousands on thousands of miles were traversed the means of transit often being of the most primitive description, and the ground to be gone over such as would test the mettle of a much younger and stronger man; but the doctor made light of it, only remarking by the way as he would come back and narrate some of his experiences, that it was interesting to find out what a strain the human frame could stand. Into every corner of Russia he penetrated with the gospel message. Permits were granted, through the influence of a Christian countess, by the head authorities, which gave him access to all the prisons of Russia and Siberia, each permit lasting two years, and then a renewal of it for another couple of years, the evangelist feeling with every extension of the privilege (enjoyed alone by him) the importance of using it to the utmost; and so journey after journey was undertaken. Bibles supplied freely by the British and Foreign Bible Society were distributed through the prisons and elsewhere by the thousand, while the gospel of salvation was sounded out with the living voice.

His sympathy and love for the oppressed won for him a way to many a heart, and the Day alone will declare the full results of such abundant labors, where the tread of the evangelist's foot was otherwise unknown. No thought of rest seemed to enter his mind even after the eightieth milestone had been passed—still he would go forth as with all the zest and energy of former days, and his record mounted up to four journeys to the Continent. On one occasion he went right through Siberia, visiting the inhospitable Saghalien Island, in the Gulf of Tartary, the Russian convict station for the most desperate of her criminals. It was a universal surprise that a servant of God should come there, but as still a part of "the world," they were the objects of divine love, and the evangelist had the gospel of grace, salvation, and peace for the worst of them. Japan, China, Singapore, and other parts were taken in in the course of his journey home.

Some twenty years before he died, hearing of communities of Germans in Canada, he booked his passage, and set out to preach the gospel to his countrymen. The Stundists of Russia, the Armenians, and others who have had his sympathy and succor in the midst of the fires of persecution, as well as many abroad and at home, whose temporal needs called forth his generous benefactions, have all lost a friend.

He caught a chill attending a two-days' conference at Clifton, and was called hence on October 9, 1906, at the advanced age of eighty-three.—D.R.

John Gifford Bellett
1795-1864

J. G. BELLETT

T HE NAME OF John Gifford Bellett will always be reverenced and his memory ever cherished by those knowing the unction of his ministry from the products of his pen.

Born in Dublin, in the year 1795, he was of an Anglo-Irish family connected with the Irish Established Church, which lost its status in 1869. He was educated at the Grammar School, Exeter, where he had as a schoolfellow William Follett, who afterwards as an eloquent advocate distinguished himself at the English Bar; and from there Bellett proceeded to Trinity College Dublin, now making the acquaintance—ripening into lifelong friendship—of John Nelson Darby. Both were strong in classical scholarship, both read for the Bar—Bellett in London, and Darby in Dublin. Each was "called" in Dublin, and practiced but for a short time, Darby relinquishing that profession when he "took Orders," whilst Bellett, who had become a decided Christian during his teens, devoted himself as a layman not only to increased spiritual self-culture but to participation in whatever religious service in those days presented itself to him as a "layman."

By the year 1827 each of these two earnest souls was attending the meetings for the study of prophecy at Powerscourt House, in County Wicklow, and becoming detached from the conventional religion of Protestants around them as they advanced in knowledge of spiritual truth. In 1828 we find Bellett "breaking bread" with some friends like-minded— Francis Hutchinson and Edward Cronin, besides J. N. Darby and, it would seem, Anthony Norris Groves, who had brought with him from England similar, yet independent, convictions. To the end of 1829 their meeting-place was a private house in Fitzwilliam Square, Dublin, but in the year following a public meeting-room was engaged in Aungier Street of that city. John Vesey Parnell (afterwards Lord Congleton) is now found in their company. As between the various names mentioned, the actual priority in giving effect to their common belief is difficult to determine.

When others were called away for active promulgation of their views elsewhere, Bellett remained in Ireland, and Dublin in particular, where his residence was fixed for some fifteen years longer.

In 1846-1848 we find him residing at Bath, and he was not again settled at Dublin until about the year 1854, but thenceforth retained his home there to the time of his passing away in 1864. In 1859 he interested himself in the great revival which took place in the north of Ireland. During all these years he exhibited a notable example of lovable Christian tenderness, often assuaging the bitterness of conflict in ecclesiastical matters by his counsel and attitude.

Bellett's public ministry, as described by one who had the privilege of enjoying it during his residence at Bath, was that of one who "talked poetry," so sweet and chaste were the sentiment and expression. The late R. Govett, of Norwich, a very good judge, who had read all the published writings of the leaders of the movement, gave as his opinion that Bellett was the most spiritual. His best known books are those on the "Patriarchs," the "Evangelists," the "Son of God," and the "Moral Glory of the Lord Jesus."

His name is dear to those who now experience exercise over the continuance of strained relations between brethren confessing common truth. J. G. Bellett's influence was all exerted in the direction of minimizing alienation, and fulfilling the injunction, "be at peace among yourselves." Happy is the memory of any with such a reputation as his, of whom it can be said that, so far as is known, nothing said or left behind produced or aided dissension but all has tended towards removal of man-made barriers and the restoration of fellowship of heart in the fear of the Lord.—E.E.W.

William Henry Bennet
1843-1920

W. H. BENNET

WILLIAM HENRY BENNET was born at Ashford, Kent, where his father was in business as a confectioner. Brought up in the Church of England, he was convicted of sin and converted to God when young, and soon manifested an earnest desire to serve the Lord. His first inclinations were toward railway life, and at sixteen he passed an examination and entered the Railway Clearing House. In a little while he returned to Ashford to help his father in the business. Here he was so impressed with the indifference to spiritual things that he commenced to distribute tracts and hold cottage meetings.

In the year 1862, at the age of nineteen, as a diligent student of the Word, with a willing heart, saying, "Lord, what wilt thou have me to do?" (Acts 9:6), he was awakened to the errors of "baptismal regeneration " at the beginning of life, and the untruthful words concerning a "sure and certain hope" pronounced in the burial service over known ungodly persons at the end of life.

Once exercised, he rested not till he fully inquired "What saith the scripture?" (Romans 4:3), and as a result was immersed as a believer, then severed his connection with the National Church, renounced all sectarian associations, and for the next fifty-eight years took his place with those who gather "together in my name" (Matthew 18:20). At this time he was privileged to become acquainted with, and be helped by, the ministry of W. H. Soltau (whose lectures on "The Tabernacle and Priesthood" he attended), J. L. Harris, author of "Law and Grace," and others who greatly helped the young disciple in the school of God.

The next move seems to have been made to Merriott to assist Mr. Gribble, whose evangelistic labors were greatly blessed in these parts. During a three months' stay in this place, in 1862, W. H. Bennet first had the joy of treading "the path of faith." His parents were not happy at their young son moving on, to them, such indefinite lines as to support or future service, but two signal proofs of answers to prayer encouraged the young man. On the way to Hampton Court on the Master's service a gentleman gave him a lift in a dog-cart. Asking his business, Mr. Bennet tried to explain, and on leaving the gentleman handed him half a sovereign. Another Sunday, preaching in the open air, one of two gentlemen who had listened at the door of an inn came forward, asked for a tract, and handed him a sovereign. Thus, when leaving home for wider service, he was able in answer to the anxious inquiry of his parents to assure them that "he had all he needed." And to the very end, although in trials oft, he was enabled to say, "My God has supplied all my need" (see Philippians 4:19).

After moving about with considerable acceptance, in consultation with R. C. Chapman and H. W. Soltau, he settled in Bow, helping in a school and abounding in the work of the Lord in the district around.

In 1863 he first visited Yeovil, and finally settled there in 1869. In 1871 he married Miss Softley, who was a true helpmeet till her departure on 8th January 1919, at the ripe age of eighty-nine. In the same year the Yeovil Conference was commenced, thus for forty-nine years he guided these profitable gatherings and was a true shepherd of the flock.

A wider field of service was first opened to our brother by the issue of *The Golden Lamp*, which for twenty-one years supplied valuable ministry. On the discontinuance of the *Golden Lamp* in 1890, W. H. Bennet was invited to join Dr. Maclean and Henry Groves in the work at Bath; thus for thirty years he took an active part in this ever-growing work, continuing to reside at Yeovil, but spending a part of each week at Bath. Ever cautious and courteous, his painstaking and prayerful judgment on any matter was greatly valued.

As a ministering brother he was known in most parts of the British Isles and in some parts of the Continent. His calm setting forth of great truths, of expositions of the Psalms, or other parts of Scripture were appreciated by careful listeners. His writings were clear and convincing. Knowing the ritualistic tendencies of the State Church, he was not slow to warn those likely to be ensnared thereby. The leading article in *Echoes of Service* often bore the initials "W. H. B." as well as many papers in *The Witness,* to which he contributed for many years, the last papers being "The Holy One of God," and another appropriately bearing the title "The Eternal Hallelujahs."

To W. H. Bennet was granted grace to begin early and well, to run evenly and well, and above all to end well. Of one known for many years we can truly say: He fought a good fight, he kept the faith, he finished his course; and now henceforth the crown (2 Timothy 4:7,8). He died at Yeovil, 13th December 1920, in the seventy-eighth year of his age.—HY.P.

—

Henry Bewley
1814-1876

HENRY BEWLEY

WHAT JOHN MORLEY was to London, that and more, Henry Bewley of Willow Park was to Dublin. "Every man hath his proper gift of God; one after this manner, and another after that." In reviewing the career of this beloved and honored servant of God, one is forcibly reminded of these words. Gifted, devoted, and useful far above the average, his main life work lay in a peculiar line. He was no great speaker, nor did he travel far and wide to spread a knowledge of the Saviour he so sincerely loved and served; and yet few men have done more to send the gospel to their own generation than he. Between four and five hundred millions of tracts, prepared and printed at his sole expense, have been circulated in English, French, Italian, Spanish, and German and other tongues, and no set of tracts ever distributed are more full of simple gospel truth and fundamentally important Christian teaching.

The spread of the gospel was the object dearest to his heart and the edification of Christians came next. He was to a considerable extent the builder of Merrion Hall, Dublin, and the mainstay of the work carried on there. He was a man of large-hearted liberality, and the kind and genial host who, for so long a time past gathered round him twice a year at the "Believers' Meetings," hundreds of his fellow-Christians of all parties, from all parts of the kingdom, that they might enjoy refreshment for soul and body and go on their way rejoicing. The blessed influences that have gone out from these meetings eternity only will unfold. His funeral, which took place in Mount Jerome Cemetery in the neighborhood of Dublin, was very largely attended by ministers and members of all evangelical denominations, thus testifying their sincere respect and sorrow for the loss of the spiritually minded servant of the Lord. Peace in the presence of a sin-pardoning God and gracious Father, and assurance of triumph over death and the tomb, won by the resurrection of Christ, and secured to us in Him, were richly realized.

He died June 28, 1876, aged sixty-two. The faith which had sustained him soothed the sorrow of those who stood around the grave and committed his earthly remains to the dust to await the glorious coming of the Lord.

F. C. Bland
1826-1894

F. C. BLAND

F.C. BLAND was born in 1826, at Derriquin, upon the Kenmare River, County Kerry, where his family had been settled for generations. His early life was spent in Ireland, and in due course he entered Trinity College, and received his degree in Arts from the University of Dublin. At the comparatively early age of twenty-three he married the lady who was in no mere conventional sense his companion and friend and fellow-helper through all the vicissitudes of five-and-forty years. On his marriage, Mr. Bland settled at Derriquin, devoting himself in part to the management of the estate, which, under his care, emerged from the barbarism in which many parts of Ireland were sunk at the time of the potato famine, and in part to the amusements and hospitalities of an Irish country gentleman in a county as noted then for its social pleasures as it is famous at all times for its extraordinary natural beauties. A man of commanding presence and charming address, Mr. Bland was a special favorite with his fellows, and among the tenantry his word was law. Throughout the estate, indeed, his rule was a "benevolent despotism." In 1859 he served the office of High Sheriff for Kerry, and at the time of the revival in the south of Ireland he held a prominent position among the gentry of the county.

Dromore Castle (where lived the well-known Christian gentleman, Mr. R. J. Mahony) and Derriquin were neighboring estates. F. C. Bland and R. J. Mahony had known each other from infancy, and their mutual affection was like the love of brothers. Early in the year 1861 some earnest words spoken by Mr. Mahony at a gathering of parochial school children at Dromore Castle made such a deep impression on some of the adults present that meetings for prayer followed. One and another became deeply anxious about eternal things, and soon an increasing company of the peasantry were rejoicing in new-found blessing. The Ulster revival of 1859, and the Dublin awakening of 1860, had failed to make any sensible impression upon the people of the south. But God was about to work among them in His own way. A friend from a Midland county, hearing of the work, paid a visit to Dromore, bringing with him C. H. Mackintosh, whose ministry by word and pen has helped so very many. A meeting was arranged, and the closing passage to the 2nd chapter of the Epistle to Titus was his subject. Among the number who attended were Mr. and Mrs. Bland, and both of them were brought to Christ by the Word.

In those bright days of the early revival there was a striking freshness and power about the testimony. As in apostolic times, the convert not infrequently became a witness and a minister at once, seemingly as the natural outcome of the blessing received. Boon companions and bosom friends in recreations of their boyhood, and in the pleasures and pursuits of their early manhood, Bland and Mahony now became united in preaching Christ to their friends and neighbors. The blessing spread among the gentry, and at the summer circuit court at Tralee eight members of the grand jury took part in public meetings for the preaching of the gospel. And the fruit of that work still lives. Many Christian homes there are in Munster where "the Kerry revival" is reckoned as the epoch of their spiritual blessing.

Towards the close of that year Mr. and Mrs. Bland visited London, intending to return for the coming-of-age festivities of the eldest son of one of the principal noblemen of the county. But God had lessons to teach them, and work for them to do. Mrs. Bland fell seriously ill, and a prolonged sojourn in the south of England became a necessity. Settling in Plymouth, Mr. Bland at once set himself to seek opportunities for evangelistic work. He invited T. Shuldham Henry to join him in this effort, and during the winter a series of crowded meetings held in the Mechanics' Institute, resulted in blessing to untold numbers of the hearers. At this time Mr. Bland was brought into contact with some of the most honored and eminent of the leaders of the old revival. From them he learned the secret of Bible study, and by their ministry he was grounded and established in the faith. When, therefore, Mrs. Bland's recovery enabled him to return to his home in Ireland, he was already a mature and steadfast Christian, deeply taught in the Scriptures.

Many who will read these words will be ready to speak of help received from him, and vastly greater is the number of those who, though perchance they never even heard his name, have profited indirectly by his ministry, some of his addresses being preserved in "Twenty-one Prophetic Papers" and smaller booklets. During D. L. Moody's well-remembered meetings at the Opera House in London, scarcely a day passed that he did not spend an hour with F. C. Bland over the Bible. "Mighty in the Scriptures" might well be written in his epitaph, not that he himself would have tolerated the suggestion. In a conversation with a worker many years ago, he indicated what he would wish to have recorded on his grave. "Just my name," he said, "and this one word, 'obtained mercy' (1 Peter 2:10). It is but one word in the original," he went on to say. "What a pity it is we can't render it simply 'mercied.'"

Mr. Bland was a singularly interesting personality. Naturally haughty, intolerant of opposition, and quick to resent an injury or a slight, grace so changed him that not a few who think they knew him thoroughly would describe him as one of the gentlest and humblest of men. Though intensely practical, impatient of mere hair-splitting, and intolerant of new-fangled doctrines, no examination of Scripture seemed too minute.

The manner of his communicating the truth to others was thoroughly characteristic of the man. There was neither effort nor artifice in any address he ever gave. If addressing a thousand people he spoke in the same natural, unaffected manner as when talking with a friend at his own fireside. There was nothing whatever of oratory about his speaking; nor of eloquence either, save that sort of eloquence which is never wanting when in apt and simple words a man gives out what he believes and feels. Pathos there was certainly, and it added a special charm to his words. And above all there was an intense reverence about him. He had great thoughts as to what was due to God. Possessed with a keen sense of humor, and a mind as playful as a child's, anything of levity in divine things was utterly repugnant to him. And yet there was no austerity about him to repel, nor a trace of asceticism. All his dealings with God were in the spirit of a man who loved and trusted Him implicitly, and who knew he was beloved.

And he loved His people too. Unswerving in his devotion to truth, and keenly alive to the importance of the minutest detail of Christian doctrine, his heart was with all who loved God, however widely they might be separated from him ecclesiastically. The testimony of his life might have found expression in the words of the 119th Psalm: "I am a companion of all them that fear thee, and of them that keep thy precepts."

Mr. Bland's last illness seized him at Weston-super-Mare, where he had spent the winter. From there he was removed to South Kensington, the residence of his son, Dr. Bland, under whose care he remained until he "entered into rest" upon 5th April 1894. His strength failed so rapidly that even the visit of a friend was generally more than he was able for. But the word of Christ dwelt in him richly and, with the full consciousness that he was dying, the calm confidence of faith never forsook him. He was a man greatly beloved.

—

George Brealey
1823-1888

GEORGE BREALEY

Gᴇᴏʀɢᴇ Bʀᴇᴀʟᴇʏ was a capital tract writer, and the "Blackdown Tracts" have been scattered far and near, and God has used them in the conversion of many souls. He was best and most widely known in the south and west of England as a willing-hearted, warm-hearted, whole-hearted evangelist, whom God had greatly owned in soul winning.

He was born of poor but respectable parents at North Tawton, Devonshire, on 4th September 1823. The family had many hardships and, strange to say, though his parents were decided Christians, he was apprenticed at the age of fifteen to an infidel uncle who in addition to being a country shoemaker kept a public house. Here he learned to drink, swear, and fight, but becoming seriously ill, he was obliged to return home.

At three o'clock on Whit Sunday, 1841, his mother found him in a public-house playing cards with two other young men. A short time previously they had taunted him with being a "Methodist." He had set to and thrashed both of them, and then took them to the public-house to prove he was no "Methodist." His poor mother finding him in such a place at such a time, fell on her knees and pleaded with God for her erring boy. He was completely overpowered by his mother's prayers and entreaties, and, turning to his companions, said, "Good-bye, mates, I shall never enter this place again, as I have done." "What," they replied, "you going to turn 'Methody.' He's afraid of his mother." This taunt annoyed him, but he was enabled to control his feelings, and quietly replied, "I am not afraid of my mother. You know I love her too well, but I am afraid of God and of my sins. Will either of you go to Hell for me?" "No," they replied, "we don't want to go for ourselves, much less for you." "Then," said he, "don't laugh at me for turning round and trying to escape." He left with his mother, and soon after obtained peace with God.

At the age of twenty-one he married and commenced business on his own account in the city of Exeter in 1861. For some years he made little if any progress in the divine life.

The Lord aroused him from his spiritual slumber partly through a conversation he had with a devoted Christian in a railway carriage, and partly through the suicide of "Old Evans," a godless man known to Brealey, who lived near him, but to whom he had never spoken on eternal matters. As he cut down the lifeless body, "the terrible thought of his accountability to God and his responsibility to his fellowmen pressed so crushingly upon him, that there and then he resolved to give himself afresh to God and His service with a determination never relinquished or relaxed." From that day forward there was a mighty change in his life, which manifested itself to all, for he became an "out-and-out" Christian. He recognized that he was no longer his own in any sense, and was willing to be anything or do anything for Christ.

Referring to this "second conversion," or restoration to God, he wrote as follows: "His love had killed my earthly desires, and I was ready to be His slave because He had made me His free man." Night and day he prayed that he might be used of the Lord in His honorable and blessed service. The trammels of shame and worldly policy having been broken, he launched out into the deep, and let down his net for a draught of souls. And God greatly blessed him. He allowed himself only five hours for sleep; and in this way, while attending to his earthly calling, he succeeded in devoting several hours daily to visiting from house to house and speaking personally to the people about their spiritual condition.

Through valuable help afforded him by various Christians, he was enabled to distribute tens of thousands of gospel tracts at fairs and races. Tract distribution on such occasions was not then common, and he experienced much opposition. Undaunted, he persevered in carrying the gospel into the headquarters of the enemy. With banner, and striking texts inscribed on it, he moved from place to place, warning the unsaved to flee from the wrath to come, and pointing them to Christ, the sinner's refuge. "Instant in season, out of season," he preached in the streets and lanes of Exeter. He also visited the low public-houses, speaking tenderly yet faithfully to the poor slaves of drink, and distributing gospel papers and booklets. Eventually he became exercised about devoting his entire time to gospel work.

After much prayer he decided to go to Demerara to preach to the negroes. Berths were taken in a sailing vessel. But the Lord had work for him nearer home. A "Macedonian" cry came from the Blackdown Hills in East Devon, and in 1864 he moved there. The "Hills" have an area of four hundred square miles, and here and there are farms, hamlets, and villages scattered far apart. The moral and spiritual condition of the people at that time was wretched in the extreme. At first he had a salary which was given by various Christian friends, but as God began to work he became troubled about his position. Numbers professed to accept Christ as their Saviour. As the young believers searched the Scriptures, they saw that in apostolic times when men and women believed on Christ, they were baptized, and gathered together on the first day of the week to break bread. They desired to obey the Lord and act out what they had learned. Some who contributed toward the evangelist's support became alarmed, and threatened to withdraw their help if he baptized the converts. What was he to do? "If I teach them absolute submission to the authority of the Scripture, must I hinder them in their desire to obey the Word of the Lord? Am I not responsible to help them to obedience?" Such were the questions that George Brealey had to face, and he decided to obey God rather than man, and carry out His instructions: "Teaching them to observe all things whatsoever I have commanded." Thus he gave up his salary and trusted the Lord alone to supply all his needs, and he never regretted taking this step.

The cottage in which the meetings were held became too small. It was subsequently enlarged, and in the course of two years one hundred and forty were baptized and received into fellowship. The work increased, and other parts of the "Blackdowns" were visited with similar results. Schools and gospel halls were built, and men and women as well as boys and girls were not only been taught to read and write, but many were saved and led on in the ways of Christ, some of whom labored for the Lord in China, India, Africa, and America, while others witnessed for Christ in various parts of Britain.

When Brealey began work in the Blackdown Hills, he asked God for a "body of iron and a soul of fire," and for nearly twenty-five years he had his desire granted. In summer he preached in the open air and in tents, and in winter in halls, school houses, cottages, and meeting-places of all kinds. He had literally a passion for souls. In later years he evangelized through the large towns of England, wherever a door was opened of the Lord. Oftentimes he was heard saying, "My parish is the world. Anywhere for Jesus I would go, and anywhere I would preach, provided I would be allowed to take the truth, the whole truth, and nothing but the truth."

Early in March 1888, he was taken home to be with the Lord. In his last address he spoke as follows of the blood of Christ: "We shall never get out of the sight of the cross, and can never do without the blood; and, may I say, never was the cross of Christ or the blood of the Lamb more precious to my soul than now—make much of the cross, make much of the blood." "He being dead yet speaketh," and the work on the Blackdown Hills is still carried on in the name of Him who plucked such trophies of grace as brands from the everlasting burning.—A.M.

John R. Caldwell
1839-1917

JOHN R. CALDWELL

~~~~~

JOHN R. CALDWELL was born in Dublin, on 26th May 1839. His parents came to reside in Glasgow when he was five years of age, where he was brought up in "the nurture and admonition of the Lord," his father being a leader in connection with the Independent Church. As might be expected from such surroundings his leanings were ever to the moral and even evangelical side of life. After being interviewed by two deacons, who inquired if he believed in the Bible and the Lord Jesus, he joined the church, taught in the Sunday School, was a member of the Y.M.C.A., and passed for a Christian by all who knew him.

At this time, in the year 1860, Gordon Forlong, a well-known gentleman evangelist, was invited by the godly elders of Ewing Place Church to have a series of meetings in the church, with the result, to use Mr. Caldwell's own words, "I felt I had not experienced the great change, and at the close of one meeting I waited as an anxious one among many, and heard from John 5:24 that 'he that heareth my word, and believeth on him that sent me, hath everlasting life, and shall not come into condemnation, but is passed from death unto life.' This was indeed good news to me. I heard, I believed, and I had everlasting life. From this time the Bible became a new Book to me, my constant and loved companion. I read it with opened eyes, and beheld in it wondrous things."

The revival in the north of Ireland in 1859 created great excitement in Glasgow. Pulpits and platforms of many churches were opened to laymen as preachers of the gospel. The old legal ecclesiastical bands were being snapped in many places. The life of the born-again element in Ewing Place seems to have overflowed its bounds. The basement of the church was utilized by them first for Sunday school work, with considerable success, then having rented the schoolroom from the managers, they launched out into an evening service on definite gospel lines. This seemed too much for the minister, for however much he had yielded to former efforts, to have a service apart from church control was too much for him; it must be stopped at once.

Perhaps it was one of the "all things," for just at this time Mr. Caldwell Senior, who was feeling the bondage of sectarianism, and Mr. Caldwell Junior, who in the days of first love was inquiring, "Lord, what wilt thou have me to do?" got into contact with godly men taking a lead in a meeting emerging from Scotch Baptist lines to what would now be called Brethren lines, though then, as now, a better definition is the "ways which be in Christ" (1 Corinthians 4:17).

Bible readings had been held in the home of Mr. Caldwell. Various doctrines were discussed, and the Scriptures were examined on themes hitherto neglected, with the result that J. R. Caldwell and his friend and partner, George Young, were immersed as believers in Christ.

A transition period of some months at this juncture would be difficult to describe, but it ended in a severance from membership in the Congregational denomination, and an adherence, which was to be lifelong, to meet in simplicity, according to the Scriptures. As he says, "He found there those with whom he had true fellowship, to whom the Word of the Lord was precious and the name of Jesus sweet."

A successful business life, a strenuous church life, and a steady Christian life does not afford points of contrast or scenes of romance to make an enthralling story, yet it would take a volume to speak of the many-sided life of usefulness of such a "brother beloved." A few phases must suffice.

Ministry of the Word may be mentioned first, as his name will be remembered by thousands of the Lord's people in all parts of the earth who had the privilege of hearing Mr. Caldwell speak. In the morning meeting, at which he ministered only at intervals, the Word was sweet, short, Christ-exalting, and worship-producing. In the Sunday school, in the gospel meeting, at the street corner, the message was quietly and reverently listened to. But his forte was ministering the Word to the saints in the continued exposition of a book—Leviticus, Corinthians, Thessalonians, and Hebrews being his favorites—or in a series of addresses on the Offerings, Old Testament Characters, God's Chosen People, Christian Duties, or similar themes; or, as was much more common, in a helpful message from the portion of Scripture or theme which had formed his private meditation during the preceding days.

His notes were merely small slips of paper with the headings and the abundant references to which he asked his hearers to turn in the course of every address. He kept scant record, if any, of where and when he had given certain addresses, and felt quite free in repeating a message if suited to the hearers. "The Red Heifer" and "Kinsman-Redeemer" were favorite subjects on which he spoke many times. "God our Father," "The Love of God," "The Church," and "The Lord's Coming," will be remembered by many as others which flowed in freshness from heart to heart.

His writings took up a great part of his time when not occupied with the extensive business of Caldwell, Young & Co., Silk Merchants, of which he was the head. One of his warmest books is "Things to Come," written in early Christian life, concise and up-to-date even today; put third on the list of "Best Books on the Signs of the Times," by Dr. Torrey, of Los Angeles. His other books, "God' s Chosen People" "Shadows of Christ," "Christ in the Levitical Offerings," "Earthly Relationships," "Because Ye Belong to Christ," and other subjects, have edified many. His volumes of Exposition of the Epistles to the Corinthians, first given as addresses to audiences of six hundred on Sunday afternoons, latter issued under the title of "The Charter of the Church," will long remain standard volumes of exegesis on the Church Epistles. Many smaller books and pamphlets, gospel tracts, and almost innumerable magazine articles; always manifesting care in preparation, moderation in statement, and aiming at the definite spiritual profit of the readers, flowed from his busy pen during the long period of close on sixty years of Christian life.

As *Counsellor* his advice was sought by brethren of high and low degree in all parts of the world. It was ever freely given, either with quiet deliberate voice or concise yet clear pen. The extent and value of this service will only be rightly assessed at the day of recompense.

His liberality, which none would have dared to speak about in his lifetime, cannot even now be told, because he strictly followed the Scriptural injunction: "Let not thy left hand know what thy right hand doeth" (Matthew 6:3). He was an earnest advocate of "systematic giving," which in his position meant a liberality considerably above what most would judge.

Sound doctrine ever found in Mr. Caldwell a loyal adherent and faithful advocate. From "Higher Criticism," the New Theology, and much of the modern familiarity with Bible truths and doctrines his spiritual instinct revolted. More than once in the pages of *The Witness*, which he so ably edited from 1876 to 1914, he reiterated his adherence to the fundamentals of the faith. The statement at the close of 1910 is typical. It reads:

"While not claiming infallibility, we rejoice to believe that a steadfast testimony throughout has been maintained concerning the fundamentals of the faith, including the plenary and verbal inspiration of the Scriptures, the perfect humanity, essential deity, glorious work and worth of the Lord Jesus Christ, the utter ruin of man, necessity and sufficiency of the atonement, present possession of eternal life by the believer, the priesthood of all saints, the oneness of the body of Christ, the immersion of believers as being the Christian baptism of the New Testament, the weekly 'breaking of bread' as the privilege of all the children of God, separation from the world and its associations, gathering together in the name of the Lord apart from sectarian titles and clerical assumption, the personal and premillennial coming of the Lord as the 'blessed hope' for which we wait, the eternal conscious punishment of the impenitent, and the eternal blessing and glory of the saved."

Continuing, he added: "It may be well to make clear our position regarding the somewhat vexed question of 'the fellowship of saints.' Apart from a period of some years, from 1876, during which the Editor was induced to advocate narrow views concerning assembly fellowship *The Witness* has continued to advocate the reception of all those who are (I) truly 'born again,' (2) sound in fundamental doctrine, and (3) godly in walk. Such was the practice of 'beloved brethren' of early days, and such the ministry by tongue and pen of many of our honored contributors now with the Lord." To such teachings he held tenaciously to the end.

The first real signs of closing years were manifest in 1905. Before leaving for France, fifty-two brethren, thinking they might not have another occasion, desired to confirm their love and return thanks for the help received, met Mr. Caldwell in a room of the Christian Institute on Monday, 20th November 1905. His health steadily failed, and latterly he was as a child resting in the bosom of his Father God, till without a murmur during all the weary months of pain and weakness he quietly fell on sleep on Lord's day morning, 14th January 1917, to awake in His likeness on the morning of the resurrection.—HY.P.

The Earl of Carrick
1835-1901

THE EARL OF
CARRICK

THE RIGHT HON. SOMERSET ARTHUR BUTLER, fifth Earl of Carrick and Vicount Ikerrin, was born 30th January 1835. He succeeded to the title and estates when his brother died in 1846. He was educated at Harrow, joined the 1st Battalion Grenadier Guards as ensign and lieutenant in 1853, and took part in the campaign in the Crimea in 1855, being at the siege of Sebastopol, for which he had the medal with clasp. The Prince of Wales, afterwards King Edward VII, joined his regiment, and was placed in his company.

He retired from the army as lieutenant and captain in 1862, after which he spent much of his time in fishing, shooting, hunting, yachting, and looking after the interests of large properties for which he was trustee in Ireland and Yorkshire. He also took considerable interest in local matters

The following is copied from an account of Lord Carrick's conversion, which was found among his papers: "I was converted in 1869, apart from any human instrumentality or any writing of man. After my conversion I set to work to study God's Word, spending hours day by day searching into prophecy, etc. In 1869 the Church of Ireland was disestablished by Act of Parliament, and I threw myself heartily into the work of reorganization for three or four years. I and another gentleman in this county were the first to call for a revision of the Prayer Book. I labored on the Revision Committee for many days, trying with four or five others to get it altered according to God's Word. In this we entirely failed, but I learned that the whole Church of Ireland organization, from the top to the bottom was unscriptural, and that it must be swept away—it could not be made Scriptural. I therefore came clean out, having no idea as to church fellowship in the future; I knew nothing about either Open or Exclusive Brethren.

I saw all denominations to be of man, and not of God; so I sat alone every Lord's day. Before this, God impressed on me Jeremiah 33:3: 'Call unto me, and I will answer thee, and shew thee great and mighty things, which thou knowest not,' and I told the Lord that if He would show me the hidden things I knew not, I would carry them out, no matter what the cost. From that day the Lord began to teach me. I saw in the Word that the Scriptural way was for believers to meet together each Lord's day to remember the Lord in breaking of bread; so I and three or four others began thus to meet, and now, after eighteen years, a meeting still goes on in this house, and then in any place where I find believers gathered to the name of the Lord seeking to carry out church order, there is my place in fellowship. Thus have I been for eighteen years seeking to obey Ephesians 4:3, the unity the Spirit has formed is that of all believers, all who are born again, are united into one in Christ (Ephesians 5:30; Romans 12:5; 1 Corinthians 10:17; 1 Corinthians 12:27). What is needed is faithful men who will teach the truth, the whole truth, and nothing but the truth (2 Timothy 4:2), and help on and encourage those of God's children who are seeking to carry out the principles and precepts of God."

His mother, Lady Carrick, was an intelligent Christian, and no doubt her prayers and example had an unconscious influence upon him.

Very many have to thank God they ever heard him preach the Word, and not only was the word from his lips blessed, but by his life he was "an epistle of Christ, read and known of all men." Since his departure, a Christian lady, well known in Dublin as an earnest worker, told the writer it was noticing his holy life and his out-and-out acknowledgment of the claims of Christ upon him that made her decide for Christ some thirty years ago (Psalm 40:3).

The last time he spoke was on 15th December 1901 at the morning meeting at Bray, the subject being "The Coming of the Lord." The last time he spoke at Mount Juliet was on the 5th chapter of 2nd Corinthians. He pointed out some of the things Paul said—"I know"—dwelt especially on the 10th and 20th verses, and explained about the judgment seat of Christ being for believers. On the 20th verse he said it was as though Christ Himself was beseeching sinners to be reconciled, and begged any unsaved sinner who might be present to accept Christ. On the 1st verse he remarked about the dissolving of the tabernacle and our bodies being raised when the Lord came, and said he did not want to die—he was looking for the Lord to come for His people. He brought in the Lord's coming in almost all his late addresses. Now he is with Christ and all the redeemed in Heaven, still looking forward to "the coming of the Lord."

We must not think that position frees those who have it from the trials of this world. The late Earl was much tried in various ways; his health was very unsatisfactory, and he suffered much in body. His troubles began when he was a boy at Harrow, and he often spoke of the grief he had at hearing that his estates, which were much encumbered by past generations, had been forced into the newly-appointed Encumbered Estates Court and sold at about seven years' purchase. He was much grieved at the cruel murder of his wood-ranger, a man for whom he had a great regard, and who was a Christian in fellowship at the meeting. His trials were many and various, but God overruled them in blessing to his soul and to His own glory, and made his ministry more sympathetic than it otherwise would have been.

Lord Carrick was a diligent student of God's Word, and believed firmly in the verbal inspiration of the original Scriptures. He was one who believed in waiting upon God in prayer, and thus he got his message from Him and delivered it faithfully. He was naturally shy and reserved, but he soon felt at home with Christians. He was very kind to children and young people, and won their confidence. The Earl never married, so that the title passed to his second cousin.

He left for County Galway to stay with his half-sister, the Dowager Countess of Clancarty, who was very ill, and he appears to have taken a chill. Congestion of the lungs followed. On Saturday evening, December 21st, he realized he was dying, and said: "I will be in the glory land before the morning;" and so it proved. At 3:20 he took some refreshment, and inquired how his sister was. On hearing she was better, he said, "Thank God, " and sank to rest, without even a sigh, at 3:30 a.m., December 22nd, 1901.

The funeral took place on Friday, December 27th, at his seat,

Mount Juliet, in County Kilkenny. It was very largely attended by all classes including the Protestant and Roman Catholic clergy from Kilkenny, Thomastown, and surrounding districts, testifying to the very high esteem in which he was held.

THE EARL OF CAVAN

1815-1887

LORD CAVAN was born in 1815, his days extending to more than three-score years and ten. Married in 1838, he was, at the time of his departure from this earthly scene, just on the verge of completing a happy half-century.

The singular manner in which the Lord in His lovingkindness drew him into His fold enhanced the happiness of his married life. Chosen in life's prime as a signal vessel of the grace of God, the person, the cause, and the reproach of Christ became his joy and his glory.

On making Weston-super-Mare his home in 1860, he built the residence which visitors see, with its dark background of woods, as the train on its approach to the town winds round the base of the hill on whose slopes it stands.

"The Lodge," around which hosts of precious memories cluster, was lent to Lord Radstock in the early autumn of 1866, with the desire that the breath of the Spirit of life might pass over the place. The Lord granted this desire by a remarkable ingathering into the kingdom of God, which is known perhaps to the ends of the world.

From the year 1864, during a continued summer residence in the north of Scotland for the benefit of the health of his family, his experience of the Holy Spirit's anointing power had been greatly deepened; and it was graciously given him to perceive how powerfully that Spirit enables those "that do know their God" to be the means of bringing multitudes to the knowledge of Christ. In Edinburgh, in 1874, he was among those who greeted Moody and Sankey in that city.

Quiet in manner, with little action, and no attempt to seem a striking preacher, with his Bible in one hand and his eyeglass in the other, confidence in the Lord gave power to what he spoke. "I am," he would say, "only a plain man; but I speak what I know." He might begin without giving the impression of much power; but after a little, with his heart yearning over those he addressed, his tender manner became full of energy,—his tones earnest, and his words very solemn. The true end of preaching was reached, his hearers felt that, whether for life of death, Lord Cavan's testimony was a message from God.

He was an evangelist from the heart, and spoke just what burdened sinners needed. He took an active interest in mission enterprise, and frequently presided at the meetings held in the town of Weston-super-Mare. Both he and the Countess of Cavan took special interest in the inhabitants of the village of Milton, near Weston, and were accustomed to visit them; and were unostentatiously charitable to the needy. Many years ago, at his own expense, he erected a mission room, there being at that time very little provision for the spiritual wants of the people of Milton. He often conducted the services; and they were generally well attended. For many years the Friday morning prayer meetings, held in the assembly rooms, were presided over by him; and he was also a very diligent worker in connection with the services held in the gospel hall, as well as in mission services in different parts of the county.

For many years the invitations of the trustees to the conference at Mildmay bore his name; and he took a warm interest in the work of the Scripture Readers' Society for Ireland. He had a great love for that poor country, but had no connection with it except by his title until, in middle life, a small and entangled estate unexpectedly fell to him, which he subsequently changed for a property in the Island of Achill, where he strove to ameliorate the condition of the people. He tried to get roads made, and to promote fisheries. By his efforts a substantial little pier was built and he endeavored to establish a steamer service, which should help the people to a ready market for their fish. For several years he and Lady Cavan spent some time there among them.

The "blessed hope" of the Lord's return, a theme on which he had always loved to dwell, was a very present hope to him, his longing for that return being only intensified by increasing bodily weakness and pain.

Lord Cavan passed away on December 16th, 1887. On the Sunday following his death warm tributes were paid to his memory in most of the Christian gatherings in the town. The body of the deceased Earl was interred at Weston Cemetery on 22nd December. Among others, Mr. Thomas Newberry gave an address, accompanied by a very earnest appeal to the unsaved.

Lord Adalbert Cecil
1841-1889

LORD ADALBERT CECIL

L ORD ADALBERT CECIL, son of the second Marquis of Exeter, was born 18th July 1841. Little is related concerning his early boyhood, but as a young man he seems to have come under the influence of the well-known missionary, Rev. William Haslam, the conversion story in one of his books entitled "Lord A——" referring to Lord Adalbert.

After his conversion to God he made rapid progress in divine things, becoming an earnest evangelistic worker and one able to minister the Word to profit. In his position he was free to devote all his energies to the work nearest his heart, and so was "always abounding in the work of the Lord" (1 Corinthians 15:58).

His desire ever was to be treated more as a member of the Heavenly family than as connected with the noble and great of earth. He mixed freely with rich and poor saints, being at home with the former, and by grace proving himself equally at home with the latter. He was thus a living manifestation of that beautiful blend so seldom seen on earth—a combination of a true gentleman by "birth" and a Christian gentleman abounding in love and lowliness by "new birth" (John 3:3).

A veteran who worshipped and worked with him gives this testimony: "Lord Adalbert Cecil was one of the most godly men we have ever known. Christ mastered his being. Rank, title, wealth, influence, society, and all that is valued in the world were cheerfully surrendered and laid down at the feet of his beloved Saviour and Lord. His intense earnestness and almost absolute devotedness to the interests of Christ, His unbounded generosity, especially to the members of the Household of Faith along with a rare combination of humility and Christlike-mindedness were conspicuous traits of a truly beautiful Christian character.

"On one occasion we were fellow-travellers. On leaving the train Lord Cecil lifted our bag and his own as well. 'I cannot allow this, my lord. It would be my duty and privilege to carry your bag.' His hearty, gracious answer was just like the man, 'Come away, brother, come away.'

"The grace of God has wrought mightily in this world. Lord Cecil was in himself a bright and noble witness and exponent of an experimental Christianity."

After some years' service in Britain he went to Canada to help further the work of the Lord. Here he was called to higher service in a tragic manner, as the newspaper report indicates:

"Lord Adalbert Cecil was drowned on 12th June, near Adolphustown, Western Canada, through the upsetting of his boat as he was crossing the Bay of Quinte to regain his camp. Lord Adalbert relinquished the attractions of aristocratic society in England and devoted himself to evangelization work in the Far West. On Tuesday, 11th June, 1889, he took a boat at Belleville, and sailed to a place where there were a number of Indian believers in whom he was interested. On returning for Picton the next day the wind blew strongly, and the boat, which had two sails, was difficult to manage. He was accompanied by a young man named Churchill, and they had nearly reached their destination, when, one of the sails requiring adjustment, Lord Adalbert stood up to arrange it, and, losing his balance, he fell overboard. He might have gained the shore, which was only about one hundred yards distant, but he continued to swim after the boat, fearing, it is supposed, that Churchill might be lost, so that in death, as in life, his thought was altogether for others, and not for himself. He had but little strength (his health having for some time been a source of anxiety), and when he sank, which he shortly did, he never rose again. His life no doubt went out at once, a life of exceptional loveliness, of self-sacrifice, and of incalculable usefulness; and having 'turned many to righteousness,' he is one of those of whom it is said, that they 'shall shine as the stars for ever and ever!'" Thus in death, as in life, Lord Adalbert Cecil manifested the true spirit of one who has truly learnt the meaning of the words, "the Son of God, who loved me, and gave himself for me" (Galatians 2:20). May many such, rich or poor, be raised up to glorify God.

Robert Cleaver Chapman
1803-1902

R. C. CHAPMAN

ROBERT CLEAVER CHAPMAN was born in Denmark on January 4th, 1803, where his parents resided at that time. His mother felt the importance of a child's early years, and taught and trained her children herself till they were nine or ten, seeking to instill high principles and a love for learning. While in Denmark Robert Chapman had lessons from a French abbe, and then he was sent to a school in Yorkshire, where he made good progress. He studied European languages, and purposed to acquire Eastern ones. He had a passion for literature, and desired to give himself to it; but though the Chapmans had been rich, the position of his father—Mr. Thomas Chapman—had in this respect undergone some change, and it was needful for the son to pursue a course that would bring remuneration; therefore, though with some reluctance, he studied law and became a solicitor. In this profession he soon occupied a good position, and had he pursued the course on which he started there is little question that the high honors to which it can lead might have been his. But God had honor in store for him, great and abiding, such as the world cannot give.

The turning point in Mr. Chapman's life came when he was about twenty. He was invited by Mr. John Whitmore—an elder and greatly valued Christian worker at John Street Chapel, Bedford Row—to hear the well-known James Harington Evans, and in a few days a great change was apparent to those who knew him.

Taking his stand at once and decidedly as a confessor of Christ's name, and owning Him as Lord, he was baptized as a believer, and attached himself to the assembly of Christians in London in which Mr. Harington Evans ministered the Word. Having learned from the Scriptures that it was the will of God that believers should be baptized, he went to Mr. Evans and expressed his desire to carry it out. With commendable caution Mr. Evans said, "You will wait a while, and consider the matter." "No," said Mr. Chapman, "I will make haste, and delay not, to keep His commandments." How blessedly he adhered to this purpose through his long life is well known.

Mr. Chapman felt that he was called of God to give himself to the ministry of the Word. When his friends told him he would never make a preacher his reply was, "There are many who preach Christ, but not so many who live Christ; my great aim will be to *live* Christ." It was by God's grace that resolution was made, and by the same grace it was kept (Philippians 2:13). That he did live Christ over seventy years, no one who knew him can question.

In the very year (1832) that Robert Chapman took up his residence at Barnstaple, with the steadfast purpose of seeking to learn and carry out all the will of God, George Muller and his friend and fellow-laborer, Henry Craik, took up their abode in Bristol. These servants of Christ had already been exercised about many things at Teignmouth, and on the evening of the 13th August, "at Bethesda Chapel, Mr. Muller, Mr. Craik, one other brother, and four sisters (only seven in all) sat down together, uniting in church fellowship, 'without any rules, desiring to act only as the Lord should be pleased to give light through His Word.'"

Early in the same second quarter of the last century some servants of Christ in Dublin and other places were moved to give themselves to the diligent study of the Scriptures and made an effort to carry out what was written. This Mr. Chapman had for some time been doing; consequently, when he and they were in God's providence brought together, they found themselves in many respects of one mind, and thus new links were formed.

In the matter of Christian fellowship he gladly went where there was room for the whole Bible, and a readiness, so far as he knew, to carry out the will of God according to the Scriptures. He would not acknowledge sectarian titles, and if the name of a religious denomination was mentioned to him he would say that it grated upon his ears. But his heart went out to all who are Christ's, and such, whatever name they bore, were welcomed by him, even as in his intercessions he embraced the whole Church of God.

Though he never failed to give baptism a high place as expressing the believer's burial and resurrection with Christ and was accustomed to baptize in the river Taw at Barnstaple until he was eighty (when he thought it well to leave this service to others), no one ever more strongly withstood the teaching that there is anything saving in it.

A hearty carrying out of the exhortation to be "given to hospitality" characterized the humble residences at Barnstaple, Nos. 6 and 9, on opposite sides of the short street called New Buildings. These abodes of peace and love are known to many throughout the world, and remembered with gratitude. No servant of Christ ever went there without finding a loving welcome and true sympathy, and few can have left without carrying away some deeper sense of the blessedness of trusting God, and seeking first His kingdom and His righteousness. No. 6 was from the beginning Mr. Chapman's dwelling, and in one of the rooms of this most simply furnished abode he who was truly "great in the sight of the Lord" breathed his last. Some time back a friend offered him the use of a better house, and desired him to occupy it as being more suitable, but he declined the offer saying he wished to continue where any Christian even the poorest could come to him without hesitation.

Mr. Chapman rose very early; but he retired early as well. For a long while he prepared his own breakfast and took it alone; but in later years he joined others at breakfast at 7 o'clock, dinner being at 12 o'clock. There was great cheerfulness at the table—words of wisdom and grace were constantly heard; but no room was given for conversation to degenerate into frivolous talk. It was also a rule of the house that no one should speak ill of an absent person, and any infringement of this rule called forth a firm though gracious reproof. After breakfast, Mr. Chapman gave an exposition of Scripture—preceded by a hymn, and followed by prayer—which was greatly valued. Guests at Mr. Chapman's table ever found a plentiful supply; but nothing was allowed to be wasted.

From his early days until he had reached a great age Mr. Chapman was diligent in open-air preaching, and through his preaching at the annual fair at Barnstaple, and still more frequently in the town and neighborhood, he became well known. But it was especially his life that told on the people of that town, and made him such a true witness for God. He was a man of considerable self-control. During his long course of service in the church he at times had great provocation, yet was he never moved, except to sorrow for those whose spirit and words were so contrary to Christ. When he was opposed he bore the opposition in patience, and when any turned from him he pursued them with his prayers and any expression of love it was possible for him to give. Those who knew him longest bear witness that they never heard a hasty or ungracious word escape his lips. A common saying at his house was, "It is better to lose your purse than your temper."

The help Mr. Chapman rendered in conferences, and in special meetings of servants of Christ before the word "conference" became so general, it is impossible to estimate. His words were always weighty; but his influence—the very atmosphere his presence created—was even more powerful. He used to say that while he gladly gave himself to intercession for larger meetings of which he heard, he specially valued those smaller ones in which it was possible really to confer over the Word of God. Many gratefully remember his help at Leominster and Yeovil. He did not cease to attend such conferences until he was over ninety and when he could no longer be present, he still welcomed notices of them for prayer, and often wrote some words of greeting and help.

One special and continuous subject of prayer with Mr. Chapman was the spread of the gospel in all lands, and visits to New Buildings were paid by servants of Christ from many countries; but in the Lord's work in Spain he took special interest. Accompanied by two brethren (Mr. Pick and Mr. Handcock, of Barnstaple), he had visited it in 1838, when it was fast closed against the Word of God, and journeyed from place to place, speaking of Christ as God gave opportunity, and praying that God would yet open Spain to the gospel. In 1863 he had the joy of guiding into that land Mr. W. Gould and Mr. G. Lawrence, whom he left there.

His "Choice Sayings" have had an extensive sale both in book and leaflet form. His "Choice Hymns and Meditations" also appeared in book form. He edited a life-record of his colleague, William Hake, under the title "Seventy Years of Pilgrim Life." His poems, "No Condemnation, O My Soul," "Jesus in His Heavenly Temple," "Author of Our Salvation," "Can Heavenly Friendships Pass?" "I Rest on Christ the Son of God," "No Bone of Thee was Broken," "Oh, My Saviour Crucified," "Show Me Thy Wounds Exalted Lord," "The Lamb of God to Slaughter Led," "With Jesus in Our Midst," and several others appear in hymn books in use today.

Until very old age Mr. Chapman's voice was heard in public, and occasionally his address was given in full in a local paper, the editor of which highly esteemed him. At the Barnstaple annual meeting in June 1901—the last he attended—he stood on his feet exactly one hour, he gave out the opening hymn from the desk, and then prayed, read several portions of Scripture, and spoke with much vigor.

On June 2, 1902, he rose as usual, but it was evident that he was poorly, and in the afternoon he fell with a slight shock of paralysis, affecting the left side. On the 12th of June serious symptoms manifested themselves, and about 8:50 that evening this loved servant of Christ, in his one hundredth year, entered into his rest, to await with Him the blissful moment when the body itself shall be raised, and he shall in every sense be conformed to the image of the Lord whom he so faithfully served.—HY.P.

John Marsden Code
1805-1873

J. M. CODE

JOHN MARSDEN CODE was born 1805. He was educated at Trinity College, Dublin, took the degree of M.A., and was ordained a clergyman of the Church of England, but soon withdrew for conscientious reasons. He had a curacy at Westfort, County Mayo, and is mentioned in the life of the Archbishop of Tuam as having resigned and joined the Brethren.

It was about that time that J. N. Darby, C. Hargrove, and others left the Established Church. Mr. Code never joined with J. N. D. in his Exclusive views, though he was much attached to him personally. He was with the Brethren at Cork, and ministered there. Later he left Ireland and settled in Bath with his family, where he remained till his death and ministered with much acceptance for many years.

He was a great Bible student and deeply taught in the Scriptures. His preaching the gospel on Lord's day evening was very impressive and much appreciated by members of the Church of England who regularly attended the meetings in large numbers. He was entirely possessed by the love of God, and though never forgetting the hatefulness of sin, used to say very often: "God hates sin, and loves the sinner."

He had only one idea in life—CHRIST!—and it was the same in his home, where he frequently burst out in some beautiful spiritual expression.

One who knew him most intimately writes: "I have never known any one more utterly possessed and permeated by Christ his Saviour." Like so many of the gifted men given by the Lord to the church in these times, Mr. Code was equally facile with his pen, and his "Notes on Romans" are veritable gems. He was a frequent speaker at the various conferences, and his presence and ministry of the Word at the believers' meetings in Dublin were always hailed with thankfulness to the Lord.

He had ever desired, if the Lord should call him home before His return, to be taken suddenly and the Lord granted his wish, for at 4 o'clock on April 16th, 1873, he quietly and quickly fell asleep in Jesus, aged sixty-eight. There was no sense of death—no pain, no farewell word. He did not seem to die. Life seemed as if simply suspended here, to be resumed in Paradise. The last words of Scripture he repeated were: "for so he giveth his beloved sleep." He was greatly beloved and much mourned.

William Collingwood
1819-1903

WILLIAM COLLINGWOOD

———◦◦◦———

AMONG THE LONG list of honored and esteemed servants of God whose names are associated with the inception of what has become known as "The Brethren Movement," none were more loved and trusted than William Collingwood, the friend and fellow-worker with most of that illustrious group of truth-loving men whose testimony has proved a blessing to thousands of God's people all over the world.

Born at Greenwich on April 23rd, 1819, he was educated at Oxford, where his grandfather was printer to the University. At Christ Church School he showed great aptitude for classics, but when he was offered a place on the Foundation of the College, he was not able to accept. His father's friend, J. D. Harding, and his cousin, Collingwood Smith, encouraged him to become an artist, and he rapidly came to the front as a painter of interiors and landscapes. In 1839 he settled at Liverpool as a teacher of drawing and, after election, to the membership of the Water Color Society.

For some time he attached himself to Dr. M'Neile, of St. Jude's, at Liverpool, a then famous evangelical churchman. Later he became acquainted with Lord Congleton, George Muller, and other leaders of a movement which aimed at the carrying out of the Scriptures in their simplicity and entirety. In 1844 he joined the late John Price of Chester, John Plunkett, Thomas Porter, and a few others in meeting simply in the Lord's name at Back Canning Street, Liverpool. Afterwards they met in the Crown Street Hall, built by Mr. Collingwood, who took a leading part till he left Liverpool in 1884. He continued to the end a strong supporter of the original principle of receiving Christians as such, and a friend and fellow-worker of all active evangelicals.

We remember hearing him recount how when speaking to a brother about the sad divisions among God's people, the brother replied: "Why, it's with a company in——you should be." He went down to see them, fully determined on no account to leave Dr. M'Neile, to whom he was sincerely attached. Welcomed at the morning meeting, it was such a revelation of the power of God and the leading of the Spirit that he returned at night to gospel meeting, and continued steadfastly so to meet till his decease.

In 1850, under the influence of Dr. Gutzlaff, he proposed to go out to China in the double capacity of artist and missionary. This was prevented by his marriage in the next year with Marie Imhoff, daughter of a notary at Arbon, Switzerland, and by family cares ensuing; but he became an earnest supporter of all mission work, and his house was the resort of many missionaries outward and homeward bound from the port of Liverpool.

In 1890 he settled at Bristol, where he attached himself to Bethesda, and joined with his old friend George Muller, spending his leisure time in writing many papers and booklets, among which were "The Bible its Own Evidence," "The Brethren: An Historical Sketch," etc. Valuable articles on "Doctrine" and spiritual themes appeared in *The Witness* over a number of years.

Mr. Collingwood's reverential love for the Word of God was a conspicuous feature in his character. So absorbed did he become in its treasures that the din of controversy and criticism scarcely reached him. In fact, the realm of controversy was uncongenial to him, for his spirit was gentle and loving, but when he did enter it he showed that he could do so with telling effect.

To those who were about him in his closing days, the spirit of contentment with the acquiescence in the will of God were very noticeable and beautiful to behold. As late as Whit Sunday, May 31, he was present at the morning meeting in Bethesda, though too feeble to take any audible part. On the following Saturday a stroke of paralysis laid him low. But his mental powers remained clear, and his spirit was bright and strong with faith and hope. A slight rally raised hopes of partial recovery, but on 25th June 1903, a change for the worse occurred, and on the afternoon of that day he fell asleep in the eighty-fifth year of his age.

Lord Congleton
1805-1866

LORD CONGLETON

JOHN PARNELL, second Lord Congleton, the eldest son of Baron Congleton, was born in London on June 16th, 1805. When studying at the University of Edinburgh he was led to accept Christ as his Saviour and Lord. From the day of his conversion he took a decided stand as a Christian among his fellow-students and friends. When asked if he had not to give up much to become a Christian, his characteristic reply was: "Give up! No, I gave up nothing; I got all."

On leaving college his father, wishing him to become a soldier, purchased for him a commission in the army. He could not, however, accede to his father's request, believing that it was not God's will that he should be connected with the military profession. Soon after this decision of his, a rich uncle left him property the annual value of which was £1200. It is needless to say that principal and interest were consecrated to God.

During the years 1827 and 1828 he was a frequent visitor at an uncle's house in Dublin. Here he became acquainted with the late Anthony Norris Groves, John N. Darby, John G. Bellett, Dr. Cronin, and other devoted and gifted Christians, who were used of God in commencing a remarkable movement for God in the world.

Mr. Henry Groves, Lord Congleton's biographer, tells us that among the truths that exercised these brethren were—first, the oneness of the church of God, involving a fellowship large enough to embrace all saints, and narrow enough to exclude the world; second, the completeness and sufficiency of the written Word in all matters of faith and pre-eminently in things affecting our church life and walk; and third, the speedy premillennial advent of the Lord Jesus.

The first public room where so-called "Brethren" assembled for the breaking of bread was hired by Lord Congleton (then Mr. Parnell), and was situated, not at Plymouth as is generally believed, but in Aungier Street, Dublin .

On September 18th, 1830 he accompanied a mission party to Bagdad in Asiatic Turkey, purposing to join Mr. A. N. Groves who was labouring there. They took with them a great number of books, a printing press, and a large medicine chest. After many rough and painful experiences, as well as hair-breadth escapes, they reached Bagdad on June 27th, 1831. Here they found almost insuperable difficulties placed in their way by the Turkish authorities. Being bigoted Mohammedans, they did their utmost to prevent the truth being spread. After toiling for a time at Bagdad and neighborhood, Lord Congleton and several others visited India, and finding open doors in that needy land remained for years, preaching the gospel to the unsaved and teaching the Word to believers.

In the summer of 1837 Lord Congleton left India and returned to England, where for forty-six long years he toiled and labored until his Home-call. Lord Congleton was a diligent and able Bible student. It was his custom, as it was that of his friend, the late George Muller, to rise early in the morning in order that he might have a period of uninterrupted meditation and study of God's Word. To him, as with Jeremiah, the Scriptures were "the joy and rejoicing of his heart." When in poor health he wrote from Cannes as follows: "As to myself, I do not know that I ever was happier. Of late I have been almost daily picking up nuggets of metal, far, far more precious than gold, out of the Holy Scriptures—the Book I have been reading daily for more than fifty years, and it seems to get newer instead of older." He was also a man of prayer. In addition to his early morning hours for prayer and communion with God he usually retired to his room at eleven in the forenoon, three in the afternoon, and eight in the evening.

He had a great love for the children of God, irrespective of sect or party, and it was a delight to him to be of any service whatever to the humblest, weakest, poorest, or most ignorant of them. He loved believers because they belonged to Christ and counted it a privilege to help them in any way he possibly could. And this was not done in a patronizing way, as it is to be feared is too often the case with some who are in "easier" circumstances than their poorer brethren. He was free from that spirit of caste which so pervades Christian society. Instead of seeking the company of the rich and the great, the refined and educated, he sought the poor and the outcast, the sick and the sorrowing, and ministered to their needs.

He was a self-denying and faithful steward of the money and property entrusted to his care. It was his constant rule to devote one half of his income to the Lord's service. Though glad to carry the gospel of God's grace—the proclamation of His mercy—into every open door, his special ministry was among believers. He delighted in expounding the Scriptures to God's people. Whilst contending for "open" ministry at the Lord's table, he did not believe in an "any man" ministry. One of his utterances in prayer often was, "May we be willing to sit silent until Thou givest us a word, and ready also to speak when we get a message from Thee."

In a booklet written by him on the "Open Meeting" some important principles are enunciated. "Everything connected with the open meeting calls for the greatest lowliness of mind. Mere sanctified natural ability and educational acquirement in a member of Christ will not suffice to edify His body; and that everybody with any experience knows. A man must have a gift in addition to being a member of Christ in order to be able to edify his fellow-members. And after that he has to wait upon Christ, the Head of the body, his Lord, for guidance as to whether, when the members are all come together into one place, he is to move. It is only the lowly ones that will wait for, or discern, or obey that guidance. And it is only the lowly ones that will submit to the judgment of others."

In the early morning of October 23rd, 1883, Lord Congleton fell asleep. "Lord Jesus, receive my spirit," was often on his lips, and he remarked that that summed up all his desires.—A.M.

Henry Craik
1805-1866

HENRY CRAIK

H ENRY CRAIK, for forty-four years the beloved colleague in ministry of George Muller of Bristol, was born at Prestonpans, East Lothian, on the August 8th, 1805. After a course of instruction in the Parochial School of Kennoway (of which his father was the master), he entered St. Andrews University at the beginning of the session 1820-21, and studied under Professor Alexander and Dr. Hunter. Here he speedily gained distinction for his proficiency in Greek. In an old memorandum book, among other entries is the following from Mr. Craik's pen: "1823-1824.—Attended Greek, Latin, Natural Philosophy, and Dr. Chalmers' lectures. Obtained a prize in the Latin, and two in the Greek the highest honor, as before. This concluded my Philosophy course, and qualified me for entering St. Mary's College, or the Divinity Hall. During all these years I had been living without God, though I read the Scriptures, and kept up a kind of formal praying, as far as I can recollect. My happiness consisted principally in my companionship; but I feel a difficulty in recalling my state of heart, except that I did not delight in the things of God."

In early days Mr. Craik's great mental powers made themselves manifest, and his own diary gives evidence of the extensive literary labors to which he devoted himself.

It was in the year 1826, and about the twentieth year of his age, that the great spiritual change occurred which resulted in the consecration of his great abilities to the service of his Lord and Saviour. This change he himself especially attributed to the conversation and society of his college companion, John Urquhart. In 1826 Mr. Craik moved to Edinburgh, where for a time he was engaged in tutorial work as well as study, and continued to enjoy the ministry of Dr. Chalmers.

In the month of July in that year he "received a proposal to become tutor in the family of Mr. Groves, a gentleman then residing in Exeter," the well-known Anthony Norris Groves. This proposal was accepted, and he took up his abode in the family of Mr. Groves, where he remained two years. His admiration of Mr. Groves was very great, and while with him

Mr. Craik commenced exposition of the Scriptures in a schoolroom at Heavitree. His time was now, and for some years onward, fully occupied with classical studies, in which he greatly delighted, and especially in the study of the original languages of the Bible.

In the year 1831 he took up his abode in Shaldon, Devonshire, and became pastor of the Baptist Church there. The same year he was married to Miss Mary Anderson, but after only a few months of married life she was taken from him early in 1832.

Mr. Craik's first meeting with Mr. Muller took place in July 1829, at Teignmouth, and thus began the friendship which led on to the association in ministry, and which remained unbroken till death.

In March 1832, Mr. Craik accepted a pressing invitation to preach in Gideon Chapel, Bristol. Crowds flocked to hear him, and the second Sunday the chapel was crammed. A week later he was joined by Mr. Muller, and the two preached alternately in Gideon, as well as in other chapels in Bristol. There were many striking conversions. On the 1st of May, 1832, Mr. Craik and Mr. Muller returned to Devonshire but soon afterwards the way was made quite clear to return and settle at Gideon Chapel. The conditions on which these servants of Christ consented to settle at Gideon were—That they should be considered only as ministering among the people, and not as occupying any fixed pastoral relationship; that pew rents should be abolished, and that they should go on as they had done in Devonshire in respect to the supply of temporal wants.

Speaking of the removal of these two ministers of Christ to Bristol, Mr. Craik's biographer says: "If the angels of God have any knowledge, as we may reasonably suppose, of the future consequence of events, they must surely have rejoiced with exceeding joy as they witnessed the arrival of Mr. Craik and his colleague, Mr. Muller, in the ancient city of Bristol; for the former, in the course of a few years was destined to take his stand among the very foremost of the ministers of the city, to become the friend and correspondent of some of the most able and learned men of the kingdom; an author eminent for his services in the cause of religion, Biblical criticism, and Protestantism, and what is more, the spiritual father of some hundreds of Christian men and women; while the latter was not only destined to serve the cause of truth by his writings and his ministry of the Word, but, more important still, to become the Founder and Director of the New Orphan Houses on Ashley Down, and also of the Scriptural Knowledge Institution for Home and

Abroad." After coming to Bristol Mr. Craik married a second time, the lady of his choice being Miss Howland.

The ministry begun at Gideon was afterwards transferred to Bethesda Chapel, and a little later Salem Chapel was also rented. In these buildings, for a long series of years, the church continued to grow and multiply, and the "little one became a thousand."

Mr. Craik was a man of true humility, self-forgetful to a fault, and exceedingly affectionate and approachable. To have known him and enjoyed his ministry is among the most precious memories of the writer. There was nothing heavy about his discourses, but verily they were solid to a degree. He was "mighty in the Scriptures," and his sermons were rich in expository wealth. One discourse of his would shed light on a large field of Scripture. His sermons on Sunday evenings usually lasted a full hour, but instead of this being a weariness or cause of complaint, it was with regret that hearers observed the approach of the time for closing the service. Rugged and somewhat careless in appearance, a stranger might at first be disappointed, but such a feeling would soon vanish before the outbursts of truly natural eloquence and the glowing fervor which habitually characterized his delivery. His readiness to enter into the spiritual difficulties of any member of the church was a marked feature, and the writer cherishes the memory of one such instance of a special kind, when he not only replied by a letter (which is still preserved), but took up the topic in question on two subsequent occasions in ministry. His removal in 1866, at the comparatively early age of sixty-one years, was an irreparable loss, and the immense concourse at his funeral testified that the loss was felt by the whole Christian community.—J.L.S.

Dan Crawford
1869-1926

DAN CRAWFORD

D AN CRAWFORD was fellow-worker and then successor to Frederick Stanley Arnot, as Fred Arnot was the true follower and successor of David Livingstone, the father of African pioneers and missionaries.

Mr. Crawford was born in Gourock, situated at the mouth of the Clyde, in 1869, and was led to Christ by a working man drawing a line across the floor of the Gospel Hall and urging him to decide before he crossed that line. He has both written and repeated the story, concluding: "At 20 minutes past 10, by grace I crossed that line."

At once he became a diligent student of the Scriptures, and a ravenous reader of good books, thus laying a good foundation, to be manifest in his labors in Africa, and in his letters to friends throughout the world. Acquaintances of early days say that from the first he manifested that out and out daring and individualism which ever characterized his service.

After a few years in his native town, during which he was diligent in service, he was led to volunteer for service in Central Africa. Meeting the stripling going forth, the veteran missionary, Hudson Taylor, reminded him of the trials ahead, but encouraged him that "whilst the Devil might build a fence around him, he could never erect a roof over his head, communication with the Holy Hill would ever remain unbroken" (Psalm 3:4).

Along with Mr. and Mrs. Arnot, Dr. Fisher, Tom Morris, Fred Lane, George Fisher, Archie Munnoch, Jeanie Gilchrist and others, he went forth in 1889, landing at Benguella on the West Coast. On the way to Bihe they had their introduction to the infamous slave caravans, "one such took nearly three hours to pass, a horde of 800 souls, all doomed to exile for life." After spending some time in Bihe, two hundred miles inland, he had many thrilling experiences before reaching Garenganze, one thousand miles farther inland, which he did just thirty-two months after leaving the homeland. Little did Mr. Crawford think that in this remote spot in the heart of Africa he would spend twenty-two years before sighting the homeland shores.

The great chief Msidi was then in power in Garenganze district. His despotic rule, five hundred wives, sickening beer drinks, butchery of myriads of natives, and unmentionable atrocities only deepened the impression that the messengers of the cross had found a needy spot, and one likely to manifest gospel triumphs.

After the death of Msidi the missionaries divided. Mr. Crawford got a grant of land from the Congo authorities and gradually formed a model African village at Luanza which has proved a center of blessing morally and spiritually throughout a very wide area.

Here he built what he termed his £30 mission house, a comfortable building overlooking Lake Mveru. In this he entertained the king of the Belgians about 1916. Dan loved to tell how, while they were sitting on a bluff overlooking the great lake, he got the desire of his heart by the king asking him to explain the difference between Protestant and Catholic missions. "For three quarters of an hour I let him have the gospel of the grace of God as plain as ever man heard it."

Concerning these solitary years in Africa, the *British Weekly* rightly points out what was probably the one recreation and safeguard from monotony of this devoted worker in these words: "The solitude of Africa had deepened a genuine gift for philosophy, so that Dan Crawford had attained at a leap and intuitively what others may at best only arrive at by the help of formal writings. His acquaintance, during all those years of willing exile in the heart of Africa with contemporary affairs in Great Britain, in Europe, and America, and throughout the world, was a constant mystery to those to whom he spoke intimately."

After twenty-three years work, which it would take pages to recount, along with his wife he came home on furlough in 1912. His first book, which he had long been preparing, entitled "Thinking Black," was issued in that year. It ran through two or three editions, was proclaimed by reviewers "a missionary classic," and we understand yielded in royalties some £2000 for native schools in Africa.

The reading of the book, the unique and soul-stirring addresses which Mr. Crawford delivered, his rush from town to town, his being lionized yet remaining unspoiled, are too well known to need description. He consorted with all sorts of persons, but usually had a word for his Master. A typical case in London: One night in the Whitechapel district, seeing a number of poor men entering a building for "a 3d. feed," he buttoned up his collar, pulled down his slouch hat, entered and dined as a down-and-out. The next night he was to address a distinguished company in the West End, probably connected with the Royal Geographical Society. Peers, baronets, and men of various titles and distinctions were present. He related with relish the contrast of the "feed" of the night before, taking care to emphasize that for poor or rich a greater banquet was alike free (Matthew 22:4).

The degree of F.R.G.S. was awarded at this time, and if anyone deserved it for enlightening the members concerning untrodden wilds and first-white-man pioneering in dark-man's-land it was D.C. He was one of the earliest to revisit the spot where David Livingstone's heart lies buried under a tree, when his body was brought home and laid to rest in Westminster Abbey. Finding the place overgrown and the memorial almost effaced, he took steps to have it put in order.

Having toured Britain, he crossed the Atlantic and visited many towns in Canada and the United States; also in Australia. In each place halls were packed and souls were stirred.

Finishing a furlough—deserved, fully utilized, and probably unique in every way—with his wife he returned to Luanza in 1913. A regular system of letters issued through a printer in Elizabethville, and reprinted in various papers on both sides of the Atlantic, kept many friends in touch with the Luanza Mission. He also issued a companion volume entitled "Back to the Long Grass." On his return he used the large sum he had collected in establishing schools in quite a number of districts around Luanza. Money was never a snare to Dan, if he got it freely he lavished it on the land he loved.

A few weeks before his Home-call he had the joy of realizing one of the greatest ambitions of his life, by finishing his translation of the whole Bible into the native tongue, for the African Christian is no lover of portions or parts, his desire is for the whole Word of his Father God.

The years since his return were filled up with consolidation, enlargement of area, a visit or two to the coast or railhead towns. Without any warning of failing health the end had come unexpectedly. A simple injury to his hand, followed by blood poisoning and the startling message: "Dan Crawford died June 3, 1926." He was laid to rest beside others in the little sacred spot in Luanza. To know Dan Crawford was to love him, and those who knew him best can most truly say: "We loved thee well, but Jesus loved thee best—farewell."—HY.P.

Dr. Edward Cronin
1801-1882

DR. EDWARD CRONIN

D R. CRONIN was born in Cork in 1801. His father was a Romanist, and he was brought up in that Church, but his mother was a Protestant. He was educated after school at Dublin University. How or when he was converted is not known, but Mr. Andrew Miller says: "He came up to Dublin as a medical student about the year 1826. He applied for communion as a visitor, and was readily received by the Independents, but when they learnt he had become a resident this liberty was refused. He was then informed that he could no longer be admitted to the table of any of the congregations without special membership with some one of them.

"This announcement made a deep impression on his mind, and was no doubt used of God to turn his attention to the truth of the 'One Body.' He paused, and after much exercise of conscience and prayer, he refused to submit to their Church order. It was a time of trial,...but the Lord overruled it for blessing." He and a Mr. Edward Wilson, Secretary of the Bible Society, after studying the Word for some time, began to see their way clear to come together on Lord's day morning for the breaking of bread and prayer.

They were speedily joined by several others. They were no doubt forced into the place of separation by the mistaken conduct of the Congregational body, but they were also led to fall back upon the sure Word of God, to act under their divine instincts and the unerring guidance of the Holy Spirit. The little meeting never formally broke up, but they united at once with those who began to break bread in Fitzwilliam Square.

Dr. Cronin's name is always associated with Mr. Darby, Mr. Bellett, and Mr. F. Hutchinson, as coming together in the winter of 1827-28, after much conference and prayer on the Lord's day morning for breaking of bread as the early Christians did, counting on the Lord to be with them.

Later on Dr. Cronin, together with his mother and sister, went out with John Parnell (Lord Congleton) and F. W. Newman to Bagdad to join Anthony Norris Groves in mission work. They had a terrible journey across the Mediterranean to Aleppo, and thence through the desert to Bagdad. Lord Congleton married Miss Cronin at Aleppo, but owing to the fatigue and unhealthy condition she died there. Mrs. Cronin died later in Bagdad when the party arrived in June 1832. On one occasion they were stoned out of a town and Dr. Cronin left for dead. The work of Bagdad proving barren of results, Mr. A. N. Groves went to India, where he spent many years, and the others returned to England to stir up the church to faith and prayer that great signs and wonders should follow in the mission field.

Dr. Cronin addicted himself to ministry of the saints and took a leading part in oversight in the London meetings of Exclusive Elder Brethren, until his independent action at Ryde in 1879 led to their deciding that they had no fellowship with his act.

Dr. Edward Cronin died at Brixton in February 1882 aged eighty-one, still holding firmly to the Scriptural principles which had governed his life, and, above all, with a simple and happy trust in the Saviour whom he had loved and served so faithfully for so many years.—C.E.F.

WILLIAM TALBOT CROSBIE

1817-1899

WM. TALBOT CROSBIE, of Ardfert Abbey, was the third of the Kerry landlords whom the revival of 1861 brought out so boldly for the Lord to serve Him in the gospel, R. J. Mahony and F. C. Bland being the other two.

Born in 1817, Mr. Crosbie was brought to Christ as a very young man. After a long minority he entered upon the management of his large estate, and aided by his young wife, a sister of the late Lord Gwydyr, set to work to rearrange the farms and instruct the tenants. After a few years came the famine, but thanks to the measures Mr. Crosbie had taken in good time, the Ardfert Estate was saved.

In the midst of such labors as these, the mighty breath of the Holy Spirit, first felt in Ulster, began to be heard and, at first through unknown men and feeble instruments, the message of the gospel came as glad tidings to many. Every part of Kerry was affected, though only as to the Protestant population. The homes of the three we have named became the centers of a divine energy which spread itself in all directions. The meetings originated then in the granary at Ardfert continued without interruption for many years. Many and wonderful were the scenes of awakening there and in Tralee, under the ministry of J. Denham Smith, T. Shuldham Henry, and many others whom Mr. Crosbie brought to Kerry and accompanied in the work.

John Hambleton, in his "Buds, Blossoms, and Fruits of the Revival," says: "I went to see Mr. Crosbie....The butler (Fidler his name) and all the servants were happy and rejoicing Christians and becoming real laborers in the vineyard. In the evening we held a meeting in the loft, and upwards of 100 converts with open Bibles listened to the expounding of the Word; and such a time of refreshing we had that it seemed Heaven had come down to earth. Every Protestant in this village seemed converted to God."

The effects upon himself of this spiritual movement were very great. A Christian before, he now received his call to a new life of liberty, of joy, of devotion to his Master, of separation from the world, and of service in the Word of God and the gospel, which constituted together a complete transformation of character and new departure in the activities of his energetic nature.

He had been prominent in county, political, and fiscal affairs. As Grand Juror and Justice of the Peace he had labored for the good of the county with an energy and capacity that fitted him to be a leader of men. But now so powerfully was he possessed by the reality and blessedness of his place in Christ, his Heavenly inheritance, and the hope—a present and real one to him—of Christ's early return to call His own to Himself, that after full consideration, and not without many a wrench and the severance of old associations, he retired from it all, resigned his deputy lieutenancy and magistracy, and gave himself to the service of the gospel and the gentle pursuits of his own home farm and the hospitalities of his Christian home at Ardfert Abbey.

It was Christian work and service that ever held the first place in his heart. With Mr. Mahony and Mr. Gordon Oswald he preached in Naples and other parts of Italy. He worked in and around Lurgan, and for many years bore the principal expense of the gospel mission there. Everywhere he went he was ready to give his testimony for Christ, and had great power and tact in personal dealing with his friends, guests, and casual acquaintances.

He had great delight in the Dublin Believers' Meetings, where for some twenty-five years he was a constant attendant and frequent speaker. He was brought up in the evangelical branch of the Church of England, but with the deep spiritual movement of 1861 came also the spirit of inquiry as to the mind of God upon many doctrines hitherto unquestioningly accepted. Among these were infant baptism, apostolical succession, priesthood, and Episcopal ordination. As the result, he and his family began to meet with other recent converts under the name of Christian only, without connection with any existing sect or denomination for fellowship, prayer, ministry of God's Word, and the celebration of the Lord's Supper.

Among his papers was found the following: "If so be that, contrary to my hope in the Lord's coming, I should fall asleep in Jesus, I desire that my funeral should be conducted in the simplest and most unsectarian manner possible, having for many years renounced all connection with any sect, believing as I do that Christianity is a higher thing than any combination based on human theology."

He also referred to himself as "a sinner saved all of grace, having no claim whatever to any merit of my own, but resting solely on the all-sufficient merits of my adorable Saviour, in whom alone I have trusted since my conversion in 1839, and who has supplied all, all my need, in spite of all my failures."

He passed away on September 4, 1899, at the ripe age of eighty-two. His body was buried in the ancient ruined cathedral of Ardfert, the services being conducted by his two younger sons and son-in-law.

John Nelson Darby
1800-1882

JOHN NELSON DARBY

J OHN NELSON DARBY, the Tertullian of these last days, was the youngest son of John Darby of Leap Castle, King's County. The year of his
birth at Westminster was 1800; that also of E. B. Pusey, who was to
champion Anglo-Catholicism; and the career of each ended in the
same year. The name "Nelson" was derived from the connection between his uncle, Henry Darby, commander of the "Bellerophon" in the
battle of the Nile, and the famous admiral, Lord Nelson. He was educated at Westminster School, then at Trinity College, Dublin, where
he graduated in 1819 as Classical Medallist. He was called to the Irish
Chancery Bar, but soon afterwards, in 1825, took Deacon's orders from
Archbishop Magee, by whom he was priested the next year. He was
appointed to the Wicklow parish of Calary, residing in a peasant's
cottage on the bog.

The Viscountess Powerscourt, from attending Drummond's Albury
Conferences on Prophecy, started like meetings at her mansion near
Bray, through which Darby met A. N. Groves and J. V. Parnell (Lord
Congleton), introduced by his friend J. G. Bellett, who was in touch
also with Edward Cronin and others like-minded in Dublin. All of
these vindicated the functions of the Holy Spirit and the Christian
hope generally neglected. Darby, constrained by the Scriptural view
of the church as independent of the state, relinquished his parochial
position in 1827, and in the next year completed his separation from
the establishment by "breaking bread" in Dublin with the above-
named associates.

He had also become acquainted in Ireland with Francis William,
brother of John Henry (Cardinal) Newman. The younger of these, who
was a Fellow of Baliol College, had so distinguished himself in the Oxford schools that, when presented in 1826 for the B.A. degree, the whole
congregation rose in his honor. He became tutor to the family of Mr. (Chief
Justice) Pennefather, Darby's brother-in-law. Thrilled by the personality

of J.N.D., Newman persuaded "the Irish clergyman" to visit Oxford in 1830, and then introduced to him a former pupil, Benjamin Wills Newton, another First Classman, who was a Fellow of Exeter. G. V. Wigram of Queen's, Lancelot Brenton of Oriel; and W. E. Gladstone (afterwards British Premier) of Christchurch, also met Darby, but succumbed to the influence of the elder Newman, who just then was select preacher before the university.

Benjamin Wills Newton, who was a native of Plymouth, brought about a visit by Darby to that town, strongly evangelical through the ministry of Dr. Hawker, and influenced by the "separation" principles of John Walker, another Irish ex-clergyman. By the year 1832 a "gathering" of believers "to the name of Jesus," the first of its order in England, was definitely formed there. James L. Harris, resigning his local incumbency of Plymstock, united with the Brethren, and started their first organ, *The Christian Witness*, to which J.N.D. contributed. S. P. Tregelles, the textual critic, who was Newton's brother-in-law, was "received" in 1836; after R. Chapman at Barnstaple, and H. Craik with G. Muller at Bristol had taken a like position. Great simplicity and devotedness marked the company in those golden days.

In the year 1837 Darby carried the "testimony" to the continent, beginning with Methodists in Switzerland, so that by 1840 several French-speaking congregations had been formed, when his lectures on the hopes of the church of God were delivered at Geneva. It was from his *Etudes sur la Parole* that the "Synopsis of the Books of the Bible" was produced.

Revisiting Plymouth in 1845, he found considerable departure from the teaching maintained elsewhere on ministry, justification, the secret rapture, etc. J. N. D. withdrew from the meeting as dominated by Newton, and an independent company was started.

After developing the work in France, from 1853 Darby labored among Baptists in Germany; and assemblies of believers arose at Dusseldorf, Elberfeld, etc., for whose use he produced the "Elberfeld Bible." Among others Fraulein von Bunsen, secretary to her father the Chevalier, united with the *Darbisten*, so-called. During meetings of the Evangelical Alliance at Berlin, J. N. D. met Dr. Tholuck (cf. "Autobiography of G. Muller"), to whom he explained his views on gifts. The Halle theologian agreed that such was the primitive system, but queried if it could still be realized. Darby's very pertinent reply was, "Have you ever tried?" He provided his French-speaking associates with the "Pau Bible," and rendered like service to Brethren in Great Britain. His English version of the New Testament, which Drs. Field and Weymouth have independently turned to account, was before the revisers in the seventies, and a complete edition of his English Bible appeared in 1890.

From 1859, besides the fields of labor already mentioned, J.N.D. ministered in Canada, the States, the West Indies, and New Zealand; also in Holland and Italy.

For fifty years he was strenuously engaged in original exposition of Scripture. The "Synopsis," recommended by Bishop Ellicott to the Gloucester theological students, acquired among J.N.D.'s adherents authority like that commanded by Wesley's "Notes" among Methodists. Professor Stokes has described it as "the standard of appeal. Every departure from that model is bitterly resented" ("Expositor's Bible," Acts 1, page 382). But nobody has protested against such use of his writings more than Darby himself, for whom truth was "a growing tree" (C.W., XXIII, page 191). J.N.D.'s ordinary style is repugnant, and in his correspondence reference is made to this as having exercised him. By contrast, his living ministry was matchless and his "spiritual songs" are powerfully beautiful. Weakness in detail was another of his limitations. Nevertheless, in his own generation he singularly served the counsel of God. His criticism of that which he deemed error is usually trenchant and luminous.

The governing idea is the ruin of the church, or apostasy of the dispensation (C. W., I, p. 192), which was his "burden" ("Correspondence," I, p. 52); but he could echo words of Calvin (commentary on Psalms 102, verse 14): "The sadder the desolation into which the Church has been brought, the less ought our affection to be alienated from her." Loof's criticism of Darby's conception of the apostolic church as "an organized visible society" (C. W., XX, 450, cf. "Correspondence," II, 245, 278), that "church" with him meant "that which the Protestant faith has always made of it" fails, because J.N.D. did not accept Augustine's distinction. He found "the essential principle of unity" ("Correspondence," I, 114) in the operations of the Holy Spirit. The Bishop of Birmingham considers him wholly wrong here; but then Dr. Gore's view of the relation of the church to the Bible is very different from that of J.N.D. No one, indeed, rightly instructed, pretends that the position —one of *weakness*, as J.N.D.

always said—is a logical one; none for that matter is to be found, *pace* Bishop Gore, outside Rome, as to which Darby held that the "historical" church is a caricature of that exhibited in the New Testament. A controversy (1866) over his papers on the suffering of Christ arose only from the objectors' failure to seize his real position.

In 1881 the theory of fellowship and discipline which he had accredited was used against him by his ablest supporter; the issue, as Darby described it, was one between "the Spirit" and "intelligence," he himself correcting his logic by his experience. The disintegration continued after his decease until, in 1908, the leading London section associated with his name, in their treatment of another provincial trouble, acted upon an interpretation of "divine principles" scarcely distinguishable from that of Kelly. Substitute Plymouth for London, and you have the metropolitan discipline of Newton! It were idle to inquire with which "remnant" of several lies "survival of the fittest." Many souls have been exercised with regard to healthier relations between brethren divided during the past years. New problems have arisen, not to be solved by reference to the past. Collective reunion is discountenanced as likely to accentuate the disease; while individual surrender of that believed to be human is fraught with blessing to those concerned. Grace may be counted upon for any endeavor to strengthen in a Scriptural way the things that remain.

J. N. D. wrote many hymns, including "Hark! Ten Thousand Voices Crying," "O Lord, Thy Love's Unbounded," "Rest of the Saints Above," "Rise, My Soul, Thy God Directs Thee," "This World is a Wilderness Wide," and others which are sung world-wide. A volume of the poems has been issued.

Of the first little band in Dublin, already Groves, Bellett and Cronin had passed away—Lord Congleton shortly to do so—when the turn came of J.N.D., on the 29th of April, 1882. In his closing days at Bournemouth he recorded that he knew of nothing to recall; that Christ had been his object. Although a born leader, he was nobly simple in habit and manner, equally transparent and trustful. He had nothing petty about him. As occasion arose he would throw off religious conventionality. His ministry was ever in close touch with his pastoral visitation, in which he engaged every afternoon. Even if weakness lurked in it, his strength of judgment came of the predominance that the moral aspect of any matter had for him. He lived in the Bible, and recommended "thinking in Scripture." May that similarly ever remain our sole spiritual food, mainstay, and weapon.—E.E.W.

James George Deck
1807-1884

J. G. DECK

JAMES GEORGE DECK was born November 1st, 1807, at Bury St. Edmunds, Suffolk, and was blessed, like Timothy, with a praying mother, one who used to retire every evening to her room for a quiet hour with God on behalf of her children, and also of her children's children, and who never punished her children without first praying with them. All of her children were early converted and consecrated to God; a blessing which has descended to the third generation. One of her daughters, Mrs. M. J. Walker, was the authoress of "Jesus, I Will Trust Thee," "The Wanderer No More Will Roam" (*Believers Hymn Book*), besides other well-known hymns.

Having studied for the army at Paris, under one of Napoleon's generals, Mr. Deck went to India in 1824 as an officer in the East India Company's service, receiving a commission in the 14th Madras Native Infantry. Even then there had been deep conviction of sin, under stress of which he drew up on one occasion a code of good resolutions, signing it with his own blood, only to find himself without strength to keep them. His youthful ambition was that, having distinguished himself in his profession, he might afterwards enter Parliament for his native town.

But God had better things in store for him, for returning to England in 1826, he was brought under the power of the gospel, and was converted "through a sermon preached by a godly Church of England clergyman whom his sister Clara, herself previously converted, took him to hear." All things became new to him, his life's passion then being to follow Jesus and win souls for the kingdom. About this time he became acquainted with and married the daughter of Samuel Feild, an evangelical clergyman, and in her he found a wife who, through grace, shared with himself the "like precious faith."

On returning to India he at once took his place as a Christian among his brother officers, and began boldly witnessing for Christ, a number being led through his instrumentality to know and trust the same precious Savior. Becoming exercised as to his position as a Christian in the army he resigned his commission with the intention of becoming a clergyman, and with this object he returned to England in 1835 with his wife and two children. While visiting his father-in-law, Mr. Feild, at the vicarage, Hatherleigh, Devon, his second son, Dr. J. Feild Deck, was born and christened. An observation made by Mr. Feild in connection with this christening against some Baptists who were troubling his parish caused Mr. Deck to examine the Word of God upon the question of the "baptismal regeneration" of infants as set forth in the Prayer Book. Not finding such teaching supported by the Bible he became exercised as to his forthcoming ordination as a clergyman, when he would have to declare, *ex animo* that he "assented and consented to all and everything contained in the Book of Common Prayer." Approaching his loved wife he said, "I have left the army to become a clergyman, but now see that the Church of England is contrary to the Word of God; what shall we do?" Her noble reply was, "Whatever you believe to be the will of God, do it at any cost." The Church of England and the promised "living" had to be given up. But, what were they to join? Plainly, what they "found written" (Nehemiah 7:5) must be the test of everything. Seeking thus to be absolutely guided by the written Word, they presently found themselves in touch with many other Christians similarly exercised at that time, and who have since become known as "Brethren." Having themselves been baptized by immersion as believers, there was henceforth no more infant baptism in their family.

Leaving the Church of England and the traditions of men, and looking only to the Lord to supply their temporal wants, a trust never disappointed, Mr. Deck began to witness for Christ in the villages of Colaton Raleigh, Kingston, Devon; seeking, like Ezra, not only to be a "ready scribe" (Ezra 7:6) in the Word of God, but likewise "to do and to teach" the precious truths so recently apprehended in it. It was a singularly godless, High Church parish, but soon many precious souls were won for God through the preaching of the gospel, and having been baptized as believers were gathered to the name of the Lord Jesus Christ in church fellowship, according to Acts 2:42, as "holy brethren" (Hebrews 3:1) waiting for God's Son from Heaven (1 Thessalonians 1:10).

It was during this period, between 1838 and 1844, that Mr. Deck wrote most of those hymns which have been his special ministry to the church of God: "Abba! Father! We Approach Thee"; "A Little While! Our Lord Shall Come"; "Lamb of God! Our Souls Adore Thee"; and "Jesus, We Remember Thee". His hymns were not evangelical, but rather hymns of worship and Christian consecration, in view of our Lord 's near return.

His sphere of ministry was chiefly in the western counties of England, residing and labouring after he left Kingston at Sidmouth, Wellington, and Weymouth; with mission visits to Otterton and to East Coker, near Taunton, being much used in these various places in conversions and also in instructing and establishing those who believed in the divine truths and principles which in the Word of God had become so precious unto himself. Whilst in Wellington the late Henry Dyer assisted in the school, and proved a loved and valued fellow-laborer in the ministry of the Word.

In 1852 he had an illness and breakdown so severe as to call for an entire cessation from ministry. The school also had to be given up. Medical men recommended a sea voyage and a complete change of occupation as essential to his recovery, so it was decided to emigrate to New Zealand.

Arriving in 1853, Mr. Deck purchased land and settled with the family at Waiwerro, near the village of Motueka, in the Nelson province, where three months later his devoted wife, after a brief illness, "fell asleep," and was laid to rest in the Motueka Cemetery. Health having been wonderfully restored, he had the joy before long of witnessing once more in the land of his adoption for his beloved Lord and Saviour.

He removed in 1865 with his family to Wellington, an effectual door of service having been opened to him in that city and province both in the gospel and in church fellowship, a large and happy meeting being gathered at Wellington and several other assemblies in the district. During this time several more hymns were given him: "Jesus, Our Life, Is Risen;" "Lord of Life, This Day Rejoices All Who Know Thee, Strong to Save." He also wrote that splendid baptismal hymn, "Around Thy Grave, Lord Jesus," and others, "Father, We Seek Thy Face," "Great Captain of Salvation," "In Love We Part as Brethren," "Jesus, Thy Name We Love," "Lord Jesus, Are We One with Thee?" "Lord We Are Thine," "O Happy Day, When First We Felt," "Oft We, Alas, Forget the Love," "The Veil Is Rent," and many others.

He paid a visit to Invercargill, the southernmost city in the colony, where his son, Dr. J. Feild Deck, was practicing and in whose house a little company of a dozen had commenced to remember the Lord in the breaking of bread, whom he much helped by his ministry.

Feeling at length with advancing years unequal for carrying on the work at Wellington, he returned with his family to Motueka where, after being for two years a complete invalid, the home-call came, August 14th, 1884, in his seventy-sixth year. On Sunday, August 17th, "devout men" laid the earthly tabernacle to rest in the Motueka Cemetery. There was a large attendance, many his own children in the faith, his own hymn, "Thou Hast Stood Here, Lord Jesus," being sung at the grave. His name is fragrant to many today, and through his hymns, "he, being dead, yet speaketh."—S.J.D.

Edward Dennett
1831-1914

EDWARD DENNETT

E DWARD DENNETT was born in the Isle of Wight, 1831, at Bembridge, and died in Croydon in October, 1914 after a short illness. His people were all in the Church of England, but he was converted as a lad through the instrumentality of a godly clergyman, and he left the church from conviction and became minister of a Baptist Chapel in Greenwich, having previously matriculated at London University.

In 1873 he contracted a severe illness through visiting one of his parishioners, and was sent abroad for a year by his people. He wintered at Veytaux, and coming in contact with "Brethren" staying at the same "pension," he had a good deal of interchange with them, which helped to clear in his mind certain difficulties that he had.

Taking no steps till his return, he explained his views and resigned his charge shortly after "breaking bread" for the first time with those gathered simply at the Lord's table "unto His name."

Mr. Dennett had the pen of a ready writer. His sphere of labor was England, Ireland, and Scotland, and he paid visits to Norway, Sweden, and America. He had pastoral and teaching gifts of a high order.

Sir Edward Denny, Bart.
1796-1889

SIR EDWARD DENNY

⟐

I T IS ESPECIALLY pleasing for the Christian to enumerate among the "poets of the sanctuary" and the sweet singers of the Master one whose advantages of birth, fortune, and title raise him above the level of his fellow believers.

And such an one was the author of "Hymns and Poems" including, "A Pilgrim through this Lonely World", "Bright with All His Crowns of Glory", "Sweet Feast of Love Divine", "What Grace, O Lord, and Beauty Shone", "While in Sweet Communion Feeding", and numbers more—all breathing loyalty to his Lord and Master, with intimate knowledge of His truth and will—dealing lovingly with His coming again and His millennial glory, with many a sweet stanza on the pilgrim's path and portion.

Sir Edward Denny, Bart., of Tralee Castle, County Kerry, was born October 2nd, 1796, succeeded his father as fourth baronet, August 1831, and fell asleep in June 1889, aged ninety-three.

The following interesting notice is culled from the *Leeds Mercury*, June 19th, 1889: "Nearly the whole town of Tralee belonged to him. He had an opportunity twenty years ago, when his leases fell in, of raising his rents to figures that, in some cases, would not have been considered extortionate had they been quadrupled. He, however, decided to accept the old rates. The result was that he was almost alone in escaping any reduction at the hands of the Land Commission. So far as he was himself concerned, a little money went a long way, but he gave liberally to poor relations and to the development of religious work in connection with 'the Brethren.' Living in a quiet way in a cottage at Islington, he devoted his time to the study of the prophetic books. His rental income from Ireland was about £13,000 a year."

In the year 1848 he published "Hymns and Poems," and ten years afterwards, a Chart, entitled, "A Prophetical Stream of Time; or, An Outline of God's Dealings with Man from the Creation to the End of All Things," also two Charts, entitled, "The Seventy Weeks of Daniel" and

"The Cycle of Seventy Weeks," and yet again, a chart entitled, "The Feasts of the Lord." These publications with many others attest his deep insight into the Word of God which he loved so well.

Sir Edward was brought under conviction of sin by reading an Irish story, "Father Clement," and soon confessed his Lord, ministering to the poor and to the saints in a most unassuming manner. He was much loved and esteemed in London, and was connected mostly with the Park Walk Assembly.

It was the writer's privilege to meet with Sir Edward at his residence in the Bolton Gardens, and in his study there to spend some time in his company. Aged, yet sweetly communicative, it was a valued time of communion as our minds reverted to scenes of the past and the Lord's gracious dealings with His people. In order to test our brother's memory, I remember repeating one of his hymns, with a slight change of words. It was detected at once, and proved there was little falling off of that loving and bright intellect, though ninety years were creeping on the aged baronet. On parting he gave me his photo, so seldom given, which is here reproduced.

In the introduction to his "Hymns and Poems," in referring to 1 Corinthians 13, he writes: "Love, then, as we read, being 'the greatest of these,' seeing that the blessed God is Himself essentially Love, our hopes should not surely come short of that day when He whom, not having seen, we love, will reveal Himself to our hearts in all His attractions; when our powers of loving will be fully developed. And this will not be till the whole family meet in the house of their Father; till the Bride, the Lamb's Wife, is actually enthroned with her Lord. 'Come, Lord Jesus!'" —A.M.E.

John Dickie
1823-1891

JOHN DICKIE

⟶∞⊂∞⟵

JOHN DICKIE, the writer of letters published in two volumes under the
title of "Words of Faith, Hope, and Love," was born in January 1823, in
Irvine, a seaport town in Ayrshire, and was early bereaved of both parents. He was a delicate boy, of a sensitive temperament, modest and retiring, but of a kind and warm-hearted disposition. At an early age he
developed studious habits, and he made such progress that he was enabled in the year 1841, by means of what he earned by teaching, to enter
Glasgow University.

About this time the great crisis of his life occurred. He became deeply
anxious as to his spiritual condition; and, his conscience being tender,
he felt sin to be an intolerable burden till, when between nineteen and
twenty years of age, he was led to accept the Lord Jesus Christ as his all-
sufficient Saviour. Yet even after this his conflicts with sinful self and
the wicked one were many and severe. The deep spiritual experiences
which he thus early passed through doubtless gave character to his after
Christian life.

Having with his whole heart yielded himself to God, he felt that he
was no longer his own, but the Lord's, and he resolved to consecrate his
life to His service. He ardently desired to become a minister of the gospel, and to this end, after finishing his university career, he entered the
Divinity Hall. But toward the close of his first session, symptoms of pul-
monary consumption began to manifest themselves, and during his second year his health completely failed. He consulted some of the most
eminent physicians whose opinions were that the case was hopeless. Under these circumstances he returned to his friends in Irvine. He gradually became worse, and for over two years his voice so completely failed
that he was able to communicate with his friends only by means of the
dumb alphabet. Subsequently he went to London to consult a distinguished specialist on chest diseases, but his opinion was the same as that
given by the home doctors.

Turning his back on the capital he said to himself: "If it is God's will, notwithstanding this verdict, I shall survive, if not, His will be done." Studying his own constitution, he adopted a system of dietetics which he believed suitable, and lived a life of extreme self-denial. This treatment was doubtless the means of prolonging a singularly useful life for a period of over forty years. After some years his health improved considerably, and for several years he found a sphere of much usefulness as a missionary in his native town.

In the year 1858 Mr. Dickie removed to Kilmarnock at the invitation of Mr. John Stewart, a well-known Christian gentleman, and a devoted laborer in the Master's vineyard. Here he remained for about twenty years, often prostrated through weakness; but with much patience he persevered in the Lord's work, counting upon the sufficiency of His grace. He identified himself with a company of God's people, gathered to the name of the Lord Jesus, who met in a building erected and maintained by Mr. Stewart. Here Mr. Dickie ministered regularly in word and doctrine, exercising the gifts with which God had endowed him.

His labors among the dissipated and openly ungodly, as well as among the poor and sick, were not in vain. God enabled him to win many trophies of grace, and pluck brands from the fire. Not the least remarkable of these was a blacksmith named Philip Sharkey, a man most profane, a drunkard, and at times a terror to his neighbors. This man Mr. Dickie sought out and, after long, patient, and prayerful effort, had the joy of winning him to trust in the Saviour; his subsequent life and triumphant departure to be with God being the evidence of his true conversion. Mr. Dickie wrote an account of this interesting case, and it was published under the title, "Philip Sharkey, the Kilmarnock Blacksmith." The circulation was enormous, one gentleman alone purchased for distribution one hundred thousand copies. He afterwards wrote many other tracts and booklets, among them being "The Devil's Cradle," "Christian Thoroughness," "Stewardship," "Divine Compensations," etc., the circulation of each reaching many thousands. He also became a contributor to several religious periodicals, and in particular to the *Family Treasury*. Besides his prose writings, Mr. Dickie wrote many poems and hymns.

In the year 1878 he became so feeble in health that he left Kilmarnock and returned to Irvine to reside with his sister and her husband, Provost Watt. For a few years after his return to his native town he was enabled to go about serving the Lord, though in much physical weakness; but in the year 1882 his little remnant of strength completely failed, and for the remaining eight years of his life he was confined wholly to his room, never having been able to leave it again, except on one occasion in the summer of 1890, and that only for a few minutes. His utter weakness and sickness hindered him from seeing any but his immediate relations, who ministered to him with all the kindness that affection could prompt.

During these eight years his sufferings were very great—much pain, constant sickness, excessive weakness and sleeplessness, together with nervous irritability of the brain, were his portion. Yet such was his experience of the sufficient grace of the Lord, that at the close of them he could say that "they were the cream of his whole life." On January 18th, 1891, he gently fell asleep. When the pangs of death were upon him, his eyes being closed, he was asked if he was sleeping. He replied, "Just musing on the sufferings of the cross," and so, conscious to the last, he passed from this place of suffering into the presence of his Lord. His mortal remains were interred in Irvine Cemetery in presence of many friends.— J.T.

William Henry Dorman
1802-1878

W. H. DORMAN

WILLIAM HENRY DORMAN was born in 1802, of humble parentage. Converted at an early age, he became a Congregational minister, eventually holding the important pastorate of the Union Chapel at Islington. After earnest and prayerful study of the Scriptures, and comparing what he found in the Word of God with the existing state of things around him, he was led to associate himself with "Brethren" about the year 1838. He immediately became recognized as a true minister with, as it has been well said, "The source of all true ministry—these two things: the love produced in the heart by grace, the love which impels to activity; and the sovereignty of God who communicates gifts as seems good to Him, and calls to this or that service—a call which renders ministry a matter of faithfulness and duty on the part of him who is called."

Mr. Dorman's accession to the "Brethren" so-called was notable in that he was the only Nonconformist minister of any real prominence in England who became connected with the remarkable spiritual movement which bears that name. He labored at Reading, where he was instrumental in leading Mr. C. E. Stuart to leave the Church of England and take his place in fellowship with the gathering of believers meeting there. He also ministered at Bristol for some years.

A very clear and concise speaker, he was closely associated with Mr. J. N. Darby for many years. But in 1866 he, together with Capt. Percy Hall, Thomas Newberry, Jos. Stancomb, and others, left J.N.D.'s fellowship, believing him to hold views which they regarded as almost identical with those of Mr. B. W. Newton.

Mr. Dorman's "Reasons for Retiring from the Dissenters" was largely used in awakening an interest in the new spiritual movement amongst the Nonconformist sects. He "fell asleep" in 1878, and was buried at Reading.—C.E.F.

Henry Dyer
1821-1896

HENRY DYER

⟨⟨⟨⟨⟩⟩⟩⟩

HENRY DYER was brought to the Lord at an early age, and first met with Christians assembling only in the Lord's name in London about 1846. Soon after he spent some years at Wellington, Somerset, and at Weymouth, in the family of the late J. G. Deck (whose hymns have so greatly helped the worship of many believers), and then was for a time at Sherborne, in Dorset.

His brother, Mr. William B. Dyer, a man of exceptional gift as a preacher of the Word, had gone to Yeovil about the year 1848, and was much used of God there and in the neighborhood. Mr. Henry Dyer, who was considerably younger, frequently visited him, and took up his abode in Yeovil about 1860, after his brother went to Kendal.

With the feeling that the occasional assembling of servants of Christ for united prayer and conference over the Scriptures was calculated to help them in their service, Mr. Dyer began a meeting for this purpose in Yeovil when such conferences were rare, and though comparatively small, it was very much valued. This meeting was held quarterly, and was the precursor of the larger and more extended annual meetings in that town. His faithful and loving service of those days is gratefully remembered both in Yeovil itself and in neighboring towns and villages, and he loved at times to speak of one and another who were brought to God through his reading the Scriptures and speaking at street corners—a work in which he was very diligent as long as he was able to continue it.

Where he remained in any locality he was pre-eminently a pastor. His tenderness in visiting the suffering and the sorrowful was very marked, and his earnestness in seeking the wandering showed how truly he watched for souls, while his readiness—at any cost to himself—to contribute to the breaking down of barriers between the Lord's people gave evidence of his possession of the mind of Christ in no ordinary measure.

During the last months of his brother's illness he lovingly ministered to him, and after his departure to be with Christ, in June 1865, he remained for some time in Kendal, where he was followed in service by Mr.

Henry Groves. After this he spent some years in Exeter, Bath, and Malvern. But, while many assemblies profited much by his visits, his specially fruitful service for twenty-five years was connected with the conferences which have become so much more general. From the beginning of the Leominster conferences "the three Henry's," as they were sometimes called—Henry Heath, Henry Dyer, and Henry Groves—gave themselves in true fellowship to the sustaining of these meetings. In other special meetings of children of God, held annually or half-yearly at Dublin, Belfast, Glasgow, and many other places Mr. Dyer's unique and powerful exposition and application of Scripture caused his presence to be much desired and valued.

A few years back, on account of weakness in his chest and throat, Mr. Dyer was advised to spend the winter in a more suitable climate than the British Isles, and this was doubtless God's way of leading His servant to many countries in the four quarters of the globe, in which scattered and solitary servants of Christ were much refreshed and encouraged by the visits of himself and Mrs. Dyer. He had long done his utmost to help forward efforts for spreading the Gospel in Romish and heathen countries, and these visits enabled him to speak still more forcibly of their deep need, and to exhort Christians of these favored lands to take their share in this great work.

His last long journey was to South Africa, which he reached in February, 1895. There, besides spending a good deal of time in Capetown, Durban, and Johannesburg, he and Mrs. Dyer took long and wearisome journeys to visit believers in out-of-the-way places. In Johannesburg they were shut up during the grave troubles in the early days of 1896, when it seemed probable that the city would be the scene of warfare, and our dear brother's ministry and example greatly strengthened the faith of many there at the time. But, while doubtless the climate helped him in some ways, the strain of all this told upon him, and when they reached England in May he was very feeble; yet it was hoped that rest and care would restore him to health, which hope in some measure was realized.

After the conference at Leominster in June they visited Malvern, where he was taken very ill, and they then went to Bournemouth. In August they left for Barnstaple, stopping en route at Exeter, where he gradually grew weaker, and peacefully fell asleep on the 15th of November 1896, in the seventy-fifth year of his age. Like "David, after he had served his own generation by the will of God, [he] fell on sleep" (Acts 13:36).

Our brother was well known as "a ready scribe" or teacher of the Word of God, the secret being that, like Ezra who is thus described, he "prepared his heart to seek the law of the Lord, and to do it, and to teach [it]." It would of necessity be known only to a smaller circle that, if possible, a more marked characteristic was his intense sympathy, the exercise of which was aided by a remarkable memory. His letters were often very helpful, and he was a most diligent correspondent, but he was also a man of prayer, and, rising early, he habitually sought to remember many at the mercyseat. The fragrance of his memory remains in the hearts of a large number who profited by his ministry.—W.H.B.

Lord Farnham
1803-1884

LORD FARNHAM

SOMERSET RICHARD MAXWELL, the eighth Lord Farnham, was born in Ireland in 1803, and departed to be with Christ in 1884. His family claim descent from Henry III and subsequent kings of England, but he ever rejoiced that he was "adopted into the family of the great King and given to be an heir of God and joint heir of Christ," and "esteemed the reproach of Christ greater riches than the treasures in Egypt," so although he served his country as M.P. for some years, having been converted in early life, he devoted himself to the Lord's work, writing and speaking for Him as opportunity offered. His presence was specially valued at the Dublin Believers' Meetings. Of a self-effacing nature, he did not push himself forward.

He succeeded his brother Henry, who was burnt in a terrible railway disaster at Abergele, Wales, in 1868, and was previously better known as Hon. Somerset Maxwell, under which name he wrote "Sacred Poems on Subjects of Paramount Importance," and also three prose works, "The Wells of Salvation," "Atonement," and "Realities."

Of "The Wells" a reviewer said: "We are drawn on and on by it until the gifted and devout author exhibits the depth and breadth of that wonderful word 'salvation' as it is rarely exhibited. We thank him for his feast of good things;" and a leading minister wrote: "I have found in a few pages of this volume suggestive matter for ten sermons."

As Hon. S. Maxwell he was one of the three trustees of Merrion Hall, Dublin when it was built. Later, in 1874 as Lord Farnham, he convened the meeting in Dublin at which the Irish Evangelization Society was formed. Thus ever with voice and pen and personal effort he strove for the Master.

James W. C. Fegan
1852-1925

J. W. C. FEGAN

JAMES W. C. FEGAN, the Boys' Friend, was born April 17, 1852, and brought up in a Christian home in Southampton. His godly training had much to do with the shaping of his future career. His parents entertained Mr. Darby from time to time both in Southampton and in London, and not long before she died in 1907, Mrs. Fegan told how she remembered Mr. Darby as a clergyman coming down out of his pulpit one Sunday and walking down the street in his black gown to join those who had been in the habit of holding what was virtually a "united communion" or Breaking of Bread each Lord's day.

In 1865 the family removed to London, and on his thirteenth birthday James entered the City of London School, where he won the approval of that prince of schoolmasters, Dr. E. A. Abbot, to whom he afterwards acknowledged his great indebtedness. Lord Oxford and Dr. Garnett were at the school at the same time. In 1869 he entered business with a firm of Colonial brokers in Mincing Lane.

On leaving school he entered a commercial office in the city, but did not care for city life. His intention was to finish with the smoke and din of London as early as possible, and retire to the country, where he could go in for outdoor life and healthful sports which he loved, and in some of which he excelled, but God had a nobler future in store for him.

Destined to rescue others, he must first be rescued "from the power of Satan to God," and this is how it took place, given in his own words: "I opened my Bible at the Epistle to the Romans, and as I read on, got deeper and deeper in realized sinfulness and helplessness, till I came to the twenty-first verse of the third chapter. There God revealed to me how the supreme need of my life that night—fitness for His holy presence—was met in a righteousness of His own providing, 'apart from the law,' 'unto all,' and 'upon all them that believe.' That moment the light of God's salvation flashed into my heart. I looked to His dear Son as my Sinbearer. I trusted God's Word that His righteousness was upon me, a believing sinner. I knew it, because I saw God said it. I lay down that night in 'peace with God.'"

Years afterwards, he added: "I have nothing more now to rest upon for my soul's salvation than I had that night— what my Saviour had done for me on the cross, and what God had said to me in His Word."

Immediately after conversion he commenced to work for his new-found Saviour, and within three days had made his first purchase of tracts, which, however, he was too shy to hand personally to individuals and disposed of them by putting them into letter boxes and under doors.

He was unexpectedly called upon one night by Gawin Kirkham of open-air fame, to say a word at an open-air meeting which he happened to pass. "From that night," he said, "I became an open-air preacher. I used to be a martyr to quinsy before, but I have never had an attack since—grand remedy 'the open-air cure' for body and soul, and church too, for many ailments with which they are liable to be afflicted."

He found his life work, however, in the rescue of poor lads. A visit to Deptford Ragged School gave him his first impulse. The sight stirred his young soul, and he commenced to devote his energies and spare time after business hours to this good work.

His next step was to take a cottage in Deptford on his own responsibility, at a rent of five shillings per week, in which he could have the boys in whom he was interested on week nights and all day on Sundays. S. W. Morris, of Coventry; Thomas H. Morris, of Walthamstow, who died in Africa; Alex. Hopkins and Rice T. Hopkins, who pioneered in Australia; Lord Shaftesbury; Charles Inglis; Joshua Poole; Lieut. Mandeville; and Arthur Austin were helpers in early and later days.

In 1872 he opened his first Boys' Home, with one boy, and by the year 1874 the work had so grown that he was obliged to leave business altogether to devote himself entirely to rescue and evangelistic work. As typical of his methods, and showing that he was the right man for the rescue of boys, we cite a night's adventure.

"After rescuing an Arab named Willie, he confided to me that in two large yards, in which a number of railway vans were drawn up for the night, a lot of boys used to sleep; but they had been frightened out of one yard through a ferocious yard-dog, and had been disturbed, and kicked and cuffed by a fresh watchman, who had not yet fallen into the easygoing laissez-faire habits of his class in the other yard, so that the most venturesome only had just begun to make it their sleeping place again.

"The next night, in company with one of my boys in uniform, I was surveying this latter yard with its boarded fence, perhaps eight feet high, when a policeman on his beat sauntered up and asked if he could be of any service.

"When I told him my quest, he pooh-poohed the idea that any boys could be sleeping out in the vans in that yard at all. 'Watchman always about, sir. Besides, fence too high, couldn't get in, sir.'

"However, I felt perfect confidence in my young informant's good faith, so I said, 'Well, we can soon settle the point. If you don' t mind stooping down, constable, I'll put my handkerchief on your coat not to dirty it, just step on your back, and be over the fence in a jiffy.' He smiled good-humouredly, and, bending down, said, 'All right, sir. Over you go!'

"From the top of the fence I could step easily to the floor of one of the vans, which almost filled the yard. Presently I could hear the heavy breathing of some boys sleeping under a tarpaulin, and every now and then the convulsive gasping for breath of others not so well protected, as they shuddered with cold in their slumbers.

"I carefully woke up the first boy I discovered, so as not to disturb the others, and gently assuring him of my friendly intentions, led him, as I thought, to the point where I had climbed over, but I had slightly miscalculated the direction in the maze of vans, so that, when I looked over the fence, I had to whistle to the constable, and whisper, 'Halloa! Look out, constable, here's one,' as I gently dropped my quarry into his hands.

"I was soon back with another, and another—till the constable was guarding eleven, ranged with official precision, when I dropped over the fence—without having caught a glimpse of the zealous watchman.

"'Eleven of 'em, sir,' said the constable. 'Well, I'm blowed! What next! How did you boys get in? How did you get over that fence? That's what I want to know.' 'Please, sir,' replied one of them on whom his penetrating gaze had lingered, 'We didn't get over—we got under—round the corner,' and he took us to a spot where part of two boards had been broken away quite close to the ground, leaving an aperture about the size of the entrance to a fowlhouse, through which a boy, by lying flat on the ground could just wriggle his way into the yard.

"Very soon I had chartered a four-wheeler—eight boys inside, three on the roof. My boy and I sat with the driver. It was a raw night, and I was cold and weary after having had a busy day's work, followed by a preaching engagement afterwards—but I preferred the outside!

"This was a most encouraging haul, and after I had got eight of these boys settled down in the Home, and had restored three of them to their relations, I fixed upon a night to explore the other yard, and took with me my superintendent and, at his urgent request, my protege, Willie."

In 1889 Mr. Fegan was married to Miss Pope, of Plymouth, who helped greatly in the expansion of the work. After some thirty years spent in the Southwark Home, a move was made to Southwark Street, then to "The Red Lamp," Horseferry Road, Westminster, which was opened in 1913.

One of the greatest ventures related to the buildings at Stony Stratford. It also shows how the Lord overruled for the good of the Homes. Looking around for suitable country premises, one of the Council suggested a building at Stony Stratford. It had been designed as a school for the sons of gentlemen, and built at a cost of £40,000. The school was a failure, the insurance company had foreclosed on the estate, and the buildings were derelict. A "sporting offer" of £4500 was made, and against all expectation, it was accepted, the purchase being made in 1900.

In this orphanage at Stony Stratford, Bucks, boys from the age of eight to fourteen are housed and educated. They go on to a training farm at Goudhurst. Here they are trained in every branch of agriculture and are then sent on to the Receiving Home in Toronto to be placed on farms in Canada. Something like £22,000 has been contributed to the work by the boys themselves who have passed through the Homes and have settled in Canada.

Mr. Fegan's work was not only philanthropic, it was evangelistic. He had ever before him, not merely the care of the body, but the salvation of the soul, and many a one, both young and old, will bless God throughout eternity for having been brought into touch with the gospel of Jesus Christ by the efforts of our departed friend.

In early days his parents removed from New Cross to Downe in Kent. During the summer of 1880 Mr. Fegan took some of his boys for a camping holiday. Before the boys returned to London they visited the home of Charles Darwin, who lived near by, and sang hymns in front of the house. Mr. Darwin expressed his sympathy with the philanthropic work being done, and gave each of the boys sixpence, evoking ringing cheers as they departed. Services were also held in the district in a tent, and when it became too late for tent services, greatly daring, Mr. Fegan asked Mr. Darwin if he would lend him the Reading Room which he had established for the villagers, but which was very slightly frequented. It was, in fact, an old school-room which he rented from Sir John Lubbock (afterwards Lord Avebury) for £10 a year. He lent it with pleasure and, emboldened by his first success, Fegan wrote again, asking if he might have it for a week's Mission as it was so seldom used. He received the following answer from the great naturalist:

"Dear Mr. Fegan,—You ought not to have to write to me for permission to use the Reading Room. You have far more right to it than we have, for your services have done more for the village in a few months than all our efforts for many years. *We have never been able to reclaim a drunkard, but through your services I do not know that there is a drunkard left in the village.* Now may I have the pleasure of handing the Reading Room over to you? Perhaps, if we should want it some night for a special purpose, you will be good enough to let us use it. Yours sincerely, Charles Darwin."

The transfer was made, and in that Reading Room, now called "The Gospel Room," services have been held continuously for half a century.

Mr. Fegan has left the following memoranda on the subject, which may perhaps be given here: "The services I held were attended sometimes by members of the Darwin family, and regularly by members of their household. Indeed, when I had a Mission in Downe, the Darwin family were considerate enough to alter their dinner hour so that their household might attend—but this was characteristic of all who served them. At the services, Parslow, the old family butler, whose name is mentioned both by Huxley and Wallace, was converted to God and brought into church membership, also Mrs. Sales, the housekeeper, was brought into the light, and others."

In "Emma Darwin: a Century of Family Letters, 1792-1896," edited by her daughter, Mrs. Litchfield, there is a letter written to her daughter from Downe in February 1881, in which there is a sentence and a footnote referring to the village blacksmith, a great character.

"Hurrah for Mr. Fegan! Old M. was a notable old drunkard, in the village of Downe, converted through Mr. Fegan, 1881."

Space forbids details of other activities, the "Camping Out" of boys which Mr. Fegan originated, the theatre services, the village missions, the visits to Canada, and the Distributing Home at Toronto, the Home Farm on Canadian lines at Great Howden (Goudhurst), including "Fegan's Orchard," all of which continue as he left them.

But for his strength of character and determination of will, he never could have accomplished what he did, and yet Mr. Fegan had a heart full of loving kindness and tender sympathy, which won for him, not only the esteem, but the affection of the thousands of boys to whom he acted the part of guide, counsellor, and friend.

He passed away on December 9, 1925, at his home in Blantyre Lodge, Goudhurst, Kent, at the age of seventy-three. May the good work carried on by our departed brother be continued to God's glory for years to come.—T.R.

Albert R. Fenn
1832-1896

ALBERT R. FENN

ALBERT ROBERT FENN was a native and freeborn citizen of London. He was born in 1832. His childhood was bright and happy; but various family trials saddened his boyhood and early manhood, which, however, in God's wonderful providence resulted in spiritual blessing. When about eighteen, he entered the Borough Road Training College, with the object of becoming a schoolmaster. Six months of his studies were carried on in Bristol, when he visited "The New Orphan Houses," Ashley Down, and purchased a report of Mr. Muller's work, which he read with interest. He was duly appointed to the charge of a school in Lincolnshire.

On one of his holiday visits home, on coming out of church, he re-marked to his father, "We have been calling ourselves 'miserable sinners' all these years, and I never felt miserable about my sins." The reply was not satisfactory, so he went direct to God, saying, "O God, I am such a fool that I never felt my sins; make me feel them." This prayer was strikingly answered, for he became deeply convicted of sin, and knew not how to obtain deliverance. Many weeks had passed, when one night, after his housekeeper had retired, he determined to make one more long prayer, and a last tremendous effort to gain salvation; if that did not succeed, he would despair. He had not been long on his knees when in the language of the leper, he cried out with all his soul, "Lord, if thou wilt, thou canst make me clean." This was evidently a Spirit-taught cry, and the same Spirit brought the reply with power to his soul, "I will, be thou clean." Rising from his knees full of joy, he searched for the Scripture so power-fully brought to bear upon himself. So great was his happiness that he wanted to die and go to Heaven. The Wesleyans, then on the alert to set young Christians to work, with much persevering persuasion induced him to preach.

Mr. Fenn early determined to make the New Testament his guide, and the words, "Owe no man anything?" called forth his attention. He had purchased his furniture from his predecessor on credit. This he paid off as quickly as possible, and never after purchased anything without the ability to pay immediately. 1 Corinthians 16:2 came next, "Upon the first day of the week let every one of you lay by him in store, as God hath prospered him." The debt being paid, he secured a box for "the Lord's portion." He did not receive money weekly, but separated the proportion he had "purposed in heart" quarterly. Where he had given a shilling before, thinking it enough for a young man with a small salary, now he could give ten, and could show kindness to needy neighbors without grudging. This proportionate giving was continued to the end, only the proportion increased with faith, and as "God prospered." The baptism of believers was the next point under consideration. Naturally he went to the clergyman about it, but got no help from him or anyone else, and the subject was shelved for a time

The character of some of those who partook of the Lord's Supper at church concerned him. He saw from the Scripture that it was an ordinance for disciples, and it was too evident that certain persons who participated monthly were not true Christians. He found out Mr. Andrew Jukes author of "The Law of Offerings" and other works, and consulted him. While entering fully into all he had to say after giving him a most hearty welcome, Mr. Jukes pressed upon him the being first and most concerned about maintaining a good condition of soul, saying, "A good condition is more important than a good position."

Early in his Christian career Mr. Fenn became an abstainer from alcoholic beverages. He had been accustomed to their very moderate use in his father's house, and naturally continued in the same until he concluded they were non-essential, and it became him as a young believer to avoid that which was such a curse to his country. In this course he persevered, finding that even in Spain, where the use at meals of the simple wines of the country is universal, its habitual use could be dispensed with. He had to mourn over two brothers who ruined their health, their businesses, and their families through drink, and he often exhorted Christian parents in England to banish alcohol from their homes.

A reperusal of Mr. Muller's report led Mr. Fenn to desire to have some part in that blessed work, and the way opened for him to take a school in Bristol, supported by Mr. Muller. A Bible Class for young men, and in the summer open-air preaching occupied some of the evenings, and evangelizing in surrounding villages the Saturday afternoons and the Sundays. While thus engaged he was led to decide to give himself wholly to evangelistic and pastoral work. Yatton, Weston-super-Mare, and Kingsbridge successively were spheres and centers, each yielding fruit, and also experiences useful in future service.

He was very frequently led to pray for Austria, Italy, and Spain, that they might be opened to the gospel, so that when Spain was so remarkably opened in 1868, Mr. and Mrs. Fenn offered themselves to God for service in that country, realizing the call of the Lord of the vineyard to go forward. Mr. and Mrs. Henry Payne had been assured of the same call, and in October 1869, they started together.

Six months were spent in Madrid learning the language; then in 1870 Barcelona was visited, where day and night schools were started, Mr. Muller undertaking to pay rents and teachers' salaries. A little church was formed of those who gave evidence of being born again. Then the second Carlist rising occurred, and disturbed the work much. Twice Mr. Fenn narrowly escaped assassination in Barcelona. In 1874 he returned to Madrid, and the history of the twenty-one years' service in the capital will be revealed in that Day. The example of a godly life, and a family of Christian boys with straightforward, truthful, and punctual transactions in all business matters, were constantly influencing people in favor of the Protestants. The education given to the children in the schools, with their daily Bible lessons, the mild and moral discipline in contrast with Romish methods, the improved behavior of the scholars at their homes, induced many parents to come and hear the preaching, and there was almost always a gathering into the mission church, not by dozens, but by twos and threes.

In April 1895, Mr. and Mrs. Fenn said farewell to those among whom they had lived and worked for twenty-one years. Mr. Fenn had had three slight seizures in Spain, and before dawn on July 29th, 1896, he had a severe one in his sleep. On August 3rd he passed away, being conscious almost to the last. Before he lost his speech he said, "I have no other hope but in Christ."—C.F.

Gordon Forlong
1819-1908

GORDON FORLONG

GORDON FORLONG was named after his grandfather General Gordon of Parkhill, Aberdeenshire. He studied law in Edinburgh, practiced as an advocate in Aberdeen, and was then, as he put it, "a very prejudiced young deist." Notwithstanding his deistical opinions nourished by the reading of the principal deistical works of his day, he actually started what he termed "the Bank of Good Character and Skill," the object of which was to help young men of good character to obtain reliable situations.

The young advocate went up to London in 1851, hoping to collect funds for his project. His conversion through this visit is related as follows by Alex. Marshall who spent some time with him in Wanganui in 1901: "Whilst in London he had occasion to call on Mr. Hitchcock, of Hitchcock, Williams & Co., St. Paul's Churchyard. On leaving, Mr. Hitchcock said to him: 'Mr. Forlong, what a pity you are not a Christian!' Unwilling to be drawn into a discussion on religion, he parried Mr. Hitchcock's thrust by saying, 'We Scotch people are well up in the Bible.' 'What a pity you are not a Christian!' was repeated by Mr. Hitchcock. The Scotchman hummed and hawed for a moment, and then said that he did not understand Mr. Hitchcock. 'If you think you are a Christian,' said the earnest soul-winner, 'sit down on that chair and talk to me about Christ.' 'I cannot do that,' replied Mr. Forlong. 'No, I knew you could not,' said the Christian merchant. 'Now, Mr. Forlong, I would be very pleased if you would be kind enough to read a small book that I have.' Mr. Forlong remarked that he read a good deal, and would gladly look over the book that he purposed giving him. The book he received was a copy of a treatise entitled 'The Philosophy of the Plan of Salvation.' As he studied it carefully, he was arrested by the words of Leviticus 17:11: 'It is the blood that maketh an atonement for the soul.' While reading these words he was saved."

Like Saul of Tarsus when it pleased God to reveal His Son to him, "immediately he conferred not with flesh and blood," but straightway preached Christ. His first public testimony was given in 1852. During

the revival years, from 1858 to 1862, he gave himself heart and soul to
evangelistic work in Scotland, often in active association with Brownlow
North and his cousin, John Gordon, of Parkhill. Enormous crowds gathered to hear the two "gentlemen evangelists." Much blessing followed in
Glasgow, Edinburgh, Aberdeen, Perth, Ayr, Dumfries, Montrose, Annan,
and numerous other smaller towns. During these years, as afterwards in
London, Mr. Forlong's Bible-readings were of immense help to the many
young converts of those soul-awakening days, the very memory of which
brings inspiration.

Gordon Forlong began his gospel work in the west of London in 1863
or 1864 preaching at first in the Victoria Hall, Archer Street, Notting Hill,
chiefly used at that time as a theatre, afterwards in Victoria Hall, which
became crowded, and necessitated the building of a large iron building,
which Mr. Forlong named "Talbot Tabernacle." Lord Congleton, the
Howards of Tottenham, and many others of note, were associated with
this movement. With loyal devotion to the Bible, he taught the converts
to receive nothing save from the Word of God.

There is one marked feature about the life and work of this faithful
servant of Christ, which it is of the deepest importance to emphasize at
such a time as the present—this was his careful and ceaseless study of
the Holy Scriptures. He was truly "a man of one Book." Referring to the
earlier days of his converted life, he tells us: "I sat down to my Bible at 10
a.m., and, except for meals, I never rose till 10 at night. This plan I pursued for years. I had not a single commentary in the house."

His preaching was striking and very powerful, bringing comfort and
strength to the people of God, but alarm and terror into the hearts of the
unconverted. Mr. Forlong was a real warrior, and delighted to stand for
the truth of God as he knew it. With him there was no compromise, no
quarter, and no surrender. He made no apologies for the Scripture, but
believed them and proclaimed them fearlessly. On one occasion he remarked that he never felt so much at home as when he was surrounded
with difficulties so that he could not see his way out in any direction.
This was an opportunity for God; and the position just suited his nature.
He had backbone and grit, and possessed principles that he was quite
prepared to fight for; characteristics, we fear, which are sadly lacking in
this present generation.

Mr. Forlong appeared to belong to the past generation rather than
the present, and his right company would have been the Puritans or

Covenanters, who held, honored, and valued the Scriptures, and if needs be, would be prepared to die for them. Although a scholar, he had no sympathy whatever with so-called Higher Criticism, now known as "Modernism."

His health giving way, he emigrated to New Zealand in 1876. He lived long in Wanganui, then at Rongotea, from which place he departed to be with Christ on August 31st, 1908, in his ninetieth year. For some time before his death his mental powers had weakened, but "the end was peace—perfect peace."

Gordon Forlong was mainly instrumental in the conversion of J. R. Caldwell, for many years editor of *The Witness*; Alexander Marshall, author of "God's Way of Salvation;" C. H. Hinman, a well-known worker in New Zealand, and many others.

Mr. Forlong was certainly a remarkable man, and worthy to take first rank as a Bible evangelist and teacher of the Word of God. He stood for the truth of God, and held firmly to all the foundations right to the end.

Samuel Trevor Francis
1834-1926

S. TREVOR FRANCIS

SAMUEL TREVOR FRANCIS was one of the most remarkable of men in that during his lifetime he heard his own songs and tunes sung by congregations, large and small, in many different lands of earth, and even joined in the singing thereof.

His name will linger as a hymn writer for he was the author of "O the Deep, Deep Love of Jesus," "Eternal Love, Oh, Mighty Sea," "Hark! a Gentle Stranger Knocketh," "Call the Weary Home," "Let Me Sing You a Song of Heaven," "Jesus, We Remember Thee," "Home of Light and Glory," "Forward, Christian, Forward," "Revive Us, Lord Jesus," "I am Waiting for the Dawning," "Oh, for the Meeting in the Radiant Air," "Safe to Land, No Shadows Darken," and numerous other pieces, some of which are found in "Believers' Hymn Book," "Hymns of Light and Love," and most other books. His story must be of interest to all.

Born in Cheshunt, Herts in 1834 and taken while a baby to Hull, Francis stayed when five or six with relatives at Cheshunt, who taught him Bible truths. When nine his father, brother, and himself joined the choir of Hull Parish Church. He soon began to produce poetry, and in a few years he had a volume of poems compiled in his own handwriting.

The family having moved to London, he spent twelve months with a doctor in Camberwell. His health failing, he returned to Hull, where a Mr. Akester asked him if "he would like to see a man buried alive," afterwards explaining that it was a baptismal service, conducted by Andrew Jukes, author of "The Law of the Offerings," etc. Thus he was introduced to a company meeting on Scriptural lines, and heard the gospel of man's ruin and God's remedy.

On returning to London one day, as he was crossing Hungerford Bridge, he halted, and a message was borne into his soul, "You *do* believe on the Lord Jesus Christ?" At once he exclaimed, "I *do* believe," and that moment took place the change called "New Birth" (John 3:3), which revolutionized all his after life. Soon after he assembled with a company in Kennington, commenced open-air preaching, which he kept up for seventy-three years in Britain and all other lands he visited.

Through his preaching during the revival of 1859-1860 many were led to the Lord. Later he was one of the most willing helpers of Moody and Sankey in their great London campaign in 1873-1874. At times he did deputy for Mr. Sankey in leading the praise. He also helped Canon Hay Aitken in several of his missions, when many churchmen and others were converted.

Impaired eyesight led to his making a tour of the world so that in his many journeys he was ever cheered by hearing one and another of the words he had penned poured forth in song, in English or other tongues.

Later in life he paid visits to Canada, Australia, Palestine, Egypt, and accompanied R. C. Morgan, the first editor of *The Christian*, to parts of North Africa.

He quietly entered into Rest, from a nursing home, on December 28th, 1925, in the ninety-second year of age.

A collection of his poems which had appeared in *The Revival, The Witness, The Christian, Word and Work, Great Thoughts, Life of Faith,* and many other papers, was produced under the title of "O the Deep, Deep Love of Jesus."

Dr. Thirtle, in *The Christian*, said: "All his poetical work, as well as his spoken word, was permeated by a realization of the love of Christ, and with a heart desire to see the Saviour's face." Now he realizes what he so sweetly penned: —HY.P.

"At Home with the Lord, what joy is this!
To gaze on His face is infinite bliss."

Henry Frowde, M.A.
1841-1927

HENRY FROWDE, M.A.

decorative divider

HENRY FROWDE came of Devonshire stock from which, he liked to recall, Froude, the historian, sprang, and he was a relative of Mortimer Collins. At the age of sixteen (he was born on February 8th, 1841), Mr. Frowde entered the service of the Religious Tract Society, and later became manager of the London Bible Warehouse, in Paternoster Row. Professor Bartholomew Price, afterwards Master of Pembroke, became Secretary to the Delegates at Oxford in 1868. His was one of the greatest names connected with the Press, and his was the inspiration to offer the management of the London Office of the Oxford University Press to Mr. Frowde, who entered upon his new duties in February 1874. In 1874 there were twenty-five Oxford Editions of the Bible current; twenty years later the number had increased to seventy-eight. Now the numbers are larger still.

The first Oxford Bible that Mr. Frowde published was a diamond 24mo, of which two hundred and fifty thousand copies were promptly sold. This was printed on Oxford India paper, which was soon to revolutionize the trade in Bibles, devotional works, volumes of poetry, etc. Some paper had been brought in 1841 from the Far East, just sufficient for the printing of twenty-four copies of a diamond 24mo Bible, not for sale. At Mr. Frowde's suggestion experiments were made to imitate this paper, with the happy results known to all book-lovers. Mr. Frowde rose fully to the occasion with the Oxford Bible for Teachers, which in 1876 had assumed a shape generally resembling its present form. Many millions of this have been sold. Mr. Frowde had a happy knack of creating and anticipating public taste. His Finger Prayer Book is a case in point; within a few weeks one hundred thousand copies were sold. Thus, undoubtedly, the name of Frowde appeared on more volumes than that of any other publisher, and if this be fame, he attained it abundantly. But Mr. Frowde was seen at his best when something out of the ordinary had to be done, when, for example, new editions of the Prayer Book had to be produced at top speed, following changes in the royal succession, or in the titles of the Royal Family, e.g., the present King, who before he became Prince of Wales, appeared in the Prayer Book as Duke of York.

Only those personally acquainted with Mr. Henry Frowde, and they were few, could appreciate his undoubted genius which was of the painstaking order. Mr. Frowde never spared himself, and his energy was extraordinary. His foresight in business was not less remarkable than his courage and organizing ability. It is true that he was fortunate in his stage—the Oxford University Press—and in the spacious times in which he labored. He was the hero of what has been called "the greatest publishing feat on record," the publication within twelve hours of a million copies of the Revised New Testament. That was in 1881, and one cannot imagine the present generation exhibiting such excitement over a Bible (it was noticeable to a less degree when the Revised Bible was published in 1885), nor bookseller selling now, as then, one hundred and fifty thousand copies in one day.

But Mr. Frowde was always proud of the Caxton Memorial Bible (1877). The printing of this began at Oxford at 2:00 a.m.; the sheets were forwarded to London, there folded, rolled, collated, sewn, gilded, bound in Turkey Morocco and delivered at South Kensington before 2:00 p.m., where the four hundredth Anniversary of Caxton was being celebrated. Mr. Gladstone described this "as the climax and consummation of the art of printing."

In 1880, Mr. Frowde was appointed Publisher to the University, taking over the publication of the classical and learned Clarendon Press books. His stupendous success with Bibles, etc., his main interest, made it possible for the delegates to arrange for the publication of works which would have taxed too severely the resources of an ordinary publisher, e.g., the Oxford English Dictionary.

Mr. Frowde was a fine judge of printing and binding, but he was not a professed scholar, much less an author-publisher; yet the honorary degree of M.A. which the University granted him in 1897 was as much appreciated by him as it was deserved. In the meantime Mr. Frowde had opened branches in Edinburgh and Glasgow, to be followed in due course by branches in New York and elsewhere, laying the foundations on which his successor, Mr. Humphrey Milford built to such striking purpose. Mention should be made of the Oxford Poets and other popular series which owe their being to Mr. Frowde and are now famous.

Not demonstrative in his religious views, all his Christian life he was associated with Brethren known as "Exclusive."

In 1913, at the age of seventy-two, Mr. Frowde retired with, as it was thought, but a short time to live. The doctors were wrong however, and the last fourteen years he spent quietly at Croydon, enfeebled, but interested to the last in the great institution to which he had devoted his unique gifts for thirty-nine years. He was called home on March 3rd, 1927.—W.B.C.

F. W. Grant
1834-1902

F. W. GRANT

F. W. GRANT was born in the Putney district of London, on July 25th, 1834. His conversion was occasioned by the reading of the Scriptures himself, and not through the instrumentality of others. He was educated at King's College School with the expectation of securing a position in the War Office. The necessary influence for this failing, he went to Canada when he was twenty-one years of age. At the time he came to Canada the Church of England was opening parishes in the new parts of the country, and he was examined and ordained to the ministry without having taken the regular college course. He left the "systems" on receiving light through the reading of the literature published by so-called "Brethren," and lived for a time in Toronto, afterwards coming to the United States, where he lived in the city of Brooklyn, and then in Plainfield, N.J., till his death. He was the leader in what is known as "the Grant party" in America.

His claim for a permanent place in the hearts of the saints rests—as it really does with any, but more ostensibly than with most—in his identification with the Word of God. Unknown to many in the flesh who have profited by his ministry with little of what may be called popularity, or the magnetism supposed to be so essential in a leader, he is lost sight of in the precious truth which it was his joy to unfold. Those who knew him personally loved him for the worth and Christian nobility of his character, the fruit of God's grace; for that wondrous mind received from Him; and for the simplicity and dignity of a true Christian man. But it is not of these things that we speak, while we would ever seek to walk in the steps of piety and faith wherever seen. We turn rather to that Word to which he held fast, and, in conscious feebleness and dependence, used so constantly. What views of the Word did he give us! What thoughts of Christ! What truths under the guidance of the Holy Spirit! These abide.

He had been for years a diligent student of the Book of Psalms. Not only did their contents attract, but the form in which they were written—their divisions into a Pentateuch, the acrostic form of a number of them, their evident relation one to another in various groups—all these things impressed him with the fact that God had written them upon a distinct plan in which the numerical significance of psalm and group and book had a clearly marked and important place. But if the Psalms were written thus, why not all Scripture? So he went on, till he found the same divine harmony throughout the inspired Word, set to work, and with unbounded patience produced "The Numerical Bible," issued in seven volumes. He was the author of "Facts and Theories as to a Future State," "Genesis in the Light of the New Testament" "Spiritual Law in the Natural World," "The Crowned Christ," and many other valuable books and pamphlets, which have had an extensive circulation on both sides of the Atlantic.

The passion of our brother's life, the desire that consumed him, was to make Christ more precious, to make His Word more loved, more read, more studied. He made a significant utterance shortly before his departure. Sitting propped in his chair, with the Word of God open before him, as was his custom through the days of weary, helpless waiting, he turned to the writer of these lines, and with a depth of pathos, glancing at his Bible, said: "Oh, the Book, *the Book*, the BOOK!" It seemed as though he said: "What a fullness there; how little I have grasped it; how feebly expressed its thoughts." Thus he passed to be "with Christ" at Plainfield, New Jersey, on July 25th, 1902, on his sixty-eighth birthday.—R.

Anthony Norris Groves
1795-1853

ANTHONY NORRIS GROVES

ANTHONY NORRIS GROVES was born at Newton, in Hants in 1795. His father seems to have been a well-to-do and generous man, only a little venturesome in his undertakings, for, besides being part owner of the famous ship "Royal George" that went down "with twice three hundred men," he laid out a fortune in draining land near the sea, which ended in nothing but heavy loss. A factory for refining salt was more successful for a time, but that too proved a failure, through a servant revealing the secret of the process to others.

It is not to be wondered, then, that Mr. A. N. Groves took after his father, and was fond of bold and daring enterprise, only not in the way of "loving his life" and amassing money, but rather in throwing his life and his money away—as it appeared to many.

He was converted at Exeter, through Miss Paget, whose name is well known in connection with the work of Messrs. Chapman and Hake at Barnstaple. As a dentist he had a practice worth £1000 a year, which he relinquished to go out as a missionary.

One of his first "ventures" was to take up a poor mason boy of the name of Kitto, who had fallen from a ladder and lost his hearing. This poor boy, with Mr. Groves' unwearied help, became well known, and after Mr. Groves had taken him to Palestine and the East, he returned to England and wrote his famous "Kitto's Pictorial Bible," was made a D. D., and afterwards pensioned for life by Queen Victoria. This investment alone surely surpassed all his father's ventures.

When Henry Martyn crossed from India to Syria, via Persia, all England was interested to hear of those countries, but Mr. A. N. Groves alone prepared to give himself to carry the gospel to them. No tempting and comfortable steamer lay at London Dock ready to take him and his family on board. A small sailing yacht was lent to him by a friend, and in this the little party sailed for St. Petersburg. Mrs. Groves wrote: "Our party consists of our little family—two boys of nine and ten—Mr. Groves' sister Lydia, Miss Taylor, and Mr. Bathie, a young man who came from Ireland." One of the little boys was called Henry, who afterwards lived to serve the Lord for many years in this country.

Trials and hardships abounded, of course, on the little yacht, and in Russia, travelling through rough, wild country in a carriage with their bag and baggage, hardships without number. Daily they were "in perils of waters, in perils of robbers in perils by the heathen, in perils in the city, in perils in the wilderness," but they were all as nothing compared to what lay before, so that it would appear almost like a waste of time to dwell upon the details of this long overland journey from St. Petersburg to Bagdad.

Bagdad is a city on the ancient river Euphrates, not far from the supposed site of the Garden of Eden, but Mr. Groves found the city to be a dreadful place, the temperature at times so hot that during the day all took refuge in the cellars under the house, and by night all slept—or tried to sleep—on the roof of the house. Nearly all the inhabitants were fanatical Mohammedans, who delighted in murder, war, and robbery. Little wonder that he found there too the dreadful plague, carrying off thousands of victims; and this with "war," "famine," and "flood" was the sum of the history of his three years' stay in that dreadful place. The most distressing and touching part of it all was when his brave and noble-hearted wife, Mary Groves, died of the dreadful plague. Family after family had been swept out of existence in the district all round about where the missionaries lived, and still the "plague came not nigh their dwelling," but when the storm seemed to have passed over, and light, and hope, and the dawn of a new day appeared to be breaking upon them, Mr. Groves makes this entry in his diary: "The Lord has this day manifested that the disease of my dear wife is the plague, and of a very dangerous type, so that our hearts are prostrate in the Lord's presence....It is indeed an awful moment, yet my dear wife's faith triumphs. The difference between a child of God and a worldling is not in death, but in the hope the one has in Jesus, while the other is without hope and without God in the world."

From Bagdad, Mr. Groves and family went on to India, and finding very many open doors for the gospel there he decided. "as much as in him lay," to preach Christ to the heathen millions of this most populous country in the whole of Asia.

After seeing the need in many parts of India, Mr. Groves returned to

England, and took back to India Messrs. Bowden and Beer, both of Barnstaple. These two missionaries settled in the Godavari district, and began work somewhat to the south of the Delta proper. For twenty years they toiled on almost alone, and with little encouragement, but others were raised up to join them—Mr. Heelis, Mr. M'Crae, Mr. Miles, Miss Taylor, and others—and now the work has spread into the Delta and over a wide area.

Mr. Groves, in those early days, was blessed to a native, J. C. Aroolappan, who travelled about among the villages some distance to the south of Godavari. Many through him believed, and churches were formed, but the work was not known to Christians in this country. Aroolappan died, and troubles came to the little assemblies. Some good missionaries wished to help them and join them to the Church of England, but the simple people could not fall into their ways. A Baptist society next tried to befriend the few native churches, but hitches occurred. They had been taught differently by Aroolappan, and when Mr. Handley Bird visited them a few years later, they received him with open arms. Can we imagine the joy of our brother in seeing in those many churches the fruit of Mr. A. N. Groves' small beginnings sixty years before?

Mr. Groves applied all his inherited ingenuity in seeking to improve the lot of the native Christians in India. Silk farming, coffee planting, and other industries were tried, involving the outlay of much of his own money, with but little success.

But years of anxiety and privation had told heavily upon him, and he was forced to return to England. He fell asleep at Bristol in May 1853, and the first number of *The Missionary Reporter* was published in July of the same year. *The Missionary Echo,* afterwards *Echoes of Service,* has followed the work of *The Missionary Reporter,* so that as we from time to time read reports of work for the Lord in India, China, Africa, and many other distant places, we are forced to remember the hero who, under God, laid the foundation of much of the missionary interest happily found throughout our assemblies.

Henry Groves
1818-1890

HENRY GROVES

HENRY GROVES, the eldest son of Anthony Norris Groves, missionary to Persia and India, was born at Exeter in November 1818. Together with his brother Frank, who was a little more than a year his junior, he had for his earliest teacher Mr. Henry Craik, afterwards so well known in connection with Mr. George Muller of Bristol, and was linked up with Lord Congleton, Dr. Cronin, and other devoted servants of God.

He was ten years old, and his brother was nine, when they accompanied their parents and John Kitto through St. Petersburg and Moscow to Bagdad. They commenced their travels in May 1829, and continued them till December. The fatigue and danger of that long journey early taught the boys to endure hardness; but those travelling experiences were as nothing to what lay in store for them at their destination. In April of the following year, the plague broke out in Bagdad, and the mortality often considerably exceeded a thousand a day. Fifty unburied corpses might be seen during a walk of five hundred yards, and the wails of naked and starving children who roamed the streets were heart-breaking. When this calamity was at its height, an inundation of the river took place. Upwards of five thousand houses crumbled, and in many cases crushed the inhabitants, but a small strip of rising ground at the end of their street saved the missionary's family from the water entering their dwelling. Mrs. Groves had died of the plague, and the stricken household presently found themselves, after the subsiding of the water, threatened with another danger—the doomed city was besieged by a Turkish army. Bullets were constantly flying overhead as they slept on the house-top, and bands of robbers broke once and again into the house, carrying off whatever they chose. During all this time the necessities of life had risen to an enormous price, and the food so dearly purchased had to be eaten at night and in the cellar to prevent its falling into the hands of the lawless and starving mob.

At length deliverance came, and also fresh missionaries from England. The boys' deaf tutor (afterwards the celebrated Dr. Kitto) returned home, and the friends who arrived took up their education to some extent, but so terrible were the experiences of those days that Mr. H. Groves said that after leaving England he cannot remember that he was a boy at all.

The brothers continued in Persia till 1834, when they went to India and joined their father in heroic efforts to establish a self-supporting mission. Converts among the Hindus becoming outcasts, it was thought by farming, silk, and other industries to give them some means of livelihood. Partly through inexperience, but more on account of the impossibility of producing profitably alongside of native labor, these schemes failed one after another.

After ten or twelve years Mr. A. N. Groves' health broke down, and he came to England in 1852, and died in the house of his brother-in-law, Mr. George Muller. Meanwhile Mr. Henry and Mr. Frank Groves had been appointed jointly superintendents of a sugar-refining factory in south India. For many years this prospered very fairly in their hands but, after 1857 (the year of the mutiny), the price of the raw material rose to double what it had previously been, and was no longer remunerative.

During that year Mr. H. Groves had visited England, Ireland, and America, and was deeply impressed with the work of revival which he witnessed. He longed to be free to give himself wholly to the work of the gospel, and the way for this was made plain in 1862, when the Indian factory was sold to a native firm without occasioning loss to the original shareholders.

The following year found Mr. Groves commencing the service on which he had set his heart in Bristol. In 1868 he paid a visit to Kendal, for a few weeks he thought, but here he settled, and though constantly travelling over the United Kingdom in the service of the gospel during the following three-and-twenty years it never ceased to be his home. In May 1890, a chill he took brought to light a serious state of vital organs in the form of a sudden paralytic weakness. After some fourteen months' illness he fell asleep on Thursday afternoon, July 2nd, 1891.

In the midst of family life, and in what he still could do of pastoral and teaching work, did he "finish his course," as he had, by God's grace and by God's special calling to public ministry, in early life begun it.

Count Guicciardini
1808-1851

COUNT GUICCIARDINI

C OUNT GUICCIARDINI was born on the 21st of July 1808. He received the highest possible education, and had as one of his fellow-students the future Grand Duke of Tuscany. When the young Count had reached his twenty-fifth year a temporal wave of progress caused Leopold II to patronize a higher standard of education than had prevailed in Tuscany, and he called his friend Count Guicciardini to undertake the organization of a better educational system. It was no easy task. The young nobleman soon found that he would require to make a new class of teachers, and give special attention to the moral aspect of the art of teaching. Books on the subject were lacking, and Count Guicciardini was in quest of a suitable textbook when one day he met a well-known literary friend. He asked him whether he could recommend any good, moral book on the art of teaching. After some reflection his friend exclaimed, "Take the Gospel." The abrupt recommendation did not remain unheeded by the Count, who examined his valuable library, but could find no copy of the Bible in Italian. He had, however, the Latin Vulgate, and he began to read it as a fit source from which at least he might translate some helpful matter on the subject of his quest. With this object in view he read on day by day.

While Count Guicciardini was thus perusing the Vulgate Bible he began to discover several serious points of divergence between it and his Church, and his educational pursuits became lost in his more spiritual researches. It was in this frame of mind that one day he was about to go out for a walk. He was descending the magnificent staircase of his palace when he observed the caretaker at the bottom reading a book, which was hurriedly hidden on the approach of the nobleman. Filled with curiosity almost amounting to suspicion, the Count informed his servant that he had noticed his surprising action, and asked for an explanation. Begging his master to keep the matter secret, he confessed that the mysterious volume was the Italian Bible, and he handed it to the Count. "But do you understand it?" "Yes, some of it," replied the dependent "Well, take it, and come upstairs with me."

Count Guicciardini and his caretaker were soon shut in a room in the palace reading and meditating together upon God's Word, and this continued daily for some time.

While the truth of the gospel was maturing in his mind, one day Count Guicciardini was saying his creed, and came to the profession of his belief in "the communion of saints." He suddenly stopped, and asked himself the question: "Who are these saints in whose communion I believe? They must be saints on earth." Before many days passed Count Guicciardini found his all in Christ, and his conversion and testimony showed this. He rejoiced to know that Christ was made unto him wisdom from God, and righteousness, and sanctification, and redemption; and now he gloried no longer in his own righteousness, but in the Lord (1 Corinthians 1:30-31).

The Grand Duke was now completely under the power of the Jesuits, and he consented to a determined and definite effort proposed by his government for the suppression of any evangelical work or worship in Tuscany. In January 1851, the services held in Italian in the Swiss Church were forbidden, and one hundred and twenty persons who had attended them received notice, under the penalty of imprisonment, to cease frequenting these or any other public or private evangelical meeting, while a special prohibition was forwarded to Count Guicciardini.

With all the nobility of his character the Count resented this tyrannical action of the Tuscan Government, and informed the authorities that if they insisted upon it he would feel obliged to go into voluntary exile. This sacrifice he proved ready to make. On the 3rd of May 1851, what he thought was the eve of his departure, he wrote to his few Christian brethren a letter which ranks as one of the noblest documents in the history of the Italian testimony. (The full text of the letter addressed to his brethren by the Count with the testimony of ten others will be found in "Heroes of the Faith in Modern Italy".)

On the evening of the 7th of May, Count Guicciardini went to the house of Fedele Betti, a Christian brother, to say good-bye. He was accompanied by a young Italian whom he had met on the way. Four other friends had arrived shortly before. The little gathering was therefore casual and informal, and in fact the host was the only one of the seven who had known all the others. The subject, however, soon turned upon the Count's approaching and regretted departure. Signor Betti proposed that before separating they should read the fifteenth chapter of John. Each verse afforded a subject for a brief and comforting comment, and while the simple little meeting was thus peacefully proceeding the bell rang, and seven gendarmes entered and arrested the seven disciples of Christ. At half-past eleven o'clock that night they were taken to the historical Bargello prison and all put in the same damp and dirty cell, in which however they were able to enjoy one comfort, the continuation of their happy meditation of John 15, for Count Guicciardini had a small New Testament in his pocket. The seven disciples were condemned to six months' imprisonment in different parts of Tuscany. Through diplomatic and personal influence, in a short time the sentence of imprisonment was so modified that Count Guicciardini and three of his fellow-prisoners were able to start for Genoa and Turin.

He finally reached Britain, where a warm welcome awaited him by the noblest Christians in the country. His temporary exile in England was a link in God's golden chain. Here he found young Signor Rossetti, and led him to Christ. Returning later to his native country, on which the day of liberty was dawning, he spent his time and means in the spread of the gospel. He visited his dear Italian brethren in their meetings and homes, and never allowed his social position to form a barrier in Christian fellowship. From the palace which bears his name he peacefully passed to be with the Lord for whom he had suffered the loss of all things, and counted them but as naught that he might gain Christ.

"By faith" he made the choice of the faithful, "choosing rather to suffer affliction with the people of God, than to enjoy the pleasures of sin for a season...for he had respect unto the recompense of the reward" (Hebrews 11:25,26).—J.S.A.

Captain Percy Francis Hall
1804-1884

CAPTAIN PERCY FRANCIS HALL, R.N.

———◦◦◦◦———

CAPTAIN PERCY FRANCIS HALL, R.N.., was one of the earliest Brethren at Plymouth, a teacher and preacher of the Word. In the year 1830 J. N. Darby went to Oxford, where he got in touch with G. V. Wigram, F. Newman, and B. W. Newton. Invited by Mr. Newton to Plymouth, he found Captain Hall in the house on his arrival, was introduced to him as one actively engaged in preaching in the villages.

The Captain had attained to the rank of Commander in the Navy, but he resigned his commission for conscience sake, although he could ill afford the loss of his pay. He set forth his reasons in a tract entitled "Discipleship," which was favored by some and condemned by others although none questioned his sincerity and devotedness. He soon became a great friend of J. N. Darby, H. W. Soltau, J. L. Harris, G. V. Wigram, and other "chief men," and was often quoted in a manuscript Diary which was long treasured as a memento of these wonderful early days.

Plymouth being the center of an assembly which at one time numbered over one thousand, attracted the ministry of the English leaders from other towns. As they steadfastly refused to accept any distinctive designation, it was almost inevitable that the communities should become known as Plymouth Brethren—"*Brethren*" being the Scriptural term in most frequent use, and "*Plymouth*" being the center of the largest gathering and most of the leaders. Finally the title became general, and is today world-wide, although then and now persistently repudiated as a nickname. The title "brethren," "Christians," "believers," "saints," etc., being used not in a sectarian or divisional sense, but as the names sanctioned by Scripture and embracive of all "children of God by faith in Christ Jesus" (Galatians 3:26).

Prophetic meetings were commenced in 1827 at Albury Park, Surrey. Lady Powerscourt who attended them was so delighted that she established similar gatherings at Powerscourt House, the lovely country seat, near Bray, County Wicklow. At these meetings Captain Hall took part along with brethren Darby, Bellett, and others. He was also one of the principal speakers at the special gathering of guides at Bath in 1848. He intervened in the interests of peace in the "Bethesda" trouble of 1849, and eventually adopted anything but "exclusive ground," for in his "Unity: a Fragment and a Dialogue," he declares, "I am satisfied that any Christian of the sundry parties around us...could say with a bold and free spirit, I meet with my fellow Christians in the name of the Lord Jesus Christ."

Of a very independent temperament the Captain did nothing by halves. He sold all his valuable possessions, and had everything in common with the poorer brethren (Acts 4:32). He had been a "dandy" in his unregenerate days and latterly, as the photo indicates, used to ruffle his hair and rumple his linen cuffs to show that he had no further love for such "vanity"! He closed his earthly course at Weston-super-Mare, on October 11th, 1884, at the advanced age of eighty, and entered upon the Heavenly, where unity in its highest and fullest sense will be unbroken and names unknown, except "the Name which is above every name."

General John S. Halliday
1822-1917

GENERAL HALLIDAY

GENERAL HALLIDAY belonged to an old Dumfriesshire family. He was the son of Mr. Thomas Halliday, of Ewell, Surrey, and was born on the 9th of May, 1822. His grandfather was Dr. Matthew Halliday, physician at the Imperial Court of St. Petersburg during the latter part of the reign of Catherine the Great.

He entered the military service of the Hon. East India Company as a cadet, and joined the 12th Madras Native Infantry at the age of sixteen. He served in various stations in the Madras Presidency until he was appointed to the Mysore Commission for the civil administration of Mysore. He was married in 1845 to his cousin, Miss Lucy Cotton, daughter of Mr. and Mrs. Cotton of Petrograd, being then a decided Christian. He became acquainted at Cannonore with Samuel Hebich, Christian missionary well known to Anthony Norris Groves, then labouring at Chittoor, from whom he derived much spiritual help.

On becoming Lieutenant-Colonel he reverted to military duty, commanding his old regiment in various stations in India and Burma, until he was promoted to Regimental Colonel in 1876, when he took up his residence in England, and lived for more than thirty years in Lee. He was promoted to the rank of full General in 1888, and was the Senior General of the Indian Army. He was an accomplished linguist, having a thorough knowledge of French, German, and Hindustani; was well acquainted with Hebrew and Greek in Bible study, and possessed an extensive knowledge of various subjects connected with science, art, and literature; and was also gifted in water color drawing.

Yet with all this he was an earnest and faithful witness for the Lord Jesus Christ, exhibiting great humility of spirit, and ever ready to company with fellow-believers regardless of social position, and was for very many years in fellowship with believers meeting at the Gospel Hall, Loampit Vale, Lewisham, by whom he was greatly beloved.

If there was one grace that shone out in his life more than another it was that of humility, and in this he was a faithful follower of Him who "humbled Himself." On Lord's Day morning, February 4th, 1917, at his residence, Church Terrace, Lee, Kent, in his ninety-fifth year, beloved General John S. Halliday departed to be with Christ.

John Hambleton
1820-1889

JOHN HAMBLETON

AMONG GIFTED EVANGELISTS whom God has raised up during the last forty years are the names of three remarkable and unique men, viz., Richard Weaver, Henry Moorhouse, and John Hambleton. The trio were well known to each other and frequently labored together—especially in their earlier days of service—in various parts of the great harvest-field. God greatly owned and blessed their labors, and it is not too much to say that thousands of sinners were saved, and thousands of saints were helped, through their ministry. During the first twenty years of Richard Weaver's preaching he was more used in conversions than any modern preacher. Mr. D. L. Moody was never ashamed to tell of the blessing he received through Harry Moorhouse's first visit to Chicago. Hambleton was not so well known as Weaver or Moorhouse, but in his own line of things he was none the less gifted. These three servants of Christ signally illustrate the truth of Romans 12:6: "Having then gifts differing."

John Hambleton was born and brought up in Liverpool. He had the unspeakable advantage of a godly mother, who early taught him to reverence the sacred Scriptures. His mother lived what she taught, and her consistent, Christ-like life was one of the links in the chain of his conversion. When a mere lad he disobeyed his mother, was drawn into sin and vice through evil companions and, at the age of sixteen, ran away from home and entered the theatrical profession. For sixteen years he travelled in Australia and America as an actor, theatrical manager, adventurer, and gold digger. Though mixing with infidels and scoffers and hearing their objections to and tirades against the Bible, he never doubted that the Scriptures were God's revelation to man. "In my own heart," he wrote, "I believed every doctrine of the Christian faith, though I was a rejecter of Christ and a neglecter of God's great salvation."

When the news of the discovery of gold in California reached him, he determined to leave Australia and go to the diggings. After reaching San Francisco, he set out for the gold fields. When in California he had many narrow escapes from death. Once his grave was dug, his companions thinking that his end had come. As he lay under a tree at the point of death, he became thoroughly aroused to a sense of his guilt and danger. Writing of that solemn occasion, he said: "As I lay upon that grassy couch, apparently upon the eve of death, my soul trembled as conscience suggested the question, 'Where will you go when the end comes?' Then the scenes of my past life rushed with fearful imagery through my mind. I thought of the home I had deserted, of my mother's heart I had broken, the talents I had abused, the grace of God which I had despised and rejected. And then I thought of the just retribution of the wicked and of the awful eternity, when impenitent sinners such as myself shall reap 'for ever and ever' what they have sown in time."

One would think that on recovering from such an illness he would become a new creature. Alas! it was not so. Through a singular coincidence he determined to return to the Old Country. After an absence of seventeen years from England, he landed in Liverpool on April 1st, 1857, and at once went in quest of his relations. After a good deal of difficulty he found his sisters, his mother having died some years previously. Before her departure to be with Christ she asked her daughter to take a sheet of paper and write upon it a declaration of her faith, viz., that God would save her son John and bring him back to Liverpool, that he might become a gospel preacher! He began to try and be "religious," but found it to be a very toilsome affair.

On obtaining peace with God he longed to be the means of winning souls to Christ, and began to witness for Him in the open air. After he had served an apprenticeship in open air work, he and Edward Usher hired the Teutonic Hall for gospel services. A very blessed work was done there, hundreds of persons professing conversion. Eventually he and a fellow-laborer, with a shilling between them, went out in the name of the Lord to herald the message of mercy in the large towns of Lancashire. In simple dependence upon God, unsent by sect, society, committee, or party, they went forth to preach Christ to the perishing. Henry Moorhouse afterwards joined Hambleton, and they visited fairs, races, shows, etc., distributing tracts and proclaiming to the masses ruin by the fall, redemption by the blood, and regeneration by the Holy Spirit.

John Hambleton was indeed a "burning and shining light," and during the forty years of his Christian career he lived for God and eternity. He was a bold and fearless ambassador of Christ, who sought to be guided solely by the Scriptures, and was willing to do God's will at all costs.

While faithful in carrying out what he saw in the Word of God, he did not make his light a standard of Christian fellowship. He loved all God's people, and could honestly say, "We know that we have passed from death unto life, because we love the brethren." It might be said of him as of John Knox: "He feared not the face of man," and refused to be led by any party or sect. Possessed of a magnificent voice, great command of language, and readiness of speech, he excelled as an open-air preacher.

When preaching at a race course, a number of "lewd fellows of the baser sort," led on by a Romanist, gave him great trouble. Hambleton told the ringleader that he would allow him to speak if he would answer one question. Persuaded by his comrades to accept the invitation, he stepped on the platform, whereupon Hambleton asked in solemn tones: "Why did Cain murder his brother Abel?" There was something in the question that laid hold of the man, for he rushed from the platform a convicted sinner, and the questioner was enabled to expound to the audience salvation through the precious blood of Christ.

When preaching at a fair, some show people, who rightly thought that their craft was endangered by the preaching and the praying, sent their clown with painted face and dressed up in fantastic attire, to ridicule the work and give away their handbills. Hambleton, ever ready, shouted, "Look here, friends, and you will see two fools, one for the Devil and the other for Christ. God made man in His own image, but look at that poor fellow there and see what Satan has done for him. By God's grace I am a free and a happy man serving a good Master, but that poor man is only serving the Devil, and will only get the wages of sin which is death. Yet the God he mocks sent His only Son to die on the cross to save sinners from eternal punishment, and I am here to declare the glad tidings that there is forgiveness of sin for all who believe in His most blessed name." The clown hurried away from the scene of his confusion, but later on in the day sought an interview with the "converted actor," and asked him to pray for him, declaring that he was miserable and wretched in his quiet moments.

For thirty years Hambleton labored throughout England, Scotland, and Ireland, in the open air, in tents, halls, chapels, theatres, circuses, etc. For a time he also engaged in Bible carriage work, as well as lecturing throughout the country on a large chart which he called "Ezekiel's Tile." The last ten years of his life were spent in Australia, where he toiled on until he obtained his home-call on December 8th, 1889 at age sixty-nine.—A.M.

James L. Harris
1793-1877

J. L. HARRIS

JAMES LAMPDEN HARRIS was born February 13th, 1793. He was one of a very large family, the fifth son of John Harris, of Radford, near Plymouth. After receiving his education and being duly ordained in the Church of England, he became perpetual curate of Plymstock. In 1832, through obtaining a fuller knowledge of the Scriptures, he gave up his living and associated himself with believers meeting in simplicity. His presence greatly strengthened the infant community whose first organ, *The Christian Witness*, was started under his editorship in 1834. *The Witness* of to-day follows more on the lines of the original than any other magazine, and regularly inserts valuable papers written in these early days.

J. L. Harris was certainly one of the chief men among early brethren as to his individual and assembly connections with B. W. Newton and J. N. Darby, as to his active part in the subsequent troublous times, and as to his writings, which fortunately remain when the sorrows are gone and continue to breathe the fragrance of the spirit of Christ possessed by their author.

For many years J. L. Harris held weekly Bible readings at Plymouth which were well attended by all classes. He was a good scholar, and had a large Hebrew Bible from which he used to translate freely. His opinion on difficult portions of the Word was frequently asked for and valued by leading students and others.

In the troubles of 1847 and succeeding years Mr. Harris was one of the leaders involved. A manuscript, purporting to be the notes of a lecture by Newton on the Sixth Psalm, lent to Mrs. J. L. Harris, was the start of the Newton Controversy, which has caused more discussion, used up more printers' ink and, with its assertions and withdrawals, reassertions and explanations, is more difficult to comprehend today than any other subject or dispute connected with the Brethren movement. Happily generations have come and gone, and "What saith the scripture?" (Romans 4:3) is becoming more and more the only "question" at issue.

Mr. Harris was one of the barriers to the strong inclinations toward clericalism in Plymouth. A settled order of ministry had prevailed at Plymouth, Mr. Newton and Mr. Harris ministering alternately. People "knew when it was Newton's day and when it was Harris' day, and took their measures for going accordingly."

In view of the developments since 1840, the following remark by Dr. Tregelles is interesting. "Mr. Darby requested Mr. Newton to sit where he could conveniently take the oversight of ministry, and that he would hinder that which was manifestly unprofitable and unedifying," and that on "one occasion Mr. Newton had in the assembly to stop ministry which was manifestly improper, with Mr. Darby and Mr. Wigram's presence and full concurrence."

As suggested, J.L.H. was a prolific writer, and his books "On Worship," "Law and Grace," "Precious Truth," "The Priesthood and the Cross of Christ," among others, are most valuable. He was a deep prophetic student, and took a leading part in the meeting held in the Freemasons' Hall, London, in May 1864.

As his second wife, Mr. Harris married the daughter of the celebrated Legh Richmond, author of "The Dairyman's Daughter," which has been signally owned of God. They lived at Plymstock for many years, then at Plympton, and then removed to Weston-super-Mare at the earnest entreaty of his old friend, Captain Percy Hall. Here he died on October 9th, 1877, leaving behind a name which will be revered as long as his writings are read.—C.E.F.

James E. Hawkins
1843-1918

JAMES E. HAWKINS

J AMES ELLIS HAWKINS was born in Bitterley, Salop in 1843. His parents were godly Congregationalists though afterwards they owned only the true gathering center, "my name" (Matthew 18:20), and built a hall at Orleton, Hampshire, for worship and ministry on Scriptural lines. His first soul concern was induced by hearing an address on "The Lord's Coming," by William Yapp. When fourteen years of age George Lawrence, a well-known worker in Britain and Spain, said to him, "James, you are quick at figures, here is a sum for you, 'What shall it profit a man if he shall gain the whole world and lose his own soul?'" The impression never left him, till four years later when Mr. Lawrence was preaching in the town he had the joy of pointing the sin-burdened soul to the Lamb of God, closing with 1 John 5:13. Thus the light dawned on April 5, 1861, and from that day till the end of his course, fifty-seven years after, he rejoiced in the possession of eternal life. The 1859 revival spirit, then so prevalent, also left its impress on his long and active career. Following the New Testament order, the young convert and others were baptized in the river flowing by the side of the town on April 28.

On April 30, on the invitation of William Yapp, he left for London to assist in the Book and Tract Depot at 70 Welbeck Street. Afterwards the business was changed to Yapp & Hawkins; the "Clapton," "Iron Room," and other series of booklets being issued at this time. In 1866 he married Clara Elizabeth Hunt, who proved to be a true helpmeet for forty-seven years, and an indefatigable worker in connection with *Golden Grain Almanac*.

In 1867 William Yapp retired, and James E. Hawkins carried on a prosperous business in Baker Street and Paternoster Row for many years. He introduced the "Mildmay Cards" and other famous series. His series of beautiful chromo booklets, including "Songs of the Dawn", "The Homeward Journey", "The Garment of Praise", "The Master's Presence", etc., have never been equaled for their chasteness and superb coloring, and may rightly be treasured by their fortunate possessors. Many volumes of spiritual truth valued today first bore the imprint of J. E. Hawkins. William

Lincoln's Expositions of Hebrews, John, and Revelation; Arthur Pridham's Expositions of Romans, Ephesians, Philippians, and other books; Denham Smith's "Brides of Scripture", "Gospel in Hosea", "Prophet of Glory", and "Papers for the Present Time"; D. L. Moody's "Wondrous Love", "The Great Salvation", etc.; and many others might be named.

For a number of years Mr. Hawkins acted as London publisher of *The Witness, The Golden Lamp* (long ago discontinued), *Missionary Echo* (now issued as *Echoes of Service*), and other monthlies.

A unique feature which might well be revived in what to visitors is often lonely London was a monthly drawing-room meeting at 36 Baker Street, which drew together well-known teachers and workers from all parts of the kingdom. Brethren J. G. M'Vicker, T. B. Miller, R. J. Mahony, F. C. Bland, John Hambleton, Harry Moorhouse, Dr. Neatby, Lord Carrick, and others whose names are revered, frequently took part. The meetings were times of refreshing from on high.

As an author, Mr. Hawkins produced "Short Papers on Prophecy" and "Lectures on the Tabernacle," both of which sold extensively and were helpful to young Christians. Also many smaller booklets, including "The Blood of the Lamb," which circulated by thousands, and was used to many conversions.

As an editor, he commenced *The Gospel Watchman*, a penny gospel magazine, in 1869 and continued it, with varying circulation, till 1895. His best known work is the *Golden Grain Diary*, which he brought out in 1868. It reached a circulation of twenty thousand the first year, has attained to seventy thousand some years, and is better known and valued today than ever before. Messrs. Pickering & Inglis acquired the rights a few years before his death, and continue to issue on the same lines as Mr. Hawkins did successfully for over fifty years.

During a visit to their home, Mr. and Mrs. Hawkins showed the writer their "treasure book" containing the signatures of hundreds of well-known Christian workers commending the *Golden Grain Almanac*. The familiar calligraphy of C. H. Spurgeon, D. L. Moody, F. R. Havergal, George Muller, Lord Congleton, Henry Moorhouse Dr. Pierson, Henry Dyer, Henry Groves, F. C. Bland, Earl Carrick, and others were readily distinguishable, amidst whole pages of names less known or less readily deciphered.

As a poet he produced both hymns and spiritual songs of no mean order. Had he had no other gifts he might well have been remembered by the initials J.E.H. after many a sweet and cheering verse.

As a speaker, Mr. Hawkins had considerable gift, and for sixty years his voice was heard in many parts of the country. He took the Oxford Music Hall, London, and had as helper, John Hambleton, "the converted actor." Great blessing resulted. His last service was at Ickenham three months before his home-call.

Many trials in business beset him in later years, but he kept to the old lines; and his forte in the selection of texts, arrangement of verses and chaste get-up of booklets, continued unabated for more than half a century. He passed quietly away on Sunday afternoon, December 22, 1918, and was laid to rest at Harrow awaiting the time when from the righteous Judge "each man shall have his praise from God" (1 Corinthians 4:4,5, R.V.).

As "members of Christ and stewards of the mysteries of God", may we seek grace to commence well, continue well, and conclude well, whether our allotted span be brief or prolonged.—HY.P.

Henry Heath
1815-1900

HENRY HEATH

MOST BRETHREN HAVE heard frequent references to "the three Henrys," a trio of Bible students and expositors whose helpful ministry of the Word is gratefully remembered. They were Henry Groves of Kendal, Henry Dyer of Bath, and Henry Heath of Woolpit, Suffolk.

Henry Heath was born at Teignmouth on 16th November 1815. About the year 1839 in the village of Tawstock, Mr. Heath was engaged as the schoolmaster in the school connected to the Tawstock church. During this time he was studying for holy orders, and while thus engaged he was introduced to Mr. R. C. Chapman of Barnstaple, who gave him an invitation to the Bible readings held in No. 9, New Buildings, every Thursday. To these readings Mr. Heath regularly came when his duties at the school were finished. He was greatly interested in the simple way of expounding the Word. The power of the Holy Spirit in unfolding the mind of Christ, through the Scriptures, so affected him that he became more and more exercised about his own position and purpose in life.

On one occasion Mr. Heath mentioned to a friend that the Scriptures had become a new power to his own soul and he was learning that the Bible was a living book, not only a theological work fitting his mental powers for study in Hebrew and Greek, but that it was the inspired Word of God, given to the church of God in all ages.

Then came the exercise of soul about obedience to the revealed will of God. After much waiting upon God in prayer he gave up his study for holy orders and obeyed the voice of God, following Abraham of old in the pathway of unreserved obedience to the Scriptures of truth (John 8:32).

The frequent visits to Mr. Chapman's humble dwelling and the simple manner of life with the deep, spiritual trust in the Scriptures followed out day by day by this man of God, caused such deep searchings of heart in Henry Heath that he said his path was the only way of peace, "obedience to the revealed will of God given in the Scriptures of truth. "This was the beginning of a lifelong friendship, and from that time (to quote

Mr. Chapman's words) "there was always Henry Heath's room at our house ready for him when he came."

About 1848 he went to Hackney, where he was for twenty-one years, and from there to Woolpit, a remote village in the heart of Suffolk six miles from a town and two from a railway station. Here this faithful servant of the Lord spent nearly thirty years of his life, putting into practice the text that came so forcibly to him many years previous: "Seekest thou great things for thyself? seek them not" (Jeremiah 45:5).

There, hidden away from the multitude, he was unseen and unheard by the many, yet through the power of the Holy Spirit was a great blessing to those with whom he came in contact. People from fifteen different villages (some of them six miles away) would come regularly to Woolpit room to have the privilege of sitting under his ministry and go away refreshed and strengthened. This room built on a squatters' claim, accommodated about three hundred, and had a residence, stables for several horses, and a graveyard in which lie many of His own.

In the year 1900 the call came for higher service in the presence of the Lord whom he had loved so long and served so devoutly. His name is revered still, not so much on account of the man who bore the name, but that blessed One of whom he spake.—C.J.H.

T. Shuldham Henry
?-1894

T. SHULDHAM HENRY

━━◇◇◇◇◇━━

T. SHULDHAM HENRY, M.A., LL.B., was the only son of the late P. Shuldham Henry, D.D., President of Queen's College, Belfast. Brought up for the English Bar, he relinquished his profession when he was converted to God in the year 1860. As he himself used to say, he "gave up law for grace." He was a care-free, thoughtless man of the world, wholly engrossed in its pleasures.

A much loved brother-in-law, an officer in the 91st Argyllshire Regiment, died in his arms, exclaiming, "I am going to Jesus." But this did not seem to affect him beyond the ordinary grief of losing one he loved greatly. But he was chief mourner, with a little nephew of four years of age; and when his brother-in-law's remains were lowered into the grave, and the words were pronounced "Ashes to ashes, and dust to dust," God then spake to his soul, and he heard, as it were, a voice saying to him, "If your body was in that coffin now, where would your soul be?" This was the arrow from God for the awakening of his soul from the sleep of death. Soon after he was induced to go and hear Mr. Denham Smith, who at the time was having a great season of blessing at his church at Kingstown, Dublin. Through him Mr. Henry was led into peace and rest. The change in him was great and genuine, and his soul was so filled with love to the Saviour that at once he commenced to work for Him.

Returning to London fresh from the memorable scenes of the Irish Revival, he was led to address children's meetings, with much blessing from God. He then conducted the "Additional Theatre Services" in the Surrey, the Victoria, the City of London, and the Soho Theatres, supplementing the work of Lord Shaftesbury's committee. Much blessing was the result of this work through the labors of Reginald Radcliffe, Richard Weaver, William Carter, and others. He then became the companion of Reginald Radcliffe, visiting many places in England, Scotland, and Ireland. They were the first English evangelists who preached in Paris where the Lord greatly blessed the Word. There is no knowing what would have been the result of this work, as the people flocked in crowds to hear about "the love of God," had not the Emperor Napoleon's Minister of the Interior put an end to these public meetings, and only allowed a limited number to meet in private houses. He and Mr. Radcliffe separated, the latter going to the call for help in Lancashire during the cotton famine in 1861 and 1862. Mr. Henry went to Plymouth where a remarkable work of God commenced; then to County Kerry where so many of the county gentlemen and their families had been converted, one of whom was Richard Mahony of Dromore Castle. For years Mr. Henry was associated with Denham Smith at Merrion Hall, Dublin; Iron Room, Clapton Hall, and St. George's Hall, London, in which latter places he continued to preach for at least two months every year, never without the Lord's gracious help and blessing in the winning of souls.

Shuldham Henry ever tenaciously held to the old paths in all fundamental doctrines of the Scriptures, and the blessed hope of our Lord's speedy return, and was never moved therefrom by modern sophistries.

In November 1893, he preached for a month in Clapton Hall. On his return to Plymouth he wrote: "It is such an honor to be a soul-winner, and a privilege—that angels might envy—to be allowed to build up His dear people." A rheumatic seizure laid him low; he lingered till January 2nd, 1894, and after uttering the words, "This mortal will soon put on immortality," he passed into the presence of the King.—C.H.

Richard Hill
1799-1880

RICHARD HILL

R ICHARD HILL was educated at Exeter College, Oxford. His first curacy was at Grade, a village in Cornwall, and later he became perpetual curate at West Alvington, Devon. He very soon became exercised
about his position in the Established Church, and, retiring from it, associated himself in its earliest days with the "Brethren movement."

As Mrs. Trotter has well said: "The inspiration came to them at first
alone, and not under the influence of large multitudes, neither did it die
out but energized and sustained them in lives of unusual toil and unusual length."

Mr. Hill lived at Plymstock, and there Mr. Darby stayed with him on
coming to Plymouth, Mr. Hill having "gathered simply to the name" before that time. Passing through the crisis of the divisions which arose
among these dear people— described as "the Lord's grief, the saints' sorrow, and the devil's glee"—Mr. Hill took his part, as many of the tracts of
that time bearing his name testify. He also wrote sacred poetry.

Mr. Hill married a sister of the well-known Mr. H. W. Soltau, and having been born on December 23, 1799, passed away on March 11, 1880, at
Bath, in an honored old age and much respected. One of his sons, also
Richard Hill, in happy fellowship with "Brethren," was from its inception and for upwards of thirty years Honorary Secretary of the China
Inland Mission. He, together with his brother Henry, a valued teacher at
the St. Mary Church Meeting, Torquay, have departed to be with Christ,
which is far better.

Charles H. Hinman
1859-1922

C. H. HINMAN

CHARLES HILLIAM HINMAN, one of the ablest ministers of the Word among the companies of believers who gather simply in the name of the Lord, was born in the village of Leigh, in the County of Rutland, England in 1859. His ancestors had farmed in the vicinity for four hundred years. After leaving school he was apprenticed to a draper in Grantham. After four years he moved to London, to one of the large wholesale houses in St. Paul's Churchyard.

A double great change in his life was effected when he made the change from England to New Zealand, and there experienced the greater change—passing from death to life. He spoke of his conversion thus: "I had been but a very short time in New Zealand when I was asked to go and hear Gordon Forlong, an ex-London lawyer and a converted Deist. I consented, and on the next Sunday went to hear what the lawyer had to say. I can now scarcely describe my feelings. He was evidently preaching what he understood, for he was telling it out with no uncertain sound. It was something very different to what I had been accustomed to listen to in the church. I was convinced that what he said was in the Bible, yet I thought it awful presumption for any one to say he knew he was saved. However, I was in such a state of mind that I wished to hear more, so the next Lord's day I was there again, anxious to catch every word. This day my interest and conviction were deepened. My false peace was broken up, and the bitterness of a guilty conscience took its place. The next Lord's day found me in the same place, and the burden of my soul was: What must I do to be saved? I had tried to leave off old sins, and turn over a new leaf, but it was no use; it gave no comfort, no peace." He expressed the latter thus: "Oh, the joy of that moment when I realized the work was *finished for me*! It was on the Monday morning May 10th, 1880, about nine o'clock that the words, 'IT IS FINISHED,' came before me. My deep trouble then gave way to sweet peace. My sins were forgiven—my soul was saved. Since the day I took God at His Word, and believed the record given of His Son, my greatest joy has been to tell out to others God's way of salvation."

After his conversion he spent the greater part of his time preaching the Good News throughout the length and breadth of both North and South Islands. Later a visit to England was blessed to the conversion of several of his relatives and many others.

Attacked by Bright's disease, he paid visits to the Old Country and the United States for special treatment with little effect. Returning to his home he partly recovered and was able to minister at intervals, but it was evident that the trouble was steadily gaining the mastery, and on Saturday, August 26th, 1922, he finished his course. With his family gathered around him, almost his last words were: "What shall the first five minutes be like in Heaven?"—HY.P.

Alfred J. Holiday
1841-1905

ALFRED J. HOLIDAY

ALFRED J. HOLIDAY was born and educated in London. He had the advantage not only of an excellent education, but of being brought up in an artistic and literary circle, and this had a life-long effect upon his character.

Brought to the Lord at the early age of sixteen, he at once dedicated his energies to the Lord's work, and from the first he was no half-hearted disciple. The manner of his conversion was unusual. One Sunday evening at church, hearing the gospel clearly stated, he believed and was saved, although he had had no previous soul exercise. After the service he said to his companion, "I am saved," and to his joy his friend replied, "So am I."

The new wine could not be kept in old bottles. At once they told their friends, a good number of whom professed Christ. Not long after this, Reginald Radcliffe, the lawyer-preacher, found him out and encouraged him to preach. This he did, and held large open-air meetings with great blessing at Primrose Hill and elsewhere in London.

The Lord thus prepared him for his life work, and nothing more characterized him than the simplicity of his gospel preaching and his joy in, as well as aptitude for, open air work, and to the last in the open air he was always at his best. The earnest young preacher was about this time introduced to the saintly Howards of Tottenham who, Aquila-and-Priscilla-like, expounded the Word of God more fully to him, and so led him out of the bondage of system into the happy liberty of simplicity of worship and privilege of remembering the Lord in the breaking of bread.

Business took him to Birmingham, where his activity in gospel work was much appreciated. In that city also the greatest event of his life next to conversion took place in his marriage to Miss Atchison, of London. The result was most happy, and he found in her a true helpmeet and one with whom he could have real fellowship both spiritually and intellectually. After a few years he removed to Bradford to become financial manager to Lord Masham, then Mr. S. C. Lister, whose good will and confidence he gained in a marked manner. The little assembly in Bradford soon felt the effect of the coming into their midst of those two warm-hearted believers; but, alas! dark days followed, and a long illness completely laid him aside and made work impossible. When he was restored he found the little company sadly reduced, meeting in a most unsuitable room known as "Uncle Tom's Cabin." But the old energy and strong faith prevailed. Active aggressive work was engaged in. In music halls and tents the gospel was preached. Messrs. Inglis, Willington, Marshall, Hopkins, and many others helped. The work went on and the assembly grew apace, but, as Willington at the time aptly remarked, speaking of the young converts "They will bide a deal of nursing." This proved to be true. So a new side of Alfred Holiday's character was brought into play, and this proved to be a very strong side, viz., the pastor. For years, wet or fine, he spent each week one long evening in visiting, seldom getting home before midnight. His gift as an organizer and his power and tact in getting others into work made themselves felt.

He was loving and generous to a fault. He taught what he believed strongly, yet never harshly, nor did he harbor unkind thoughts. With him it was easy to forgive and forget. It may be mentioned as characteristic of the man that one year when there was special distress in Bradford, in order to encourage simple habits, he himself went without meat, the money thus saved being given to the poor. He was a most generous giver, and did not offer that which cost him naught, going again and again without things lawful, and in the eyes of some needful, that he might have the more to give away. He could not save or put by for a rainy day while he knew of present need.

For the last thirteen years of his life he lived at Featherstone as manager for Lord Masham's estate and colliery there. He was used to build up a vigorous assembly in that place, there being none when he first went to live there.

As a gifted teacher, able to express himself in a clear and forcible manner, his ministry at Conferences was much valued. Assemblies in difficulty seemed naturally to turn to him for counsel, and he must have travelled thousands and thousands of miles on such errands, giving up many hours of sleep in his efforts to smooth over difficulties and bring brethren together.

Mr. Holiday's end on February 8th, 1905, was not only peaceful but triumphant. The outer man perished, but the inner man waxed strong. During the last four hours, notwithstanding great physical weakness, his spiritual joy increased so that it seemed that he had a sight of the Glory. Amongst other words, he said: "I have had many happy, happy years of service for the Lord down here, but now I am to be promoted higher, higher, higher." —W.H.S.

John Eliot Howard
1807-1884

JOHN ELIOT HOWARD

JOHN ELIOT HOWARD, the son of Luke Howard, the eminent meteorologist, was born in 1807. After he left school he went into his father's business at Stratford, and he was a member of the firm of Howard & Sons, the well-known quinine makers and chemical manufacturers, up to the time of his death.

He was brought up as a member of the Society of Friends and about the year 1835 the earnest study of the Scriptures and the perusal of a little work entitled "Jehovah-Tsidkenu the Watchword of the Reformers," were the means of opening his eyes to the doctrine of justification by faith. His baptism, and that of his beloved wife, took place on July 28th, 1836, and in October of the same year he resigned his connection with the Society of Friends.

On the 4th of December he partook of the Lord's Supper at the Baptist Chapel, Tottenham. From this time he began to preach the gospel going out to the surrounding villages. He was nearly thirty years of age. In 1838 he began a regular evening meeting in Tottenham, and on the 4th of November the first meeting for worship and communion was held. This was in a small room in Warner Terrace. In 1839 he built the room in Brook Street; in 1842 there were eighty-eight in communion.

In the early days of "Brethren" J.E.H. was actively engaged in the controversy amongst "Friends," and many publications issued from his pen. He was also writing on Scriptural views connected with "Brethren" so-called, with whom he was associated until the end of his life.

For over forty years he was a faithful minister of the gospel. His ministry was greatly owned of God in the conversion of sinners and the edification of believers and he was widely beloved both at home and abroad. The cause of foreign missions was very dear to his heart, and he was warm in his sympathies and generous in pecuniary help. He corresponded for many years with some beloved servants of the Lord in foreign lands, and they deeply felt the loving sympathy of his heart, so warmly expressed in his correspondence with them.

He was faithful, fearless, and independent in his expression of what he believed to be the truth. Gifted with a powerful mind, of quick perception and rapid thought, he eagerly made himself master of the religious and scientific literature of the day. He devoted a great deal of time and thought to the study of some of the scientific questions that in these days perplex so many minds, and his clear insight enabled him to unmask much of the scientific and religious philosophies that are now so prevalent, one of his best known religious works being "Lectures on the Scriptural Truths most Opposed by Puseyism."

In 1865 he wrote a volume of lectures on "Scripture and Science," which has been much valued. He rendered great and lasting service both to religion and science by showing in many learned and interesting papers that there is, and can be, no conflict between science and religion—between the facts of nature and the Word of God.

He was known in scientific circles as an eminent quinologist, and was elected a Fellow of the Royal Society in 1874. He was also a Fellow of the Linnaean Society, and of many other scientific bodies at home and on the Continent.

In 1883 he purchased the lease of the lecture hall in the High Road, Tottenham, and the meetings were transferred there from Brook Street. He preached there as usual, twice on the Sunday before his death, with much solemnity and power on the words, "For God hath not appointed us to wrath, but to obtain salvation by our Lord Jesus Christ, who died for us, that, whether we wake or sleep, we should live together with him." His words deeply impressed his audience, though they little deemed they were hearing his last discourse. "Yes, that is the central point," he said; "Christ died for us, and we live through Him. What matters it, then, whether we wake or sleep? We live and shall live together with Him." Those who listened to him with delight had little thought that it was the last time they would hear the well-known voice.

He was taken ill on November 20th, 1883, but no danger was apprehended until Thursday morning when he gently fell asleep in Jesus at his residence, Lord's Meade, Tottenham.

CAPTAIN T. H. HULL

1809-1880

THOMAS HILLMAN HULL was born in 1809 at Marpool Hall, Withycombe, Raleigh, Exmouth, the family estate, being Lord of the Manor. He entered the Indian Army as a young man where he became a distinguished officer. He had to leave the army through ill health, but God's purpose was that he should become "a good soldier of Jesus Christ."

He was brought to know the Lord through the agency of Mr. and Mrs. Anthony Norris Groves of Coonoor, S. India. These devoted servants of God received into their own house the broken-hearted young husband and his young wife who was dying of consumption, and they were the means of the conversion of both, so that the young wife died in perfect peace.

Captain Hull returned to England, invalided from the army, but henceforth to live for Christ. Later on he married again, one who was also a devoted Christian, and settled in Exmouth where he was greatly used of God. He was an accomplished scholar and a clever and effective speaker. For many years he gathered large audiences in the Exeter Road Room, which had been built by his brother for the use of the assembly of Christians gathering there. It was a common sight to see a queue of people waiting for the doors to open when he proclaimed "the unsearchable riches of Christ," and many were brought to the Lord, and led on in the Christian life by his teaching. He was prominent and active in preaching the gospel in the open air. The "common people heard him gladly." He was also busy in teaching and instructing the saints in the various local assemblies, attending most of the annual and quarterly meetings in the north and south of Devon, ministering the Word. It would be impossible to speak of the many whom he led to Christ; and he was always seeking opportunities for service in train, on race course, and tract distribution. God graciously used His dear servant to the conversion of many. He was always very humble, esteeming others better than himself.

On April 18th, 1880, at 8:00 on the Lord's day morning, he peacefully "fell asleep" after a short illness. He had greatly valued, just before this week's illness, a visit of a few days from Mr. R. C. Chapman of Barnstaple, a friend of many years. To one who was caring for him he said: "I am not dwelling on what Heaven will be like; I am swallowed up with the thought of seeing Jesus." Two, if not three, of the earlier generations of Hulls lie buried in an allotted portion of the yard at the east end of the ancient church of St. John; but William, Squire Hull, and Thomas Hull are buried in a small enclosed cemetery at Withycombe, given by the former for the use of Christians meeting in the Exeter Road Room.

Miss M. A. Hull, the authoress of that well-known and popular hymn, "There is Life for a Look at the Crucified One," was a sister. A well-known evangelist writes: "Whenever I pass Marpool Hall, now occupied and owned by others, I am always reminded of the Hulls and the Haldanes of Scotland. The devotion, self-sacrifice, and whole-heartedness to the cause of Christ of these two aristocratic families were remarkable, and should cause deep searchings of heart."

FRANCIS HUTCHINSON

⟨◦∞◦⟩

1802-1833

FRANCIS HUTCHINSON was the son of Rev. Sir Samuel Synge, Archdeacon of Killala (who assumed the additional surname of Hutchinson on succeeding his uncle). He was born on January 18th, 1802, and fell asleep in Jesus on April 3rd, 1833. He married the sister of the Earl of Donoughmore and left two sons and one daughter. His eldest son succeeded his grandfather in the Baronetcy.

Francis Hutchinson deserves a special niche in any work of reference to the "Chief Brethren," for not only was he one of the first who met together for "the breaking of bread" according to primitive custom, on the first day of the week, but it was at his house, No. 9 Fitzwilliam Square, Dublin that the little company were led to come together in the name of the Lord Jesus, owning the presence and sovereign action of the Holy Spirit in their midst. The brethren continued to meet for some time in Fitzwilliam Square, and others were gradually added to their number. The gospel was preached with a clearness and fullness and power unknown since the days of the apostles. Books and tracts were written and widely circulated. The grand doctrines of the church, the operations of the Holy Spirit, the blessed hope of the Lord's speedy return were brought out with great freshness and power to the uplifting of many hearts, and to the eternal blessing of hundreds of precious souls. Great interest was awakened, and those who ventured to their meetings were struck by the fact of hundreds of people assembled together without a minister, so-called, and yet there was no confusion, but "all things were done decently and in order."

One after another becoming affected by the truth, were received into communion. The numbers so increased that in little more than a year the house of Mr. Hutchinson was found to be unsuitable for the meetings and a large auction room in Aungier Street was hired for the purpose. From then on, as Mrs. E. Trotter writes, "the teaching and testimony of the men of 1828 not only directly animated and inspired the great evangelistic movement of 1857, but gave a new character to the missionary enterprise of the century and antedated, in its fresh and unfettered study of the Scriptures, much truth which is now a common heritage of the church of God." The old evangelicalism had become to a large extent a negation. Here was a vision; this was the burning secret at the core of life transforming it from within to without.

> I have seen the face of Jesus,
> Tell me not of aught beside;
> I have heard the voice of Jesus,
> And my soul is satisfied.

In this light all other lights paled. Among the men affected by it were men of brain, born leaders, men of birth and of large means, scholars and students who would have made their mark at any time and in any walk of life; lawyers of acute critical judgment, officers of promise in both services, large landowners with the cares and responsibilities of property.

The inspiration came to them at first *alone*, and not under the influence of large multitudes, neither did it die out, but energized and sustained them in lives of unusual toil and unusual length. Many of those principles for which they contended, and for which they suffered, have become over the years more or less a common heritage.

Theodore B. Jones
1827-1920

THEODORE B. JONES

⟫⟪

THEODORE BROOKE JONES, a patriarchal saint, passed into the presence
of his Lord on October 21st, 1920, at the ripe old age of ninety-nine
years. We know few details of his early days, but of this we have assurance that he was saved by the grace of God among the Wesleyan's in his
boyhood.

He could remember the days when London was lighted with oil
lamps, and when the omnibuses began to run in that city. His business
as a chartered accountant took him into the society of many a wealthy
and noble family, but he never failed to own his Master. In the origina-
tion of the Y.M.C.A. movement in London, under Sir George Williams,
Mr. Jones was a member of the first committee, and it was the perception
by him of the possibility of the Lord's people meeting in such an undenominational way that led him to seek the fellowship of saints gathered
in His name alone. But it would be impossible for us to note all the connections which he had with great men of God during the middle years
of last century. Of these we may note that the saintly Dr. Andrew Bonar
officiated at Mr. Jones' wedding in March 1880, and he treasured a letter
which that noted servant of the Lord sent to him immediately after the
event. On removing to the Clapton district Mr. Jones came into touch with
Mr. John Morley (brother of Sir Samuel Morley, M. P.) and with the Christians meeting in the Iron Room, from which they moved at a later date to
Clapton Hall, built by Mr. Morley.

A remarkable incident regarding the beginning of this fellowship is
told in "Footsteps of Truth" (March 1896). One evening at a meeting of
Christians in Mr. Morley's house, the latter, addressing Mr. Jones as a welcomed newcomer, begged leave to remind him that it was understood
among them that no one would enter on the controversial subject of believers' baptism. To this Mr. Jones in his quiet but forceful way answered,
as he held his Bible in one hand and struck it with the other, "Well, Mr.
Morley, if there is any subject within the covers of this Book which is to
be systematically ignored by us I can have no fellowship with you." So

impressed was Mr. Morley that with candor he immediately replied, "Jones, you are right." Soon afterwards Mr. and Mrs. Morley were immersed as believers, and a baptistery was put into the new hall at their expressed wish.

Some fifty years ago Mr. Jones resolved to go to Harrogate to live where there was no meeting. Before long his shining light drew several Christians together, and they met on the first day of the week at his home to remember the Lord's death in the breaking of bread. From that nucleus arose the assembly in that place. It was not long till the standard of the cross was also unfurled there through his instrumentality, and till his later years, when physical disability forbade it, his heart and soul were in the active work of the Lord.

Mr. Jones was neither a preacher nor a teacher, but the patient, unobtrusive labor which he undertook, the gracious comfort which he imparted, the permeating godly influence which all felt, and personal and financial burdens which he quietly and ungrudgingly bore for the Lord's sake are known only in full to Him for whom his all was laid upon the altar. He could remember, with lively interest, conversation with the world's great men, including Mr. W. E. Gladstone, but it never affected him for ill. He was a man filled and clothed with humility and grace. To the castle of a great client he was invited that he might tell of his confident trust in God and his sure hope for the world to come. In business, as one of his business friends wrote, his glowing characteristic was his contempt for filthy lucre.

Residents and visitors alike bear testimony to the experience of his beautiful, ever cheerful personality and his walk with God. The children used to run to him when he was walking in his last days to hear the kindly welcome and his words of love, and on every one with whom he came in contact of all classes and creeds, he left one impression, "He was a true man of God." When his daughter asked whether he "minded being old," he answered beautifully and characteristically, "Why mind, my dear, my steps are ordered by the Lord." Here is the secret of the Christlike life; he lived in the consciousness of the Father's loving smile and presence.— W.K.

William Kelly
1820-1906

WILLIAM KELLY

W ILLIAM KELLY—the title pages of whose writings generally bear only the initials "W. K."—was born in the north of Ireland, in 1820. Being early left fatherless, he was already supporting himself by tuition with the family of Mr. Cachemaille, rector of Sark, when in 1840 he made the Christian confession, and shortly afterwards embraced the views of the church characteristic to "Brethren," with whom he then at once united. He retained a close connection with the Channel Islands for thirty years, residing chiefly in Guernsey, but for the latter half of his Christian career his home was at Blackheath.

He was a graduate, in classical honors, of Trinity College, Dublin, and was recognized as not merely a sound, erudite scholar, but a controversialist of formidable calibre. Besides aiding Dr. S. P. Tregelles in his investigations as a Biblical textual critic, Mr. Kelly himself published in 1860 a critical edition of Revelation which Professor Heinrich Ewald of Gottingen declared was the best piece of English work of the kind that he had seen.

Such studies were carried on concurrently with the editing of a periodical entitled *The Prospect*. He took up the editorship of *The Bible Treasury* in 1857, and continued till his death fifty years after. As editor of the *B. T.* he was brought into correspondence with such men as Dean Afford, Dr. Scott the lexicographer (whom he convinced of the true force of the word unhappily rendered in the Authorized Version of 2 Thessalonians 2:2, as "is at hand"), Principal Edwards (who confessed to Mr. Kelly his conversion to the premillennial standpoint), with Professor Sanday of Oxford and other living theologians.

After the capitulation of younger ecclesiastical associates to the Higher Criticism, Archdeacon Denison spoke of Mr. Kelly's periodical as the only religious magazine any longer worth reading—so steadfast was the editor in his rejection of what he believed to be Christ-dishonoring views of the Bible.

His simplicity and self-suppression may be illustrated by the reply he made to a Dublin professor who had expressed an opinion that, if Mr. Kelly did but settle there as a teacher he would make a fortune—"For which world?"

His supreme delight was in ministering in things spiritual to those whom he described as the "few despised ones of Christ's flock." To such service he gave untiring energy put forth to within two months of his decease. He identified himself whole-heartedly with the body of doctrine developed by the late John Nelson Darby, whose right-hand man he was for many years, till he severed his connection and formed a party which for long bore his name.

The "Collected Writings" of J.N.D. were edited by Mr. Kelly, who has done much by his own expositions to give currency to the views enshrined in them. His own merits were manifest alike in oral and written ministry. Mr. C. H. Spurgeon, judging by the latter, has applied to Mr. Kelly in the "Guide to Commentaries," the words of Pope, "born for the universe." In the list of his writings will be found lectures or notes on all the books of the Bible.

How long he retained his clearness and vigor of intellect comes out in the fact that several of his best expositions appeared during the last fifteen years of his life. Within the lifetime of J.N.D. (1800-1882), Mr. Kelly was already well known to outsiders by his lectures on the Pentateuch, the Gospel of Matthew, the Revelation of John, the Church of God, and the New Testament doctrine of the Holy Spirit, besides notes on Romans, etc., recommended by Professor Sandy. Since 1890 he has put forth "In the Beginning" (Genesis 1:2), commended by Archbishop Benson; and exposition of the prophecies of Isaiah, of the Gospel of John, of the Epistle to the Hebrews, of the Epistles of John; a volume of six hundred pages on "God's Inspiration of the Scriptures;" and his last words on "Christ's Coming Again," in which he vindicates the originality of J.N.D. in regard to the "Secret Rapture;" which had been impugned by an American writer.

The last prominent survivor of the first generation of "Brethren" fell asleep on March 27th, 1906. Shortly before he passed away, W. K. said to one by his bedside: "There are three things *real*—the cross, the enmity of the world, the love of God." An aged clergyman, who had long resorted to him for counsel, on hearing of his decease, wrote: "He was pre-eminently 'a faithful man, and feared God above many' (Nehemiah 7:2)."—E.E.W.

Captain R. F. Kingscote
1811-1893

CAPTAIN
R. F. KINGSCOTE

OF THE OLD family of Kingscote of Kingscote, Gloucestershire, Captain Kingscote was in the Royal Lancers, but on his conversion he left the army. He was a great friend of the late Duke of Cambridge, the cousin of Queen Victoria. Captain Kingscote was the writer of several tracts and little pamphlets, and a series of addresses given by him at Park Street, London, on "Christ as Seen in the Offerings." This was printed and published in one volume and helped many.

Capt. Kingscote took part in the private service at the funeral of J. N. Darby, held at the house of H. A. Hammond in Bournemouth, at which over one hundred brethren were said to be present. Captain Robert F. Kingscote was born in 1811, and departed to be with Christ in 1893.

William Lincoln
1825-1888

WILLIAM LINCOLN

WILLIAM LINCOLN was born in 1825 in the east of London, and converted to God at the age of seventeen; his soul having been convicted of sin through reading Doddridge's "Rise and Progress of Religion," though the book did not bring him into peace. Desiring to serve the Lord, he first thought of missionary work and was a year studying under the church missionary society, but was refused on account of his parents having died of consumption. He then entered King's College, London, of which he became an associate; was ordained at Preston in 1849 by the Bishop of Manchester; labored in the establishment there and at Pudsey; and finally came up to London as curate at St. George's, Southwark. While there he preached mostly at a district church in the London Road, drawing very large numbers; and in 1859 obtained the appointment as minister of Beresford Chapel, Walworth. Here his preaching was very attractive and the place was soon filled to excess.

But his soul began to be exercised about his position in the Church of England, though he preached and published a sermon on infant baptism, seeking to refute Mr. Spurgeon's memorable discourse on baptismal regeneration. But he continued more and more to realize that his position was a false one, and the remaining copies of the sermon just mentioned were carefully burnt. In 1862 he finally broke his connection with the establishment. He read out his reasons for so doing on a Sunday evening to a congregation which crowded the building to the utmost. The effect was, of course, at once manifested in the reduced attendances, though large numbers still continued with him, a few, however, dropping off by degrees.

Immediately after his secession, he wrote the "Javelin of Phinehas," in which he exposed by the Word of God, the evil of the union between church and state. The work at Beresford continued to progress, though the changes were gradual; one step at a time, we may say, just as light was given. Many attempts were made to get Mr. Lincoln to join one or other of the various denominations; but his expressed determination always was, "never to join anything or any party," but to cleave to the Lord alone. His purpose and joy ever was to press the truth of gathering to the Lord's name *alone*, making Him the one center, and going forth *"unto him without the camp."* None preached more faithfully the doctrine of separation, and to Jesus only; and we may add that he practiced what he preached.

For the sake of allegiance to his Lord, and obedience to His Word, he surrendered worldly prospects and emoluments of no ordinary character. He had his reward in seeing many believers walking according to the truth; and one by one the old practices were abandoned, and worship according to its Scriptural simplicity was established at Beresford. Week by week the saints began to assemble together to break bread in obedience to the command of the Lord as gathered unto Him alone, and submitting to the Spirit to guide as He pleased.

While giving open ministry its due place, Mr. Lincoln never failed to press godly order and rule in the assembly, and opposed the spirit of democracy and communism having any place in the church of God. He was also very careful to maintain the value of ministry in teaching from the Word of God by those whom God had sent as teachers; and the time of service was made half an hour earlier, in order that, while time was given for worship and ministry in connection with the breaking of bread first, there might be special opportunity after for the ministry of the Word. All who have had experience of this would confess its value; and the benefit to the assembly has been incalculable. And thus helped and kept by God in His grace, the work went on at Beresford for twenty-eight years, though loud were the prophecies at the outset that it would not last a twelvemonth.

It was in this ministry of the Word that Mr. Lincoln was so powerful an instrument in the hand of God. He presented Scripture in its broader features with a clear grasp of principles by which the saint was to be guided in filling in details. In this way his ministry was most useful, as it put the hearers in the way of gaining instruction for themselves from the Word. In prophecy also he was much used, especially in connection with the Lord's coming for His church, and the apostasy of Christendom. He loved to press the truth of the Lord's imminent return, and lamented much what he thought was a growing coldness in respect to it. Earnestly he warned against the spreading darkness in the professing church, and pressed the truth of separation from evil.

Always accessible to any who came to him with difficulties and questions, he was used to the help of many in all parts of the world; and his answers were always remarkable, as was his teaching, for clearly presenting and pressing fundamental principles. As to the source from which he himself drew the knowledge he had, though with large opportunity of studying the writings of others, he often confessed himself as "the man of one book;" drawing what he gave to others from the fountain head—from the Word itself. His own writings were not very numerous, and we may mention the principal of them: "Joseph and Jesus" and "Four Lectures on the Second Advent," published before he left the establishment; "The Javelin of Phinehas," published immediately afterwards (difficult now to obtain); and, subsequently, "Lectures on the Hebrews," "The Epistles of John," "The Book of the Revelation," and "Typical Foreshadowings in Genesis;" with a series of lectures and leaflets on some fundamental truths in the Word of God.

Mr. Lincoln's heart was in the work at Beresford, to which he considered the Lord had specially called him, though many have objected and thought he should have extended his service more for the benefit of other assemblies. However this may be, a serious obstacle to it was his condition of health, and few probably had any idea of his continued sufferings for about the last twenty years of his life. It is a marvel that he was able to continue to study and teach so constantly as he did; but his nervous system was gradually undermined.

The last time he spoke was on September 18th, 1887, and, remarkably, it was upon the early verses of 2 Corinthians 5. The last time he was present at the breaking of bread was on December 11th. But though the outward man was perishing, the inward man was renewed, and his joy and peace continued unclouded. His remark, as he left the meeting for the last time was "It is all well; the Lord reigneth."

Life's sand ran slowly out, and the body grew weaker and weaker; but his spirit was stayed upon God, and he could say, "I'm full of praise and joy." And thus the end came, and the last answer he could give upon earth when asked if he were happy was "Yes in the Lord," and in a few brief hours he was "with Christ, which is far better." He quietly fell asleep, without any apparent pain, early on the morning of the 25th of April, 1888.

We can but admire the grace of God displayed in his unswerving and unfaltering faithfulness to the truth of God. Whenever he saw a thing to be right he persisted in it, no matter what the consequences to himself or others. And yet he was not a man of extremes, for one of the great lessons of Scripture he ever sought to impress was the balancing the truth of God, and never to push one side of truth to the disparaging of another. A simple verse which he passed on to Mr. J. R. Caldwell truly indicates his aim and spirit: —H.Y.P.

> Lord Jesus! make Thyself to me
> A living, bright reality;
> More present to faith's vision keen
> Than any outward object seen;
> More dear, more intimately nigh,
> Than e'en the sweetest earthly tie.

Dr. Robert M'Killiam
1837-1915

DR. ROBERT M'KILLIAM

ROBERT M'KILLIAM, son of Basil M'Killiam, was born at Aberdeen in 1837. His mother's godly life and prayers had great influence over him, and he was converted at an early age. He studied medicine, and passed examinations at too early an age to engage in practice taking, however, his M.D. degree at Aberdeen University at the age of twenty-one, and subsequently his C.M. degree at the same university. He practiced as physician and surgeon at Old Meldrum, Forgue, and Huntly, leaving the last named in 1880.

The doctor engaged in active Christian work when quite a young man, and because of his outstanding Christian principles was made an elder of the Free Church of Scotland at a comparatively early age for such an office. His Biblical teaching, particularly that connected with the second coming of Christ, was, however, too pronounced for the Free Church, and owing to much persecution and opposition he left that body. Several left with him, and an undenominational Christian work was then commenced at Huntly, greatly blessed and owned of God in the conversion of many and in blessing to God's people.

Dr. M'Killiam longed for London as a sphere of labor, and in 1880 the way was made clear, so he succeeded to the practice of the late Dr. Tate, of Blackheath. In a short time an assembly of believers was formed at Blackheath. The Alexandra Hall was taken, and up to the time of his last illness the doctor continued to preach the gospel and minister the Word there, and very many will have cause to thank God for his faithful ministry. His activities were not confined to Blackheath, as he travelled much all over the country and labored for the Lord most assiduously. He was editor of *The Morning Star* from its commencement in January 1894, and continued so till the time of his death—thus covering over twenty-one years. Through this paper, which was "a herald of the coming of the Lord Jesus Christ," his name was known and his teaching appreciated and blessed in many parts of the world.

The doctor's favorite theme was the personal and premillennial coming of the Lord Jesus. With his dying hand he penned these words for the readers of *The Witness*: "The 'Blessed Hope' cannot much longer be deferred. The full choir shall soon fill the heavens with music that even the Archangels shall delight to hear; and you and I, my brother, my sister, saved by His grace, however unworthy, shall add our little strain to the full acknowledgment of His worth. Mine shall still be: 'I'm only a sinner saved by grace.'"

After two serious operations, which meant many months of intense suffering, the beloved physician was called to a well-earned rest in the heavenly home on February 7th, 1915, at the advanced age of seventy-eight.—W.W.H.

John G. M'Vicker
1826-1900

JOHN G. M'VICKER

———◦◦◦———

JOHN G. M'VICKER was born in Belfast on March 15th, 1826, and died in London on January 5th, 1900, at the age of seventy-three. For more than forty of those years he knew that God was his salvation, and in that knowledge he served Him—chiefly, at first, in the north of Ireland, and later in London. He was in his early years a Presbyterian minister. Having ceased to be so, he continued until the end disclaiming any denominational name to teach and preach Jesus Christ.

It was during the awakening of 1859 that he was brought into the light which lightened him through his after days. A man so living as he was, large of heart and sympathetic, could not, and did not, fail to suffer. For suffering he had a great capacity, and his trials were many. God "acquaints His comforters with grief," and Mr. M'Vicker was one who, having suffered, could, deeply feeling, console those needing comfort. They are very many, and they are everywhere to be found.

He loved Scotland, and often visited this country. Who that has heard him speak in the meetings in Glasgow, or perhaps especially heard him pray, will forget him? He spoke once on, "Sirs, be of good cheer, for I believe God, that it shall be even as it was told me" (Acts 27:25). Let that stand as expressive of the man and of his ministry. "I believe God." Certainly he did that; it was his personal characteristic. "Be of good cheer...it shall be even as it was told me." Such was the tenor of his ministry. "Be comforted; not one word shall fail, for the guarantee of fulfillment is the character of God."

He was preaching in Clapton Hall, Stoke Newington, during December, and brought his service to a close there at the end of the month. On Sunday morning, 31st December, he gave out the hymn of which the first verse is:

> Away with our sorrow and fear
> We soon shall have entered our Home
> The City of saints shall appear
> The day of eternity come.

On Friday, January 5th following, he was occupied in visiting during the afternoon, went home, and after tea retired to his room. There, suddenly, at about eight o'clock in the evening, the end came and he fell asleep.

He was of a strong frame, not tall, but compactly built and solid. He had been black-haired and black-bearded when young; latterly his hair was iron-grey and his beard white; eyebrows bushy and over large, dark eyes. The face, when in repose, had a sad look as the countenance of one who had known pain and sorrow, His heart was of the warmest and most capacious. There the flame glowed continually. He had a most hearty appreciation of what was good, or beautiful, or well said. A brief, hearty laugh would break from him when he was pleased, which was not seldom. He was of a strong intellect, and adequately furnished by education. He had read considerably within certain limits, his range in that field being restricted by the fear of God. In thinking he was exact, and in expression accurate. His mental processes might be called severe. There was no slovenliness about him. His attire was plain, and his handwriting was, to the end, of a clerkly neatness and clearness. God was in all his thoughts, the rock of his strength and his refuge was in God. The Word of God, continually meditated upon, fed him, and by constant recourse to God in prayer his strength was continually renewed.

The loving are the beloved, and such was Mr. M'Vicker. God's grace is manifold and it is bestowed upon many. We shall see other gracious and gifted men, but those who knew him will agree in saying that we shall not see one exactly his like again. They will also agree that. if poorer by his loss, they are lastingly enriched in the memory of what, through grace, he was.—A.S.

Charles Henry Mackintosh
1820-1896

C. H. MACKINTOSH

·~≫◦◦≪~·

CHARLES HENRY MACKINTOSH, whose initials "C.H.M." are known world wide, was born in Glenmalure Barracks, County Wicklow, Ireland, in October 1820. His father was a Captain in the Highlanders' Regiment, and had served in Ireland during the Rebellion. His mother was a daughter of Lady Weldon and of a family long settled in Ireland. At the age of eighteen the young man experienced a spiritual awakening through letters received from his sister after her conversion, and obtained peace through the perusal of J. N. Darby's "Operations of the Spirit," being specially helped by words to the effect that "it is Christ's work *for us*, not His work *in us*, that gives peace."

Entering a business house in Limerick, the young Christian "gave attention to reading," and diligently applied his mind to various studies. In 1844 he opened a school at Westport, throwing himself with much enthusiasm into educational work. His spiritual attitude at this time may be inferred from the fact that he aimed at keeping Christ enshrined in the citadel of his life and making Christ's work his chief concern. At length, in 1853, he feared that his school was becoming his primary interest and accordingly he gave it up.

In the meantime his pen had been busy with expository notes on the books of the Pentateuch. At intervals over a period of forty years the volumes of "Notes by C.H.M." were issued, one each upon Genesis, Exodus, Leviticus, and Numbers, and two upon Deuteronomy. These works, which are characterized by a deep-toned evangelical spirit, have been published in large, successive editions. The preface was signed by his friend Andrew Miller, who helped to finance their issue, and who correctly says of the teaching: "Man's complete ruin in sin, and God's perfect remedy in Christ, are fully, clearly, and often strikingly presented."

As an expositor, "C.H.M." had a perspicuous style and presented his views with stimulating strength, loyalty to God's Word, and unswerving trust in Christ.

After ceasing scholastic work, "C. H. M." went to Dublin, where he began speaking in public. For many years he boldly stood forth in defense of the gospel and to proclaim the truth, and God owned his labors in a remarkable degree. When the revival swept over Ireland in 1859-60, he was very active, and some account of his labors may be found in the early volumes of "Things New and Old." He was a man of great faith, and was ever ready to testify that though God had often tried him He had never allowed him to suffer want in the matter of life's necessities while engaged in gospel work and without material employment.

During the last four years of his life he resided at Cheltenham, and when unable through the weakness of advancing years to do much on the platform, he still continued to write. His last series of tractates was entitled "Handfuls of Pasture." The influence of his writings cannot be estimated. He was continually receiving letters from all parts of the world acknowledging the satisfying character of his teaching of the books of Moses.

His first tract in 1843 was on "The Peace of God." When in 1896 he despatched a manuscript to his publishers on "The God of Peace," his hand was stayed and a few months later he entered into rest. His "Miscellaneous Writings" have been published in several formats.

He peacefully fell asleep on November 2nd, 1896, and devout men carried him to his burial in Cheltenham Cemetery. His remains were laid by the side of those of his beloved wife in the presence of a company gathered from many quarters. Dr. Wolston, of Edinburgh, discoursed on the burial of Abraham, from Genesis 25:8-10 and Hebrews 8:10. Before dispersing, the company sang J. N. Darby's beautiful hymn:

> O bright and blessed scenes,
> Where sin can never come;
> Whose sight our longing spirit weans
> From earth where yet we roam.

Dr. J. L. Maclean
1830-1906

DR. J. L. MACLEAN

JOHN LINDSAY MACLEAN, of Bath, was born on October 23rd, 1830 at Nassau, the capital of the Bahama Islands where his father, an officer in the Commissariat Department, was serving. When John Lindsay was about four years of age his father was ordered to Sierra Leone, and had to go there alone, as that settlement in those days bore the ill-omened, but well-merited name of "the white man's grave." So mother and family (two sons and a daughter) were sent to Dysart in Fifeshire, the father's birthplace and family residence. After five years' continuous service in Sierra Leone, promotion and a year's furlough were granted to the father, whose next station was at Hobart, Tasmania, at that time Great Britain's convict settlement. After the Crimean War, Commissary-General Maclean was made a K.C.B., and of course was known as General Sir George Maclean. The father died in 1861, the mother (Lady Sarah Maclean) died in 1889.

As it was settled that John Lindsay was to follow his elder brother's example and enter the army, he was sent home to the Royal Military College, Sandhurst. The course of study required from three to four years. He obtained his commission after three years and on leaving the College carried off the "General Merit" prize, the highest distinction open to a cadet. He was posted to the 69th Regiment, now designated the 2nd Battalion of the Welsh Regiment, and with it served abroad, first at Malta and then in the West Indies. Entering with characteristic keenness into his profession, his zeal was quickly rewarded by his being made Adjutant of his regiment at an unusual age and after an unusually short period of service. In the matter of promotion he was also fortunate, obtaining by purchase his Captaincy in his regiment.

At Malta the Colonel of his regiment was interested in him and took him to a Bible-reading in a private house. Struck with the evident earnestness with which those assembled dealt with the Holy Scriptures, searching them as those who believed them to be the very words of God, he continued going and was led to a personal knowledge of the Lord Jesus Christ.

While serving in Barbados he had yellow fever followed by a relapse when recovering. Several of his companions were carried off, and his life so hung in the balance that the army chaplain went to his bedside, read Hebrews 13, and left without another word. His fine constitution stood him in good stead and his life, by God's providence, was spared.

One day in a railway carriage in England he was bearing witness for his Master, when a lady said she could not understand how one who sought to spread the gospel of peace could carry a sword. This caused him to consider his position, with the result that it ended in his conviction that the life of a soldier was incompatible with that of a professing Christian. Acting on this belief, he sold his Captain's commission and quit the army. He took his medical diploma at Edinburgh in 1861, married in 1863, and in June of that year went to reside at Leominster where Mr. and Mrs. Yapp were living.

This special work of helping missionaries was begun at Leominster in fellowship with William Yapp. The earliest notes of gospel work in Italy were from the pen of Count Guicciardini. The first sheet that has been preserved is dated 1860. The earliest in which Mr. Yapp's name was linked with the Count's is 1863. The first which bears the name "William Yapp and J. L. Maclean" is 1866, and from 1867 onward Signor Rossetti was a frequent correspondent.

In the latter part of 1874 Mr. Yapp was called to rest, and in 1875 the sheet, *The Gospel in Italy*, was signed by "J. L. M'Lean" alone, but the signature follows the statement: "My friends, Mr. H. Groves of Kendal, and Mr. H. Dyer of Exeter, I may mention, will be glad to join me in receiving offerings." The last paper mentioned was issued from 10 Widcombe Crescent, Bath. J. M. Code had recently been called from Bath to be "with Christ," so Dr. and Mrs. Maclean moved to that city partly to render help in the meetings, and partly for the sake of the education of their only child (a youth of great promise who died in 1876 at age twelve).

In the year 1871, when in Glasgow, Henry Groves of Kendal, and William Bowden of India called on Thomas M'Laren to consult about starting a missionary paper *The Missionary Reporter*, a three pence quarterly then defunct. A half pence monthly was suggested, and *The Missionary Echo* was begun in 1872. The names attached to it were H. Groves and J. L. Maclean, while the fellowship of H. Dyer continued to the close of his service on earth.

In 1885 *The Missionary Echo* gave place to the present larger paper,

Echoes of Service, which was again enlarged in 1891. God was pleased to use this paper to stir up interest in mission work. Many were moved by reading its pages to give themselves to the work, and still many more were stirred to fellowship in helping it forward by their gifts. At the time of this writing there were about 1000 workers in many parts of the five continents. In addition to *Echoes of Service*, he and Henry Groves edited *The Golden Lamp* until 1889 when, on account of Mr. Groves' failing health, it was undertaken by W. H. Bennet and edited by him till discontinued in 1890.

Towards the end of 1890 W. H. Bennet of Yeovil became more definitely linked with Dr. Maclean in service. In 1891 Henry Groves was taken home. In 1894 R. E. Sparks, B.A. of Belfast, resigned his position as solicitor to the Ulster Bank that he might assist in the furtherance of the work.

The well-known Leominster Conferences were begun by William Yapp, with the assistance of Dr. Maclean, in 1874, and though Mr. Yapp was called to rest towards the end of that year, they were continued for years.

Many speak of consecration. Dr. Maclean exemplified it. He yielded himself and all he possessed to the Lord and His service. We often hear of a "self-denial week;" he had 365 days of self-denial in the year, and an extra one in leap year. Dr. Maclean's knowledge of things in general was very extensive; his memory was remarkable; his letters, which were full of wholesome counsel, were greatly valued by those who received them. He never was a fluent speaker, yet his words were always weighty. Whatever he did must be done thoroughly. He had his judgment about most things, which was not easily affected, and a persistency in carrying out what he began which seldom failed. One special trait of his character was genuine humility.

The Bible was Dr. Maclean's constant companion, and his marks and notes, especially in earlier years, show how truly he studied the Scriptures. He had a deep sense of the need and the value of prayer, which he often expressed. In his ministry he dwelt much on the example of the Lord Jesus, but no one could hold more tenaciously that only those who know the forgiveness of sins through His blood (Ephesians 1:7) can rightly consider and in any measure follow the example of His most holy life. He accepted the Bible fully and completely as the Word of God. No reasonings of higher critics troubled him.

The malady—Bright's disease—which at last proved fatal, began to make itself seriously felt early in 1906, when he went to Yeovil, then to Leominster—the residence of his sister-in-law, Mrs. Yapp—for the sake of rest and change. Any hopes of benefit by this movement were soon dissipated and, after spending the summer months there, a return was made to Bath.

On October 19 he spoke an affectionate word to his wife, as if he knew that he was going, and soon after one o'clock he peacefully fell asleep, within a few days of his seventy-sixth birthday. Those who knew him best would testify most that he was "a good and faithful servant."

Richard J. Mahony
1827-1892

R. J. MAHONY

RICHARD J. MAHONY, of Dromore Castle, County Kerry, is often spoken of as the Jonathan to F. C. Bland's David, and he is referred to in that dear friend's life, but he had a personality of his own and well deserves a place with the "Chief Men Among the Brethren."

Mr. Mahony was born in 1827, and succeeded to his father who died very suddenly in the year of the potato famine. Although marked out for a public career, and fitted by natural gifts for almost any position, he devoted himself to promote the good of his tenantry and neighbors, and thanks to his efforts Dromore became a pattern estate, even to the extent of winning the highest praise from the Dublin *Freeman's Journal*, a paper flagrantly hostile to the landed gentry of Ireland.

Mr. Mahony married, in 1856, Miss Waller of Limerick, a true helpmeet in every good work. The Ulster Revival of 1859 had run its course and waned, without extending to the other provinces of Ireland. A few words in a brief heart-stirring address, when he spoke of the love of God and the redeeming work of Christ at a meeting held in his great hall in January 1861, led to a great and widespread revival.

An extract from a circular letter written in March 1861 says, "It pleased God to bring some of us together near the beginning of the year to ask Him to give us the true saving knowledge of Him in our hearts...There are now nightly meetings throughout the parish for prayer and praise to almighty God, and there are men who a short time since never spoke or thought of religion...yet now stand up with burning hearts to tell of what great things God has done for them."

Following a meeting addressed by C. H. Mackintosh, Mr. and Mrs. Mahony rejoiced in the truth of eternal life in Christ, and from that hour set themselves to spread the glad tidings among their friends throughout the country. A lifelong friend writes: "To treat in detail of the far-reaching effect of the work begun through him would need a volume; nor would it be expedient to name the many gifts to the church whose conversion might be traced directly or indirectly to the work begun at Dromore."

Mr. Mahony's health led to a long absence from home. He preached in Edinburgh and then went abroad, in every place finding opportunities for preaching Christ, and in fashionable hotels not a few of the rich and noble were brought to God. A man of striking presence, he combined a commanding dignity with exquisite gentleness and courtesy and intellectual gifts of no common order, with the guilelessness of a little child. The *Times* truly said: "He possessed in a marked degree the special graces of Irish oratory, without any of its extravagancies." Behind all this was a heart aglow with the love of God, and a life entirely devoted to His service. No wonder that his meetings were crowded and that God owned his ministry in a special manner.

He had gifts as an author, and the little he wrote gives proof how much the church of God has lost from his using his pen so seldom. "The Real Presence and the Royal Priesthood," a gem "From Age to Age," and a touching little tract "Father Martin," are examples. "He served the Lord Christ" may be written over his life to its very close. In the summer of 1892 his speech became affected, and his inability to preach was at first very bitter to him. But soon recovering himself, he calmly repeated over and over again, "The good Lord knows best;" at times, "Someday! Someday! The good Lord knew best, and some day we shall understand it all." Thus ended a noble and beautiful life. Mr. Mahony departed to be with Christ on December 22, 1892 at age sixty-five..—C.E.F.

Alexander Marshall
1847-1928

ALEXANDER MARSHALL

———————

A LEXANDER MARSHALL was born in the town of Stranraer, Wigtownshire, a county rich in covenanting traditions and in memories of revival blessing. His father, who carried on business as a clothier, was known as "Holy Marshall." He was an elder in the Evangelical Union Church, a church which at that time was not only evangelical, but evangelistic. His mother was an eminently devoted and godly woman, and Alexander had the inestimable advantage of a godly upbringing and Christian example.

He left home at the age of eighteen to fill a situation in the warehouse of Arthur & Company, Glasgow, and it was two years after that before the choice was made which changed the course of his life. These two years were years of dissatisfaction and of endeavor to stifle the strivings of the Spirit, during which he was never free from anxiety about his soul. Entering a circus in Ingram Street, where Gordon Forlong was preaching, he heard two great truths: (1) "The blood secures;" (2) "The Word assures;" and believing them, entered into rest.

Early in his Christian life he was brought into contact with a number of earnest Christians, who were gathering in New Testament simplicity to carry out the Lord's commands, and Mr. Marshall, convinced of the Scriptural character of their mode of meeting, joined himself to the disciples. His passion to win souls was such that, after the day's business was over, he gave his evenings to preaching. In church, or chapel, or in the open air, wherever there was an open door, he delighted to tell out the good news, often travelling long distances to accomplish this. During the first memorable Moody and Sankey campaign he did valuable work in the inquiry room and at after meetings.

At length the strain of doing double duty began to tell, and he was forced to choose between continuing a business career or giving himself wholly to the work of the gospel. This choice was made, not without considerable exercise and searching of heart. A tempting offer to join a Christian friend in business, and pressure from his friends to take up the ministry in the Evangelical Union Church, were some of the things on which he turned his back.

In the year 1876, at a meeting in Union Hall, Glasgow, he was commended to the Lord for the work of the gospel. Then followed active campaigns in many cities and towns of Scotland and England in which the Word was singularly blessed, and great numbers led to the Saviour. In the year 1879, moved by the need of Canada, he went out to the province of Ontario. Here God owned his service in a remarkable way; many, who afterwards were ardent soul-winners, being led to the Lord at that time.

After his marriage to Miss Tate, in 1882, they settled first in Toronto, then in Orillia, and threw themselves into the work, with the result that many companies of Christians began to gather on New Testament lines and continue to be a witness for God. Altogether seven years were spent in this district, then followed visits to the Pacific Coast, to the United States, and finally back to Scotland. Years of unceasing toil in tents and theatres and halls began to leave their mark, and in 1896 his health broke down, and insomnia forced him to restrict his activities. A visit to New Zealand and then to California in search of restored health followed, and after a prolonged sojourn abroad, he returned to this country in 1904, ultimately making his home in Glasgow, then in Prestwick, Ayrshire.

But the urge of the gospel was ever present. Visits to the Faroe Isles, to Barbados, to Norway, to Switzerland, to Russia, and frequently to Canada and the United States, were interspersed with active campaigns in Scotland and England. At the age of seventy-one, in the darkest days of the war, he was in France succouring the soldiers and telling them of a Saviour's love. When the war was over and the Bolshevist horrors in Russia followed, he did much both in this country and in Estonia to get succour and the news of salvation to the sufferers.

Mr. Marshall's pen was as active as his lips. He was an indefatigable tract writer. His booklet, "God's Way of Salvation," has been translated into many languages, has been circulated by millions, and has been under God the means of salvation to very many. Messages from his pen have gone into all parts of the world, and many in that day will call him blessed who have, by means of his written ministry, been led into life.

When in Toronto he opened a book store, and his interest in the circulation of gospel books was in keeping with his preaching and writing. He was the greatest tract distributor I ever knew. His pockets always bulged with gospel booklets, and his message in season was always ready. During the last few years of restricted preaching activity, from the sanctuary of Redcroft he continued to send out the soul-saving message, and when no longer able to carry the tracts to the people, he kept others supplied in order that the work might go on. He never ceased to be an evangelist, and will always be remembered for his clear and Scriptural presentation of the work of Christ as the propitiation for the sins of the whole world, and for his large-hearted love for all the Lord's people. A man of great transparency of character, of simple and unaffected faith, he was most like his Master in that "He gave." He found his greatest pleasure in giving, whether it was a large part of his income, (and how much that was only the Lord and those to whom he sent it knew), or a gospel tract, all were given with the same cheerfulness and with the same ready mind.

He had attained the ripe age of eighty-one years, over sixty of which were spent in devoted and unstinted service for the Lord Jesus Christ. His gospel activities only ceased when his life ended, for before the last message of mercy, made up by his own hands and despatched by post, could reach their destination, the ambassador had been recalled, and was at home with the Lord. His last day on earth was spent in dispensing the Lord's bounty, and in sending messages of cheer and encouragement to fellow-laborers in the gospel, then followed a few hours of restlessness and suffering, after which the earthly course was ended on August 9th, 1928.—J.H.

—

Albert Midlane
1825-1909

ALBERT MIDLANE

O N JANUARY 23RD, 1825, there was born in the town of Newport, in the parish of Carisbrooke (famed for its castle), in the Isle of Wight, one who was to cause myriads throughout the world to sing of "The Friend of Sinners," and to allure many to the "Home Above the Bright Blue Sky."

Albert Midlane never knew the blessing of a godly father, but admitted that he owed much to a spiritually-minded mother and a devoted sister. He commenced life as printer, but after three years left "the art preservative" and became an ironmonger's assistant, for long years being in business on his own account. One who mourned his decease was in the employ of his firm for over fifty years.

In his boyhood days he was brought into touch with Thomas Binney, the author of "Eternal Light!" from whom he may have received some impetus to persevere in the poetic line. After many youthful attempts he had the joy of seeing published a hymn, written at Carisbrooke in 1842. His first hymn to be used was "God Bless our Sunday School," to the tune of the National Anthem, written in 1844 when he was nineteen years of age. Since then hymns and poems to the number of about one thousand have flowed steadily from his pen. These include the popular revival and prayer meeting hymn sung in all lands: "Revive Thy Work, O Lord." He also wrote the glad evangelistic refrains: "Oh What a Saviour Is Jesus the Lord," "Salvation, Oh, Salvation, Endearing Precious Sound," "Oh What a Glorious Truth Is This, Jesus Died," "How Vast, How Full, How Free, the Mercy of Our God," "Hark! The Voice of Jesus Calling," "I Am Not Told to Labor," "Oh What a Gift the Father Gave," "All Things Are Ready, Come," and "Passing Onward, Quickly Passing." His hymns of adoration and worship are still sung in many assemblies: "Sweet the Theme of Jesus' Love," "Without a Cloud Between," "Thine, Jesus, Thine," "Bound for Glory, Pressing Onward," "He Comes, He Comes, the Bridegroom Comes," as well as many pieces on various themes.

But Mr. Midlane was best known and will live longest in memory in connection with his children's hymns, the favorite of which, "There's a

253

Friend for Little Children Above the Bright Blue Sky," has attained universal and deserved popularity though some authorities, including *The Times*, maintain that "A Little Lamb Went Straying" is of equal merit. The favorite hymn and the tune which beautifully blend were both written under striking circumstances.

.The hymn was composed on February 7 in the revival year 1859. An interviewer writes: "Stimulated by a passionate desire to write a special message for the little ones Mr. Midlane, after a busy business day, settled down in the quiet of the evening to what proved the great task of his life, and by two o'clock in the morning his supreme effort in hymnology was completed. But it was achieved at the expense of great physical fatigue, which was most marked after a hard day's work in his business, and he recently told the writer that he was found in a state of collapse and had to be medically attended. 'But the hymn was completed,' added Mr. Midlane with a radiant smile."

The standard tune, "In Memoriam," to which it is often sung, was composed by Sir John Stainer under the following circumstances: "The committee engaged on the music of 'Hymns Ancient and Modern' (enlarged edition, 1875) was meeting in London, and when the hymn came up for consideration it was found that though they had several tunes before them none were considered satisfactory. It was suggested that a new tune might be written by one of the committee, and Sir Henry Baker, the chairman, proposed that Sir John Stainer should retire to Sir Henry's bedroom, and try what he could do. Sir John complied with the suggestion, and in a very short time returned with the present tune which was at once adopted." The tune, which first appeared in "Hymns Ancient and Modern," was named "In Memoriam" in connection with the death of Sir John's little son, Frederick Henry Stainer who died on December 30, 1874. Thus, love for "little children" inspired both words and music. As originally compiled the verses ran: "There's a rest, home, Friend, crown, song, and robe," but most people will agree with Dr. Julian, the noted authority on hymnology, that "the re-arrangement produces a better sequence and gives greater unity to the hymn."

Sent as a contribution to "Good News for the Young," a little paper for children edited by C. H. Mackintosh, and first printed as the concluding article to that monthly for 1859 under the heading of "Above the Bright Blue Sky," the hymn at once attained popularity. It has found its way into over two hundred hymn books; is sung in China, Japan, India, all over

Europe, America, Africa, Australasia, and in most unlikely parts of the world, as well as being translated into more than half-a-hundred languages, and giving promise of continuing to be sung "while the earth remaineth."

The author lived to see the celebration of the jubilee of his best-known hymn on February 7, 1909. On that day he had the pleasure of hearing three thousand children assembled in St. Paul's Cathedral, London, blending their voices in "There's a Friend for Little Children." In the same year he attended an open-air service in his native town. There his voice was heard in public for the last time as he earnestly spoke concerning eternal things to the crowds of old and young who had assembled to honor their fellow-townsman.

Hymn writing brought Albert Midlane into touch with many eminent personages. Lord Tennyson, the poet laureate, encouraged him greatly, and Dr. Parker, the famous City Temple preacher, said: "I had rather been the author of 'There's a Friend' than of my most eloquent sermon." C. H. Spurgeon incorporated a good many of his hymns in the Metropolitan Tabernacle hymn book, Mr. Midlane often referring to a time spent with the prince of preachers. Mrs. Luke, authoress of "I Think When I Read the Sweet Story of Old," resided for long in Newport, and the two "children's poets" had much in common. Edmund Peel, the author of "The Fair Island," was an intimate friend. Queen Victoria graciously accepted several volumes of his compositions, and the Prince Consort purchased a number for circulation among his friends. He corresponded with other notables in various spheres.

Unlike most authors, Mr. Midlane never took out a "copyright" for any of his hymns, and never derived any monetary benefit therefrom. After half a century of plodding labor in connection with his ironmongery business he found himself a bankrupt for £500 through having become guarantor for a friend. His misfortune was made known to the public, and Sunday-school friends throughout the country subscribed generously, with the result that Mr. Midlane was able to pay all his creditors and get his bankruptcy annulled, and an annuity was secured which relieved the veteran hymn writer and his wife of further anxiety in this respect.

In the earlier part of his Christian career he was associated with many of the well-known leaders of "Exclusive" Brethren, but had been associated with the "Open" party. His poems on "Union," "No Sect on Earth But

Christians Only," etc., indicate his longings for the true heart unity of all saints.

On March 20, 1901, Mr. and Mrs. Midlane celebrated their golden wedding anniversary. On January 23, 1909, the *County Press*, to which he had contributed many pieces, contained one of his last poems entitled, "On My Eighty-fourth Birthday," which indicates his being "made meet for the inheritance." Two of the verses were as follows:

> What is the world to one whose hopes
> Are fixed beyond the skies?
> What can impede the charioteer
> Just near to grasp the prize?
>
> Enough! One's cup is brimming full,
> All earthly struggles o'er,
> Beneath the shadow of His wings,
> In bliss for evermore.

On Thursday morning, February 11, he was stricken with an apoplectic seizure from which he never rallied, passing away quietly in his sleep just as the morning of Lord's day, February 28, 1909, was approaching.

The body was carried from Forest Villa, so long his abode, to Carisbrooke Cemetery, and laid to rest with the singing of his own hymns, "Star of the Morning, Rise!" and "One Lasting, Long Amen," concluding with a number of children's voices uniting in "There's a Friend for Little Children." A pathos was put to the scene by the interment of a little child not twenty yards away while the last verse of the children's hymn was being sung.—HY.P.

Andrew Miller
1810-1883

ANDREW MILLER

―――⊶◦◦◦⊷――――

ANDREW MILLER was born in the village of Kilmaurs, Ayrshire, on January 27th, 1810. As a young man he entered the firm of Smith, Anderson & Co., Glasgow eventually taking up the London Branch of the firm, afterwards changed into Miller, Son & Torrance, of Cannon Street.

While supervising a large London business, Mr. Miller was for a considerable time the voluntary pastor of a Baptist church in William Street. As light from the Word of God was followed the sectarian principles were left behind, and the believers gathered on Scriptural lines. Mr. Miller continuing to labor as an honored brother among them.

As a warm-hearted evangelist, the best of the man was ever visible. He was greatly used in the conversion of souls, both among old and young. It was no uncommon thing for the preacher to bathe his impassioned appeals with tears while he pleaded the claims of the Master he loved. In fact, he was called by many "the Rutherford of brethren."

As an author his name will be remembered as long as his valuable "Papers on Church History" or his meditations on the Song of Solomon, the Psalms, and other themes continue to be read. If they were more known they would be more valued. He encouraged the writing, wrote the introduction, and largely helped to finance the issues of C.H.M.'s "Notes on the Pentateuch," the most popular and extensively circulated of all the varied volumes connected with what is known as "the Brethren movement."

Telling how he had been led to cast in his lot with those who thus gather to the name of the Lord Jesus and to break bread every Lord's day, he said he had been a member of a church for some time previously, when one day he was invited by a Christian gentleman to attend a Bible reading which was held in his drawing-room each week. "I accepted the invitation," he said, "and went, but such a stranger was I to that kind of thing that I went in full evening dress, and found myself the only one so attired, which made me feel very uncomfortable. We were invited into the dining-room for refreshments, and then adjourned to the drawing-room for the Bible reading. After prayer a passage of Scripture was reverently read, and a deeply interesting conversation followed. As I listened to the unfolding of the Inspired Volume I began to discover that the Bible contained such wonderful truths, to which I was an entire stranger, that I soon forgot my 'evening dress,' and made up my mind to attend the next weekly Bible reading if the host would invite me. This he did, and I attended week by week, learning more and more the wonderful truths of God, and becoming better acquainted with the great purposes of redeeming love and grace. Thus I was led to cast in my lot with the so-called 'Brethren.'"

On another occasion he told how he was led to begin to preach and to speak publicly. Having to visit the north of Ireland in connection with business matters during the revival of 1859-60, he had been an eye witness of some of those wondrous scenes of spiritual blessing when many men and women were stricken down to the ground under the convicting power of God's Word, and were constrained to cry out publicly for mercy. Souls were saved, backsliders were restored, and believers were revived and blessed. On returning to London, Mr. Miller could not help but tell his friends what he had seen and heard. These friends at once said: "We must not keep these good things to ourselves, but we must invite our friends and neighbors together that they also may hear of this marvellous work of grace." Drawing-room meetings were convened, and Mr. Miller was invited to give an account of the revival work in the north of Ireland. In this way he was led out into public service for his Lord.

He had a passion for souls and was a true evangelist, as well as a spiritually qualified teacher. He saw the multitude and his soul was stirred. Rarely ever did he preach the gospel without tears, and he told me how it grieved him to his heart to find the growing apathy in gospel work among the saints in the different assemblies he visited.

"In labors more abundant" for half a century, in suffering scarcely less so near the end, Andrew Miller fell asleep on May 8th, 1883. In the eventide of retirement, as he looked back upon the past, around on the then present, and forward to the future, he exclaimed with great emphasis of soul, "*Nothing counts but Christ.*"—G.H.

T. B. Miller
1840-1905

T. B. MILLER

THOMAS BLAIR MILLER, son of Dr. Andrew Miller, whose volumes of "Church History" and expositions have been enjoyed by thousands of the Lord's people in many parts of the world, was associated with Christians meeting at Salisbury Road, High Barnet. Although head of the successful city firm of Miller, Son & Torrance, he devoted a considerable part of his time to the work of the Lord. He not only had a heart for the gospel but, like his father, was a Bible student. Especially strong was his interest in all that had to do with the Word of God; his addresses both to Christians and the unconverted consistently showing a deep love for the Bible, and many thoughtful and reverent expositions of Scripture were given by him in the meetings at St. George's Hall, Langham Place, and later at Portman Rooms, Baker Street.

As a business man he was held in the highest esteem, and his kindly sympathy with those in trouble of any kind won for him the loving respect of all who knew him.

Mr. Miller was chairman and treasurer of the Royal National Mission to Deep Sea Fishermen from its inception in 1885 until the time of his death. Having a thorough knowledge of fishermen and fisheries, he took a deep and practical interest in all matters affecting their moral and spiritual welfare. On one occasion, when describing the work of the mission, Mr. Miller emphasized the fact that the primary aim is spiritual, adding, "We keep this first, because it is the main or supreme object of our enterprise. Though we repair broken legs and heal wounds, irrespective entirely of whether a man holds our doctrinal views or has any views at all, yet our own services held aboard the mission ships, and in our various halls, and also aboard the trawlers, are always of an evangelistic nature."

In July 1905, he paid a visit to the fishermen in the North Sea, speaking at many meetings with much blessing. In all his services he sought earnestly to glorify God and win souls for Christ. He also contributed the Bible studies which appeared in the fisherman's magazine, *Toilers of the Deep.*

Ever a welcome speaker at conferences of Christians in various parts of the British Isles, he was advertised to take part in the large Half-Yearly Meetings of Christians at Glasgow in the autumn of 1905, but was called to join the larger company in glory before the time of conference arrived.

On Saturday, September 9th, he had a slight apoplectic seizure, but recovered sufficiently to take part in the meetings on the following Lord's day. On September 11th, 1905, he set out for Skegness for a few days' rest, and while there was seized with another shock from which he did not recover.

Henry Moorhouse
1840-1880

HENRY MOORHOUSE

———◦⊶⊶◦———

HENRY MOORHOUSE, or as he was more familiarly called, "Harry Moorhouse, the English Evangelist," was born in the city of Manchester. When very young he was sent to jail on more than one occasion, afterwards joining the army and trying the life of a soldier, being bought off by his father at considerable cost.

Passing the Alhambra Circus in Manchester, where Richard Weaver was preaching, hearing a noise within and thinking a fight was going on, Henry buttoned his coat and rushed in, ready for the fray. As he entered he was arrested by one word—"JESUS." The glorious name shot from the preacher's lips went home as a bullet and as balm to the heart of the wanderer. His early childhood, reckless career and awful danger rose vividly before his vision, the "glorious gospel" (2 Corinthians 4:4) message went home to his heart, and he who had entered to fight remained to praise and pray.

Thus suddenly and soundly converted to God, he entered heartily into the service of his new Master. His first services were chiefly in the open air, at local and national gatherings, and in special places of concourse. From morning till evening his joy was to spend his time distributing tracts, speaking personally with individuals wherever he got an opportunity, or crying aloud in the street or market-place, urging multitudes to "flee from the wrath to come."

Like the apostle of old, he had visions of God. Upon one occasion he saw in his sleep three young men in Manchester, each strangely attired in a white jacket, on which were the words legibly written, "These men are going to Hell!" The place appeared to be near the infirmary, and before them was a deep burning lake of fire unperceived by them. Henry called aloud for them to stop, but they took no heed, until he fell down upon his knees and cried to God, saying

"Lord, it is not by might, nor by power, but by Thy Spirit." The men then turned back in haste, having discovered their danger. This dream was on Friday night; and on the Sunday evening following, when Henry was preaching in the Alhambra Circus, those three identical young men came into the place and before the meeting closed they were all on their knees crying out for mercy and were brought to accept the Lord Jesus Christ and the pardon of their sins.

The revival stream, which had begun to flow in 1854, was in full tide in 1860, when Moorhouse was converted. Thus he was early brought into touch with the enthusiastic spirits—Richard Weaver, from the coalpit, whose style he largely followed; John Hambleton, the converted actor; Edward Usher, a dockyard laborer; William Carter, the converted sweep; Henry Varley, a butcher, and afterwards valiant champion for the truth; Reginald Radcliffe, the Liverpool lawyer; Brownlow North, the man of wealth and fashion; Joshua Poole, better known as Fiddler Joss; J. Denham Smith, a devout expositor; C. H. Spurgeon, of the Metropolitan Tabernacle; H. Grattan Guiness, of the "Regions Beyond", and many others. D. L. Moody and Ira D. Sankey afterwards became his special friends.

Henry's special call to devote all his time to the work of the Lord came through an enthusiast known as "the hatless preacher." One evening when Henry was engaged in crying his wares as auctioneer of "Notions," and rapping for bids, the hatless man suddenly appeared before him, and cried aloud, "Thou oughtest to have thy Bible in thy hand out amongst the people, and not that hammer for the devil," and immediately departed. That short, terrible speech was like a thunderbolt falling on Henry, and the words gave a harder blow than he could stand. He at once dropped the auctioneer's hammer, went to Liverpool, sought out Hambleton, and entered with him on an evangelistic tour through the provinces. Since that date Henry labored in the special work of evangelizing without a fixed salary or human promise of support. A trio consisting of John Hambleton, the preacher; Edward Usher, the singer; and Henry Moorhouse, the young and fervent disciple, attended the tercentenary of William Shakespeare at Stratford-on-Avon. They bore aloft textboards bearing the words, "Christ for Me! Praise the Lord! Mercy's Free!" and created no small stir, with fruit which shall abound in "that day."

Recorded in "Buds, Blossoms, and Fruits of the Revival" are stories of these heroes: their visits to race meetings, haunts of vice, sinners in the slums, and public executions (then not uncommon); their theater services (sometimes fourteen theaters were filled in London on one Sunday night); their labors among Romanists in many parts of Ireland; and their "labors more abundant."

Through incessant labors in Britain, Henry Moorhouse, never strong at the best, began to show signs of sadly needing rest and change. Hence he set out for the United States, arriving in Philadelphia in 1868. His welcome was so hearty, and his ministry so appreciated, that he paid five visits in the following ten years. How he became "the man who moved the man who moved the world" is best told in D. L. Moody's own words: "In 1867, when I was preaching in Dublin, at the close of the service a young man, who did not look over seventeen, though he was older, came up to me and said he would like to go back to America with me and preach the gospel. I thought he could not preach it, and I said I was undecided when I could go back. He asked me if I would write to him, as I did not know whether I wanted him or not. After I arrived at Chicago I got a letter saying he had just arrived in New York, and he would come and preach. I wrote him a cold letter, asking him to call on me if he came west. A few days after, I got a letter stating he would be in Chicago next Thursday. I didn't know what to do with him. I said to the officers of the church, 'There is a man coming from England and he wants to preach. I am going to be absent Thursday and Friday. If you will let him preach on those days I will be back on Saturday and take him off your hands.' They did not care about his preaching, being a stranger; but at my request they let him preach. On my return on Saturday I was anxious to hear how the people liked him, and I asked my wife how that young Englishman got along. How did they like him? She said they liked him very much. 'He preaches a little different from what you do. He tells the people God loves them. I think you will like him.' I said she was wrong. I thought I could not like a man who preached contrary to what I was preaching. I went down on Saturday night to hear him, but I had made up my mind not to like him, because he preached different from me."

After graphically describing the six nights Moorehouse preached on John 3:16, Moody concludes: "In closing up that seventh sermon, he said, 'For seven nights I have been trying to tell you how much God loves you, but this poor stammering tongue of mine will not let me. If I could ascend Jacob's ladder and ask Gabriel, who stands in the presence of the Almighty, to tell me how much love God the Father has for this poor lost world, all that Gabriel could say would be, that 'God so loved the world, that He gave His only begotten Son, that whosoever believeth in Him should not perish, but have everlasting life.' I have never forgotten those nights. I have preached a different gospel since, and I have had more power with God and man since then." Ever after he was a close personal friend and helper of Messrs. Moody and Sankey. Fleming H. Revell, the American publisher who died in 1931, was present at these services and confirms the story as here stated.

During the last few years of Moorehouse's life he found work something akin to that of his early days in preaching and selling Scriptures from a Bible carriage. In two years he sold over 150,000 Bibles and Testaments, and gave away millions of books and tracts.

In 1876 his service was evidently closing, his last year of labor was one of much suffering. The doctors said his heart was twice the size it ought to be, yet he was ever bright and happy. Near the end he said, "If it were the Lord's will to raise me up again, I should like to preach from the text 'God so loved the world.'" On December 28th, 1880, in his fortieth year, he passed Home to receive the "Well done," and to enter into "the joy of his Lord."

The two veterans, Richard Weaver and Henry Moorhouse, lie not far from each other in Ardwick Cemetery, Manchester. John 3:16 is engraved on the memorial to Moorhouse.

John Hambleton, in relating his farewell interview with Henry, aptly summed up his life: "Calling to see him on Monday last, before he left us, I grasped his arms, as his face betokened that the enemy death was doing his last work, and said, 'Harry, we shall soon meet up yonder.' He replied, while gasping for breath, 'Sure, sure, sure!' How plainly visible is the work of God in putting into such a little frail vessel as our brother such a treasure, showing us all that the excellency of the power is of God."

Henry's last letter aptly summed up his own life. "Ask prayer for me to suffer for Christ better than ever I preached for Him; I ONLY WANT TO GLORIFY HIM."—HY.P.

John Morley
1807-1896

JOHN MORLEY

JOHN MORLEY was born at Homerton, Hackney, London, June 4th, 1807, and resided in the same parish until his home-call when close on ninety. He was the eldest of three brothers, the others being Samuel Morley, M. P. for Bristol, whose biography has been written by Edwin Hodder; and William Morley, of Bow, all of whom are now reunited The gracious love and courteous demeanor of his mother and the unblemished character and cultivated mind of his father had great weight in molding the early life of their son.

Well-known Christian preachers and workers ever found a welcome in the parental home, thus the sons were privileged to enjoy the personal friendship of Dr. Binney, Dr. John Pye Smith, John Clayton, James Parsons, and many others.

On leaving school in 1823 he joined the world-renowned firm of I. & R. Morley, Manufacturers and Wholesale Drapery Warehousemen. Integrity and assiduity marked the thirty-two years which he devoted to the upbuilding of the "House of Morley," which, through the exertions of the parents, John and Robert Morley, and their sons, became one of the most prosperous and highly respected in the world's metropolis. His influence over the young men of the house was always very great, and throughout the establishment he was regarded with the greatest respect and affection. On his retirement in 1855 he sent a unique letter to each of the employees, gave £100 to increase the volumes in the library, a family Bible to the porters, etc., in addition to monetary and other tokens of interest in the temporal and spiritual welfare of the various members of the establishment.

Freed from business, Mr. Morley devoted his time to the furtherance of the Lord's work, visiting many parts of Britain and Europe. During one of these tours, in the eventful year of 1859, he paid a visit to Ireland. He was met at Kingstown by J. Denham Smith, who had been a guest at their hospitable home in London, and who remarked: "You will surely go to the north and see something of the revival," which at that time was spreading like wildfire through many parts of the Emerald Isle. Mr. and Mrs.

Morley promised to consider the matter, and next day they set out on what proved an eventful visit. In the midst of the manifestation of the power of the Holy Spirit, they saw the foundation truths of Scripture in a new light, learned much of the Word and will of God, and returned home with purpose of heart to devote more fully time, talents, and all to the service of such a Master.

These remarkable years, '59 to '63, were seasons of gathering in of many men to be afterwards used mightily in the Lord's service, including R. J. Mahony of Dromore Castle, W. T. Crosbie of Tralee, F. C. Bland of Derryquin, George F. Trench, Alfred Trench, Townsend Trench. and T. Shuldham Henry, several of whom were afterwards associated with Mr. Morley in work in London.

Mr. Denham Smith was soon invited to London, and had many fruitful drawing-room meetings in the homes of John and Samuel Morley. Freemasons' Hall was next taken for larger gatherings, and rooms in Wood's Hotel for more private readings. These readings were published under the title of "Life Truths," and have been helpful to thousands, including D. L. Moody.

Special meetings were also arranged in Brighton, Bath, Croydon, St. Leonards, Liverpool, Shrewsbury, and other large towns in England, as well as Paris and other centers on the Continent. The "Times of Refreshing" Hymn Book owed its birth to the spirit abroad at this time.

In the outreaching to others Mr. Morley remembered the Saviour's injunction, "Go home," so had the Iron Room erected in Upper Clapton. Opened in 1867, it became the birthplace of very many souls. Many men whose names are well known—Denham Smith, Shuldham Henry, C. Russell Hurditch, Howard Johnston, Herbert Taylor, J. G. M'Vicar, Wm. Lincoln, Rice T. Hopkins, H. W. Soltau, Henry Heath, Trevor Francis, and several others—gave help at the services, which continued to be crowded for several years. Then Mr. Morley erected the substantial and more centrally situated Clapton Hall, in Stoke-Newington. Messrs. Denham Smith, Lincoln, Dyer, Morley, and others took part in the opening services in February 1880. Mr. George Muller, of the Ashley Down Orphan Homes, visited the hall and helped in ministry.

Though not a great speaker, Mr. Morley's intense devotion to the Lord's work, especially in the Iron Room and Clapton Hall, where his genial smile, friendly handshake, kindly inquiry after body and soul, words of counsel and cheer, and little gospel booklet have borne fruit, the real har-

vest of which will only be known in eternity. For many years he kept
the roll-book, which in early Iron Room days had three hundred names
on its pages, running up at one time to eight hundred in Clapton Hall.
Two or three friendly hives-off and other circumstances have reduced
the total, but a goodly number still hold forth and abide loyal to "God
and the word of His grace."

Strange to say, for a number of years the question of baptism had not
much exercised the mind of Mr. Morley. A remark by Mr. Theodore Jones
so impressed him that he searched the Scriptures and saw it to be the
will of God. Along with his beloved life-partner he was immersed at
Tottenham, receiving John 12:26 as his text. Needless to say, a baptistery
formed part of the new Clapton Hall, and many have more fully realized
the truths of death, burial, and resurrection (Colossians 2:12) through
being immersed therein.

Regularly found in his place "upon the first day of the week, when the
disciples came together to break bread" (Acts 20:7), Morley realized the
true center. One Lord's day morning in the Old Iron Room he remarked
to Mr. A. M. Kyd, "We don't come here to remember one another, or to
remember our work, but to remember Him."

In addition to encouraging oral ministry of gifted brethren and her-
alding forth the gospel message, Mr. Morley loved to scatter the printed
page. Enormous quantities of books, leaflets, monthly papers for saved
and unsaved were sent forth. Many thousands of the *Herald of Salvation*
have been scattered over close to forty years, during which the monthly
numbers have been regularly supplied. Such plentiful sowing must produce a rich harvest. Nor did he leave the scattering to others. Personal
testimony and dealing with souls were classed amongst his greatest joys.
He used to quote his favorite text—John 3:16 —and then say, "God loved—
God gave—I believe—and I have."

Years continued to fly past. The death of Mr. Samuel Morley in 1886,
Denham Smith in 1889, Shuldham Henry in 1893, Dr. Lazeron in 1894,
followed by F. C. Bland and other veterans, left a deep impression upon
our brother. For two or three years his health gradually failed until the
opening moment of the year 1896, when he "slept in Jesus," his last words
being, "My Saviour, my Saviour!"

On 8th January the mortal remains were laid beside those of his
brother and other members of the Morley family in Abney Park Cemetery, awaiting the victor's "shout" and resurrection "reunion" to be "for-
ever with the Lord."—HY.P.

George Muller
1806-1898

GEORGE MULLER

GEORGE MULLER was born in Prussia, and designed by his father for the clerical profession. His youth was spent in utter ungodliness, even surpassing many of his age in sin and folly. His conversion was strangely sudden. It was not through deep conviction of sin or clear gospel preaching, but simply by finding himself for the first time in the company of praying people. Yet it was indeed a new birth. His life was at once turned wholly to God, and he rapidly grew in the knowledge of Him. His devotion to the ministry of the Word, on which he now entered, became a reality.

He desired to be a missionary to the Jews, for which his study of Hebrew seemed to fit him. By a striking providence he was pronounced, under medical examination, incapable of military service, and was thus set free to give himself to that of the gospel; and he came to England with the prospect of employment under the London Jews' Society. There, however, he found himself hampered by conditions to which he could not conscientiously consent. Leaving London, he was led to Teignmouth in Devonshire, where the Lord so used him that he settled there for a time, and became associated with Mr. Henry Craik in an uninterrupted fellowship until the decease of the latter in 1866. Then in 1832 they came to Bristol, where they found an open door and their united ministry, chiefly in Bethesda Chapel, was exceedingly fruitful.

Already in Devonshire they had learned to lay aside the traditions of "Congregationalism," such as infant baptism, pew rents, a separate ministerial order, and a stated salary; and they saw that the Lord's table was for all believers, irrespective of denominational views and distinctions.

While the work at Bristol was growing in their hands, Mr. Muller's heart was led out to care for destitute orphans. From a small beginning, a second and a third house were rented for their reception. At the first he had laid down for himself the rule that, beyond making known the existence of the institution, he would never apply in any way to man for help, and further that he would never reveal to any human being, outside those associated with him in the work, the state of the funds however pressing the need; for the aim he set before him was not merely the benefit of the orphans, but much more that it might be a witness to all that God is, as ever of old, the hearer of prayer.

Encouraged by God's manifest help, he sought to enlarge this sphere of usefulness. As means were supplied (for he never under any circumstances would go into debt), he built a large house on Ashley Down for three hundred orphans. To this he added a second, then a third, and finally two more— five in all,—with accommodation for over two thousand orphans and the staff of helpers.

Great as the work had become, and needing a yearly income of about £30,000, so steadfast was his purpose to trust in God alone that from the commencement in 1834, Mr. Muller and his helpers have never been known to depart from their rule. However pressing their trials the need has been told to God only. Nor have they ever advertised the institution. Only once annually (in early years not always so often), the results have been published some two months after the close of the financial year to show how the Lord has dealt with them, never failing to meet their needs though for long periods together the supply was often only by the day, or even by the hour.

The volumes of "The Lord's Dealings with George Muller," now compiled into one volume, and the reports issued annually, are a continuous record of answers to prayer in circumstances of varied trial. Did our limits allow of extracts, these would speak louder than anything that can be said concerning them. One incident, coming under the writer's notice, may serve as a sample. He had been spending the night at Mr. Muller's house, and at the simple breakfast there was no appearance of lack. On parting he handed Mr. M. a small sum, having no idea how matters might stand with him. When after two years a report was issued, he found at that date an entry to the effect that "a brother had been staying the night with them, and they had enough to put on the table for breakfast not only for themselves but for their guest, but there was nothing left to purchase the next meal. The brother, on leaving, put——into his hand, and so their wants were supplied for the time."

Financial matters were but one kind of need in which, as it arose, God alone was looked to and found to be a very present help whatever the trouble. As when in cold winter time the boiler by which the large building was warmed throughout was discovered to be irreparably worn and had to be replaced, prayer was answered in giving warm weather so long as the operation lasted, and in the men, unasked, offering to work by relays through the night to hasten its completion.

Facts like these, of constant occurrence, spreading over so large a space of time, and the deliverances invariably wrought, are such as to silence all the cavils of unbelief, and to prove that it was God hearing and answering prayer. And this Mr. Muller constantly pressed as applying to every circumstance in which God's children are placed—that He can be trusted to hear and answer prayer from an honest heart, not on the ground of our own merits but in the name of Jesus, if we will wait His time and let Him do it in His own way.

The money that passed through his hands for the orphans in answer to prayer considerably exceeded a million sterling. Besides this, he received similarly in donations to the extent of some £397.000 means for circulating Bibles and tracts supporting Scriptural schools and aiding missionaries.

Leaving his son-in-law, Mr. James Wright, in charge at Bristol, his later years, from 1874 to 1892, were spent mainly in travelling over Britain, the continent of Europe, North America and Canada, Australia, India, China, and other countries, preaching the gospel and building up believers in faith and love, often addressing large numbers of ministers and students wherever he found an open door (and it was freely accorded him in all parts, for he loved all who love the Lord by whatever name they are called), sharing widespread blessing wherever he went. Early experience in preaching had led him to abandon all attempt at pulpit oratory, and to aim rather at extreme simplicity, so that his speech was not with enticing words of man's wisdom; but it was in demonstration of the Spirit and in power.

The secret of his useful life was his simple faith in God and in His Word. He loved the Bible, read it not only at stated times, but whenever he found moments of opportunity, believing it, acting upon it, and finding it true in his experience. And the burden of his teaching was that if we would so read it and act upon it we might all enjoy the same experience, each in our own station of life or sphere of service. This indeed is what many another can bear witness to; and many such have been helped to learn it by the testimony and example of George Muller.

Often he would say, "I am a happy man." While himself "a Hell-deserving sinner," Jesus was ever his "adorable Saviour." On his last

Sunday he dwelt with peculiar feeling on the joy of seeing Him in His beauty, and "kissing His dear feet."

Early in the morning of March 10, 1898, in his ninety-third year, this man of God was suddenly called from his service on earth to the presence of the King above. The previous day had seen him busy at his ordinary occupation, and in the evening he had taken his usual part in the prayer meeting. The summons was momentary and painless, as if changed "in the twinkling of an eye."

Of the Lord's bounty sent him for personal use he was found to have given away over £80,000, and when his will was proved his whole property amounted to about £60 and the furniture of his apartment. He is gone to his rest but his works do follow him, and his life will be a standing witness for God to the end of the age.—W.C.

Dr. Thomas Neatby
1835-1911

DR. THOMAS NEATBY

THOMAS NEATBY was born at Worsborough, near Barnsley, August 1st, 1835. His parents were fervent Christians, connected with the Methodists. The Methodists were preaching the gospel with no little power among the villages of South Yorkshire, and during a mission held in the Wesleyan Chapel at Worsborough Bridge, both Thomas then only nine years old, and his elder brother professed their faith in Christ. About 1846 the family settled in Barnsley, where the father had taken over a timber merchant's business. Here friendships, destined to be cherished sixty years later as some of the choicest blessings of life, were formed with two men whose names are imperishably linked with the beginning of the gospel in inland China—Hudson Taylor and Benjamin Broomhall.

At the age of seventeen Thomas began to preach in the Wesleyan Reform connection, but before long he was associated with Christians who became widely known as "Brethren." In those early days he shared young Hudson Taylor's ambition for gospel service in China, and it was with this in view that he began the study of medicine.

He was apprenticed to doctors in Hull and Banbury, and afterwards studied at Edinburgh University and St. Bartholomew's Hospital. He graduated M.D. at St. Andrews University about 1861. By that time he had become closely associated with the work of the Christians known as "Exclusive Brethren" in London, and he gradually abandoned his plans for China. His medical practice began in Camden Road, but he removed his residence to Hampstead in 1866, remaining there until 1894, when he retired from his profession after nearly thirty-three years' most enthusiastic pursuit of it.

Even during the period of laborious professional life, half his great energy was given to the ministry. His association with J. N. Darby came to an end in 1881, but his connection with so-called "Exclusive Brethren" extended to January 1887. The interval was filled with a period of co-operation with William Kelly in a movement that marked a certain reaction against the more extreme tendencies of J. N. Darby's system; but in the end he found the entire "Exclusive" discipline a burden to his conscience. Thenceforward his services were freely at the disposal of all Christians, and he took part in many an undenominational convention; the bulk of his ministry, however, was happily exercised among the believers commonly known as "Open Brethren."

For the last twenty-six years of his life he was partially crippled by a paralytic seizure, and the extent and vigor of his labors in itinerant evangelization and Bible teaching were very remarkable indeed in the circumstances. His spirit never flagged, and his zeal for the work was keen at the last.

He was the author of one book, "Our Lord's Coming Again," published in 1877, though some of his choicest addresses are to be had in a little volume entitled "From Glory to Glory." The end came peacefully on Sunday morning, November 12th, 1911, after a few days' illness.—W.B.N.

Thomas Newberry
1811-1901

THOMAS NEWBERRY

◦◦◦◦◦

THOMAS NEWBERRY often praised God for the blessing of a Christian mother and a godly elder sister for through them, like Timothy of old, he knew the holy Scriptures from a child; and it pleased God to reveal His Son to his soul as Saviour and Lord at an early age, so that he knew the blessed experience of being "born again" (John 3:3), by the incorruptible Word of God, which "liveth and abideth for ever" (1 Peter 1:23). And his Christian life commenced with a love and reverence for the holy Scriptures, which were his food and "the joy and rejoicing of [his] heart" (Jeremiah 15:16) throughout his long and active life, so that he became "mighty in the scriptures" (Acts 18: 24), and one of the most reliable and profitable expositors of the Bible.

During the early years of his Christian experience he was but an ordinary reader of the Word of God for comfort and instruction; but soon he began the diligent study and searching of the Scriptures in the original Hebrew and Greek languages. Pursuing these studies for twenty-five years, he felt constrained to commence that which will be one of the best memorials of his valuable life, "The Englishman's Bible," which is now widely known and greatly prized by Bible students as one of the best helps ever published for enabling ordinary readers to discern the beauties of the original sacred Scriptures.

This work has been highly commended by competent scholars, who express admiration at the immense labors bestowed upon the book, and the valuable and reliable information given in its marginal notes, which help Christians to understand somewhat of the precious treasure which God has given in this, His own Word.

Diligent Scripture study drew Mr. Newberry into association with a remarkable revival which took place in the British Isles early in the last century, when the Spirit of God led many eminent Christians to search the holy Scriptures in relation to their ecclesiastical associations. The conviction was forced upon many of their souls that much of the teaching was not in harmony with the Word of God; that many of the customs were based upon expediency rather than conformity to "the law and the testimony" (Isaiah. 8:20); that principles and practices (which were plainly recorded in the Epistle to the Corinthians and other Scriptures, as characteristic of the churches of God as founded by the apostles after the divine pattern given to Paul, ("the wise masterbuilder") were not being observed, although 1 Corinthians 1:1,2 said they were binding upon "all that in every place call upon the name of Jesus Christ our Lord."

Great searching of heart took place about the year 1828-1830, leading godly men to act as those did in Malachi's day: they spoke "often one to another: and the Lord hearkened, and heard it, and a book of remembrance was written before him, for them that feared the Lord, and that thought upon his name" (Malachi 3:16). Events of deepest interest resulted from these meetings, for as the conclusion was forced upon their souls that they were not able to preach, teach, and practice all they found written in God's Word, and as they were in associations where parts of that Word were violated and ignored, they must separate from such surroundings (as taught in 2 Corinthians 6:14-18; Revelation 18:4; Isaiah. 1:16; and Jeremiah 15:19). They should occupy a position where it was possible for them to keep the ordinances of the Lord as they were delivered (1 Corinthians 11:2), and to conform to all things they found written in the law of the Lord. They were to separate to where they could exercise those gifts which were bestowed upon them by the Lord Jesus Christ for the mutual edification of fellow-saints (see Ephesians 4:11-17; 1 Peter 4:10,11; Romans 12; 1 Corinthians 12:14, etc.) without human appointment, sanction, or restrictions.

Acknowledging the supremacy and authority of the holy Scriptures, and setting aside the creeds, rules, and regulations which men had devised, and which had become sectarian barriers to the communion of saints, they regarded it as a cardinal principle of God's assemblies that the Word of God should be their sole appeal for all matters of doctrine and practice. The decisions of the Word of God were binding upon all in their fellowship; that there should be liberty to preach, teach, and obey all that they found in the Bible.

Mr. Newberry's lectures and writings upon the tabernacle and the temple have been of spiritual profit to thousands. He constructed a model of the temple of exquisite beauty and quite unique in its design and workmanship, the result of great research in the original Scriptures, so that it might convey some idea of that gorgeous temple which Solomon built from the pattern given to his father David by the Spirit of God, as Moses also constructed the tabernacle from the pattern which God gave to him in the holy mount. This model, with various writings in connection with it and its bearing upon other subjects, will be lasting memorials to the value of his Bible research. For long years he expounded the Scriptures in many parts of the British Isles, gave numerous lectures on the model of the tabernacle, wrote valuable papers for *The Witness* and other magazines. He conducted an extensive correspondence with Bible students in various parts of the world, and sought to be a helper to the saints in every possible way, falling asleep at Weston-super-Mare on January 16th, 1901, at the ripe age of ninety.

Volumes of "The Englishman's Bible" "Notes on the Temple," "Notes on the Tabernacle," 'The Parables of Our Lord," "The Temples of Solomon and Ezekiel," "Solar Light," and other books have been extensively circulated. The Bible was issued in three sizes: *Library* or bold type; *Portable*, or middle size; and *Pocket* size. Early Portable size copies are valuable and scarce.

In conclusion, we quote the earnest testimony of this departed scholar written in his old age: "As the result of a careful examination of the entire Scriptures in the originals, noticing and marking where necessary every variation of tense, preposition, and the signification of words, the impression left upon my mind is this, not the difficulty of believing the entire inspiration of the Bible, but the impossibility of doubting it....The godliness of the translators, their reverence, the superiority of their scholarship, and the manifest assistance and control afforded to them by the Holy Spirit in their work is such that the ordinary reader can rely upon the whole as the Word of God."—B.

Harrison Ord
1833-1928

HARRISON ORD

H ARRISON ORD was born in Middlesbro', Yorkshire on March 11, 1833. As years rolled on, young Harry developed a physique of splendid proportions and, during his engineering apprenticeship and subsequently through daily contact with a group of hard-headed men in the same workshop, he gained a strong, manly independence of character, which continued with him to the end of his earthly course, giving him during many years of gospel work an influence with men of a similar stamp, which many others might not wield.

Until about twenty-four years of age he lived for present things alone, although evidently bearing an excellent reputation for steady uprightness and strict morality. A successful career was his ambition, drinking freely of "Egypt's misnamed pleasures," as he pressed on toward the attainment of his object. He had moved to, and was settled in London at the time when the whole city, from its center to its suburbs, seemed to throb with the name and fame of the young preacher, Charles Haddon Spurgeon. The month of February 1857, had dawned, when, on a certain Sunday morning our stalwart engineer formed a unit in a crowd of ten thousand surging on toward the Surrey Gardens Music Hall.

That morning the arrow of conviction reached him, and continued to rankle in Ord's conscience until—in a prayer-meeting not long after when special supplication was made for him—the tale of God's love to him was told: the finished work of Christ and His willingness and power to save. That day the Saviour and the sinner met, the Saviour was trusted by the sinner, sorrow and sighing fled away, and joy and gladness filled his heart to overflowing. The grand old hymn was at once struck up by the company, "O happy day that fixed my choice," the voice of the young convert, as of "a son of thunder," completely drowning the combined voices of all the rest. Assured salvation, settled peace, were his from that memorable moment onward, not the shadow of a doubt ever finding a place in his mind as to "the great transaction done."

He at once came out boldly on the Lord's side, made rapid progress in the knowledge of Christ, and of the Scriptures which testify of Him. A passionate love for the souls of his fellows possessed him, and he soon gave evidence of marked ability in preaching the gospel, much of the eloquence and force of his worthy father in the faith seeming to be inherited by the son, the voice of each being a wonder to many.

It was not long before the bench of the engineer was forsaken for the platform of the preacher, and Harrison Ord, through his gift and grace, was speedily accorded a place in the very front ranks of the band of devoted evangelists raised up and thrust forth by the Lord of the harvest in those early days of widespread revival, to "gather in from the fields of sin" golden sheaves by the thousand to the garner of the Lord. For some eighteen years the United Kingdom was his parish, going up and down the land in labors abundant preaching "Christ, and him crucified" in buildings, tents and the open air, the Lord giving through His servant testimony to the word of His grace. Many were the seals of his ministry among the unsaved, and as the teacher became blended with the evangelist, much helpful instruction from the Word of God was imparted to Christians, young and old. He turned his mechanical skill to account, and, guided by the pattern shown to Moses in the mount, produced a fine model of the Tabernacle in the wilderness, from which he, in his lectures, unfolded much precious truth concerning Christ to be found enfolded in those types and shadows.

After a protracted tent campaign in 1875, followed by a continuation of the work in Somerset Hall, Bath—where he, with his family, then resided—our brother's strength gave way, and his wonderful voice was reduced to a whisper. Added to this trial was a deep sorrow occasioned by the loss of his dear wife and the mother of his four children. As medically advised, he decided to embark for Australia, trusting that the long voyage and change of climate might prove beneficial to general health and the restoration of his voice.

Heartily commended to God by many friends in Welbeck Hall, London, he sailed with his eldest daughter, on February 7, 1876, for Melbourne. A fifteen weeks' passage had the desired effect so that, as the writer found when they met in Melbourne by arrangement some six months later, he was able to re-engage on a moderate scale in his loved work of preaching the gospel, while awaiting the arrival of his co-worker. Arrangements were then made for a three months' evangelistic effort in

Melbourne, when the Assembly Hall, Collins Street, was crowded from start to finish, the final gospel meeting being transferred to Wilson's Circus, when four or five thousand were estimated to be present. Other parts of Victoria were visited by one or both, and altogether the Australian work was very fruitful. Early in November, the pair crossed to Tasmania, preaching mainly in Launceston and Hobart. New Zealand came next, Dunedin being the starting point, with large gatherings during a month of Sunday evenings in Prince's Theatre, and meetings in other halls during the intervening weeks. Christchurch and Nelson were visited, and testimony borne in both. In the latter, nestling among the hills, the Drill Hall was packed with hundreds outside—truly a specially blessed season. Auckland came last, when the Theatre Royal was engaged for three Lord's day evenings. "After-church services" were held, and a work begun which was taken up by friends on the spot, and carried on in the same place for some five-and-twenty years, until the building was sold for business purposes. The Day will declare the full results.

Mr. Ord visited "the Old Country" in the summer of 1880, remaining on this side till early in 1881, After some years, devoted largely to work in Melbourne and vicinity, Tasmania, and New Zealand being revisited, he removed to Geelong, and there for many years continued to minister the Word—open air and indoors—as long as strength allowed. The end—on the night of January 1, 1907—was reached in perfect peace, and Home was welcome. Writing on December 4, 1906, he said: "Sometimes it seems as though to depart and be with Christ is imminent—with not a care." In four brief weeks he had his heart's desire granted, and was with Him whom, for close on fifty years, he had trusted, loved, and served.—D.R.

Richard W. Owens
1842-1928

RICHARD W. OWENS

RICHARD W. OWENS was born at Enniscorthy, County Wexford, Ireland, in December 1842, and was brought to know Christ as his Saviour and Lord in the great 1859 revival. When a youth he was apprenticed to the drapery trade in Dublin, and was associated for several years with believers meeting in the Merrion Hall. During his stay in the Irish metropolis he abounded in "works of faith and labors of love." Among those with whom he was then associated in worship and service was Dr. Thomas Barnardo, the friend of destitute children, whom God so greatly blessed and honored. Mr. Owens and the doctor labored together among the "down and outs" in the slums of Dublin.

In 1871 Mr. Owens went to the city of New York, and in December of the same year was united in marriage to Miss Marion Bunn, a Dublin lady, who was his true helpmeet for fifty-six years. On arriving in New York City, Mr. Owens identified himself with a small and feeble Assembly of believers meeting simply in the Lord's name.

He had the true pastor's instinct and heart, and amid much to depress and discourage, he acted the part of a faithful and tender shepherd. For over fifty years he steadily and persistently sought to encourage and strengthen believers and help them on in the path of faith. As the work spread, and assemblies increased in number in and around New York, his counsel and advice was often sought and valued. The "sheep mark"—"by this shall all men know that ye are my disciples, if ye have love one to another" (John 13:35)—was abundantly manifest in him.

It was looked on by Mr. and Mrs. Owens as a privilege to be of any service that they could perform to God's beloved people. They "received" or welcomed believers, not on the ground of whence they came, but because of what they were—children of God. Mr. Owens desired "outlets" for truth not "limits," and sought to "do good unto all men, especially unto them who are of the household of faith" (Galatians 6:10), and his services were much appreciated. He had a great heart for the gospel. He was "instant in season, out of season" in proclaiming it; and he did so wherever doors were opened for him of the Lord. In halls and chapels, in tents and meeting rooms of all sorts and kinds, as well as under the blue canopy of Heaven, he delighted to make known the glad and glorious gospel.

Mr. and Mrs. Owens were greatly "given to hospitality," which was extended to many servants of Christ from various parts of the world. Among these were the late beloved Harry Moorhouse, Donald Ross, Donald Munro, Alexander Marshall, and numerous others. No more hospitable home ever existed. Then, as to his share of meeting believers at the steamers, guiding them through New York, helping them in a hundred ways, who can count up time and talents thus devoted?

On the occasion of their golden wedding anniversary, in 1921, in appreciation of their long and invaluable labors, a service of praise and thanksgiving was held, at which Mr. Owens was presented with a purse of gold. As one of his old Dublin friends wrote: "He will be missed by thousands of people in all parts of the world."—A.M.

John Jewell Penstone
1817-1902

J. J. PENSTONE

JOHN JEWELL PENSTONE, of London, was truly an able Bible scholar and Christian poet. His poem on "The Servant's Path in a Day of Rejection" has been of spiritual help to believers in all parts of the world.

From the time of his conversion to God, while quite a young man, he continued to serve the Lord diligently. The record of his life was truly the history of the (so-called) Brethren. Taking a prominent part in the revival of the early "forties," he was intimately associated with Robert and John Howard in the work of God at Tottenham. From the opening of Brook Street Chapel he continued to be closely associated with the work of God carried on there, and afterwards at Bruce Grove Hall. While he was known and loved all over the country, the Tottenham meeting had a special place in his affection.

An incident in his early Christian life is worth recording for the benefit of young preachers (and many old preachers, too.) When he commenced to preach the gospel, he used to fear he would soon lack subjects for his discourses and he was led to communicate his fears to a converted relative, who was then a prominent member of the Society of Friends. The advice received was: "Let the Book speak to thee Johnnie, then thou wilt have no difficulty in speaking to the people." This advice was very closely followed throughout his long and laborious ministry, and was, no doubt, the secret of so much of the success and blessing that attended his work.

There were two things about John Jewell Penstone which even anybody enjoying only a slight acquaintance with him could not fail to notice; a deep reverence for, and knowledge of, the Word of God, and a strong personal loyalty to our Lord Jesus Christ. Very few were better acquainted than he with the history of our English Bible, and probably fewer still had more of its contents committed to memory. Yet it was noticed that all his Bible reading had increasingly only one object in view, namely, a better knowledge of his Lord and Master, Jesus Christ.

Those who were privileged to know Mr. Penstone in his home life appreciated best his deep, personal loyalty and love to Jesus Christ. All who loved his Master were welcome, and his wealth of experience and knowledge was unreservedly held at the disposal of any who sought advice or counsel. When he said, "I will pray for you," one felt that he was among those who had power with God and prevailed, and went home from such a visit strengthened and encouraged.

Endowed with a powerful intellect and gifts which fall to the share of but few, he cast behind him selfish aims and ambitions, let go that which could raise him to merely worldly eminence, and without reserve laid all at the feet of Jesus, content himself to be nothing. He passed into the presence of the One whom he had so often delighted in "exalting" on May 12th, 1902, at the advanced age of eighty-five.

Captain William Graeme Rhind
1794-1863

CAPTAIN W. G. RHIND

———◁◦◦◦▷———

C APTAIN WILLIAM GRAEME RHIND, R.N. was born at Gillingham, Kent, December 18th, 1794, and fell asleep March 17th, 1863. His father, William Rhind, R.N., died suddenly when he was only two months old. So many members of his family having been naval men and some having attained to high rank in the service, he was early destined for the navy, and his name was actually enrolled as a first-class volunteer at seven years of age. At twelve years he entered actual service as a midshipman, and before thirteen years had rolled over the head of the child he was witness to the horrors of real war, being present at the action between the American ship "Chesapeake" and H.M.S. "Leopard." He was also engaged in the terrible and bloody fight between the American ship "United States" and the "Macedonian." The American ship being superior by nearly one-half in tonnage, crew, and weight of guns, the British were cut to pieces and Mr. Rhind and the few survivors taken prisoners to America, where he remained two years.

Afterwards in the West Indies he was brought near the brink of eternity by yellow fever. In the winter of 1816-17, peace having been proclaimed, he retired from active service as First Lieutenant, and afterwards from seniority obtained the rank of Commander. He took up his abode at Plymouth and, happening to enter a place of worship where an aged servant of Christ was preaching the gospel, he was pointed to "The Lamb of God, which taketh away the sin of the world." The entrance of that word gave light, and he found rest in Christ Jesus.

Christ was now all things to him, and he delighted in service for Him. He used to say: "Whenever I meet a man, I see one for whom I have a message." Becoming a diligent student of the Holy Scriptures, he contemplated entering the ministry of the Established Church soon after his conversion. So in 1822 he entered Sidney Sussex College, Cambridge, where the Reverend Charles Simeon was a great help to him. He also met with Mr. Alexander, a Jew, and was the first to take him to a Christian place of worship, and had the joy of seeing him brought to the saving knowledge of Christ. Mr. Alexander was subsequently appointed Bishop in Jerusalem.

After three years he left the university, his health having broken down. Following a serious operation he recovered his strength and again devoted himself to the Master's service. Buying a sailing boat, freighted with Bibles and tracts, he visited the boats and ships and vessels of war in Plymouth Harbor. He also preached in the open air, a work for which the Lord admirably fitted him and in which He graciously used him.

He planned a Bethel for Sailors at Plymouth and a Reading Library for invalid seamen in the R.N. Hospital. The Duke of Clarence (afterwards King William IV) visited Plymouth and asked Mr. Rhind what employment he would desire (Mr. Rhind's father having been the Duke's instructor in navigation). The true-hearted soldier of the cross replied: "Your Royal Highness, to remain as I am." Having put his hand to the plough, no prospect of worldly advancement could induce him to look back.

In 1832 he was invited by John Synge to Ireland, and until 1838 he visited, dispensed medicine, and preached the gospel with good results. It was then he became acquainted with Lady Powerscourt, at whose house large meetings of Christians were held, some of whom had left the communion of the Church of England for the simple and Scriptural mode of coming out from among the unconverted, and meeting simply in the name of the Lord in dependence on the guidance of the Holy Spirit.

His mind being exercised about ministry and the separate character of the church, he could not conscientiously become a minister of the establishment, and declined the position which was pressed upon him. After his return to England with his wife and family, he resided for nearly four years in the city of Hereford. Having from conviction embraced the views held by those Christians who meet simply as brethren in Christ, he met every Lord's day with those in Bridge Street for the breaking of bread (Acts 20:7). He taught and exhorted with authority and weight, and as an evangelist no one could set forth more clearly than he did that all was of grace through faith.

In 1843 he became a resident in Ross. A little room was rented at Wilton Road, and at first ten persons met together to remember the Lord Jesus as in early apostolic times; but very soon the room was too small, and over one hundred met in happy fellowship. Mr. Rhind made preaching tours in various parts of the kingdom, speaking to large and fashionable crowds at Cheltenham and other places. A great personal soul-winner, whether traveling by rail, coach, or steamboat, he would immediately present every one he met with a tract. This he called "showing his colors at once." He taught much and often of the return of the Lord Jesus, more and more to him the "blessed hope." God made this, His dear servant, to be not only a clean vessel, but a large one, and then filled him to overflowing with love. This was the secret of that happy, beaming countenance, the result of communion with Him whose presence ever imparts light and gladness, and which caused children to call him "Mr. Gloryface!"

Such was the esteem and affection felt for him by the early "chief men" that he was one of the specially selected guides who met at Plymouth in 1845 in the interests of peace at the time of the strife between Darby and Newton. He wrote books which have been much valued, such as "The Tabernacle in the Wilderness," "The Testimony of the Times," etc., and also a very useful book for the young "The Six Days of Creation," all of which passed through several editions.

He passed away at Weston-under-Penyard, two miles from Ross, on March 17th, 1863. His remains were taken to the burial ground attached to the Barton Meeting Room, Hereford. A service was held in the presence of many hundreds who surrounded the grave.

John Ritchie
1853-1930

JOHN RITCHIE

JOHN RITCHIE, for thirty-seven years the editor of *The Believer's Magazine*, was born in the village of Old Meldrum, Aberdeenshire, on September 10th, 1853. He had in his personality a good deal of the "granite" for which his native county is famous.

As a lad he had the advantage of sitting under the ministry of a good man, Mr. George Garrioch of the Free Church of Scotland, who often visited his home, and talked with him of the necessity of "the new birth." A young doctor, Dr. Robert M'Killiam, well known in later years in London as the editor of *The Morning Star* and an able teacher of the Scriptures, who had recently begun to practise in the village and cared for the souls as well as the bodies of his patients, had taken up a Sunday school class in connection with the church. Among the scholars who were deeply impressed by his earnest words was John Ritchie.

Teacher and scholar met fully forty years after these early days at a meeting in Devonshire House, London; this time the "scholar" gave the address and the "teacher" closed the meeting with prayer and thanksgiving. Needless to say it was a happy reunion.

In the years 1859-60 there came the memorable revival which swept over Scotland like a mighty flood, carrying thousands into the kingdom of God. One result of that movement of divine grace was the raising up of a band of lay preachers and evangelists drawn from various walks in life. Some were landowners, like Hay MacDowall Grant, the Laird of Arndilly; some were working men, like Duncan Matheson and James Turner, but all alike fired with gospel zeal and love for perishing souls. Under the preaching of these men and their immediate successors, the "dry bones" of Scottish Presbyterianism began to shake.

In 1871 Donald Munro and others had meetings in the town of Inverurie, Aberdeenshire, where Mr. Ritchie was then employed. Tremendous opposition was encountered; personal violence was attempted on the preachers, but the Spirit of God was working mightily, and in one week twenty or more young men and women confessed faith in Christ, including "J. R.," who never hesitated to avow his spiritual birthday as April 2nd, 1871.

After the departure of the evangelists, the young converts, who failed to find food for the new life begotten within them in the ministrations from the pulpit, used to meet together for prayer and study of the Scriptures, and gradually came to see that the teaching and practices of the early believers as revealed in the Acts and the Epistles was the path they should follow. Hearing that special meetings were being conducted by Donald Ross and others in the adjacent village of Old Rayne, and that believers were there meeting to remember the Lord according to the pattern in the Book, a number of the young Christians walked over on a Lord's day morning, and for the first time saw the observance of the Lord's supper in its original simplicity.

They were "convinced of all" (1 Corinthians 14:24), and not long afterwards they too publicly obeyed the Lord in baptism, and commenced meeting to show forth His death.

It soon became evident that the young grocer's assistant was endowed by the Holy Spirit with the gift of the evangelist. Beginning in a quiet way to open his mouth in testimony for his Lord at kitchen meetings, in barns, and in joiners' shops, fitted out as meeting places, he "increased the more in strength" (Acts 9:22), until his gift made room for him in wider spheres. His avidity for the Word of God, his wonderfully retentive memory, his fluent and flaming appeals to the consciences of his hearers, his indomitable zeal in the service of his Master, combined to mark him out as "a vessel unto honor." Soon the claims of spiritual work necessitated the abandonment of his material duties, and with the benediction of his brethren he gave himself entirely to the Lord's work.

In June 1877, he was united in marriage to Miss Liveston, of Forfar, in the house of a mutual friend in the town of Kirriemuir, finding in her a true "helpmeet" for forty-six years of married life. Her Home-call in March 1924, was a severe blow from which he never fully recovered. The young couple set up their first home in the village of Dalmellington, Ayrshire, where Mr. Ritchie had been in the midst of a gracious work of God, and where over sixty young believers required his care.

From thence, in 1879, the home was moved to Kilmarnock, where a great ingathering of souls had taken place under the preaching of Rice T. Hopkins and Alexander Marshall, and where it was felt his help would be invaluable. Here also he found a convenient center for his activities in preaching the gospel, and also in ministering the Word to believers—another gift which now came into prominence.

Here, too, in Kilmarnock, there came into use the "pen of a ready writer," which was destined to carry his ministry to almost every part of the world. From the little home in Kilmarnock, *The Young Watchman* appeared forty-seven years ago. These were the days when the editor acted as his own clerk and packer, while one of the rooms of the house was converted into a temporary despatch room; and where on the day of issue another very young "watchman" (the present writer) supervised, as he thought, the processes of wrapping up, addressing, and stamping the various parcels of literature. Then followed *The Sunday School Worker's Magazine*, *The Little Ones' Treasury*, *The Believer's Magazine*, with others still later, and all the while in Scotland, England, Ireland and Wales, the ministry of the living voice, fraught with so much blessing to many souls, was continuing. The results of this prolific and world-wide ministry the day of Christ alone will declare.

"Of making many books there is no end" (Ecclesiastes 12:12), the wise man said, and certainly the adage seems to be true of Mr. Ritchie. In his fertile mind, guided by the Spirit of God, one after another they were begotten in rapid succession. Pithy, pungent, and powerful in their appeal to the hearts of God's people; simple in diction, spiritual in tone, steadfast in their adherence to Holy Writ, suited especially to the needs of young believers, these earlier books such as "The Tabernacle," "Egypt to Canaan," "Foundation Truths," have run into many editions, and some of them have recently been translated into continental languages. Over two hundred volumes and booklets, besides hundreds of tracts have come from his pen.

In the years of young manhood the preaching of the gospel was his forte, and there were few who excelled him in holding the attention of an audience by his incisive presentation of the foundation truths of the faith, illuminated as his addresses were by striking phrase, illustrated by telling incidents, interspersed by frequent flashes of homely humor yet always thrusting for the consciences of his hearers. "J. R." was a born organizer, and had the happy knack of inspiring courage and confidence in young men who had a heart for the service of the Lord.

The summer work in the villages, which for several successive summers he organized, and in which he got young men on holiday to join him, resulted in systematic house-to-house visitation, and open-air campaigns in the counties of Ayr, Stirling, Dumfries, Wigtown, Cumberland, and elsewhere. Fred. S. Arnot and Charles A. Swan of African fame, and James Imrie, of Glasgow, were among the early helpers in this fruitful work.

In the active years of middle life, when he felt called to give himself more closely to the rapidly increasing work of writing and publishing, he yet gave freely of his time in ministering to the people of God. In his home assembly at Kilmarnock he was for many years the acknowledged and trusted leader, and some of his Sunday afternoon addresses, as well as week-night Bible readings for young believers, will be remembered with a thrilling and thankful joy by many of us while life shall last. Far afield, too, he travelled in response to urgent invitations from various parts of the country; a conference here, a series of meetings there, oftentimes taxing his physical and mental powers to the uttermost.

As life passed the meridian he was compelled to go slower. "The books [and] especially the parchments" (2 Timothy 4:13) claimed his chief attention, and long after the day's work should have been done, he burned "the midnight oil" to light the lamp of truth in others.

With a sigh, as of relief at his escape from "the last weariness—the final strife," he quite unexpectedly passed swiftly over "to the other side" on the afternoon of March 19th, 1930, and is now "at home" with the Lord.

In a shaded corner of the cemetery at Troon, we laid the tired and weary body to rest beside that of the devoted life-partner until "the Morning." In the words of the hymn he loved so well, and which he so often asked us to sing on the quiet of a Sunday evening in the old home we say:

> For ever with the Lord
> Amen! so let it be.

—JOHN RITCHIE, JR.

TEODORO P. ROSSETTI

1825-1883

TEODORO PIETROCOLA ROSSETTI was born on the 26th of November 1825, of pious parents. He was brought up most religiously, and more than one good Catholic friend ventured the prophecy that the lad would become a saint. In the true and real sense of the word the prophecy was fulfilled! He made rapid progress in his classical studies, and with his fellow students enjoyed many a walk in the country, reciting and discussing the Latin and Italian poets. Poetry is not an aftergrowth: it is innate, and appears early in the springtime of life. So in Rossetti. His early compositions showed how rich was his poetic vein.

The young student was now nineteen years of age, and among his companions was a priest, a few years his senior. They had arranged to take a long walk in the country one Sunday morning after mass. Rossetti arrived early that morning at his friend's house, purposing going with him to the solemn sacrament. When he entered the young priest's room he was shocked to find him enjoying a hearty Italian breakfast, which consisted of ham, figs, and wine!

"What are you doing?" exclaimed Rossetti. "Are you not going to say mass? And here you are eating!" "What harm is there?" asked his reverend companion. "Why, it is a mortal sin to eat before receiving the Lord," remonstrated Rossetti. "Who says so?" indifferently retorted the young priest. "Why, the holy mother church," replied Rossetti, indignantly.

"Oh, my son," answered his free-and-easy sacerdotal friend, "if you believe all that the holy mother church teaches, you will believe many things that are not true. Give me that book (pointing to the Vulgate Bible). Read here what it says: Luke 22:19, 'This is my body which is given for you.' Do you believe that it is possible to do anything in remembrance of a person who is present; or that a person can have two bodies at one time, which would have been the case if the bread had become the body of the

Lord? If you believe this, then you must believe that He is a vine and a door." These statements of the young priest came as the first great shock to Rossetti's faith in the Church of Rome.

At the age of twenty-one he went to Naples and entered the university. That was in 1846, in the very throes of political agitation. The love and longing for freedom had laid hold upon the youth of the country, and with his fellow students young Rossetti was drawn into the rapid current of the national cause. But he soon found that it was dangerous in those days to say a word against the Bourbon government, and it was only his manifest natural ability that caused his political enemies to bear with his views in the hope of gaining him over to their party. This hope proving vain, and Rossetti's fervor growing stronger in the cause of freedom, he was sought for by the government of Ferdinand II, and made his escape to France. His literary gifts soon found him many friends among the French nobility, but he found his freedom was again in danger, and he was just in time to cross the channel and reach the hospitable shores of England at the close of 1851.

He received a most cordial welcome from his uncle Gabriel, and through him was soon introduced to many literary personages in London. With a rich store of classical poetry, fired with the love of liberty, he had no lack of matter for his ready pen.

But there was One who was following the steps of that ardent youth in the land of exile, One who knew the longings of his unsatisfied soul, and He was about to reveal to that heart seeking rest, a liberty never attained to nor obtained by any of this world's reformers. So it was one of God's links in the golden chain of His grace that Rossetti should go to Teignmouth to teach. Here Count Guicciardini was staying, and the two Italian exiles met. That was a historical meeting! As they walked slowly along the shore, the Count calmly put the question to Rossetti: "If you were to die to-night, what would become of you?" "If I were to die to-night? Indeed, I do not know what would become of me," replied his friend, taken by surprise with a question so unexpected and of such a solemn personal import.

"If I were to die to-night I know where I should go," peacefully said the nobleman. "Excuse me, Count, but to say what you say, one must be either ignorant or presumptuous," retorted Rossetti. "Well, let it be so. I may be ignorant and you learned, but all the same I know where I am going and you do not," repeated the Count with perfect assurance.

No more was said on the subject, but the arrow remained fixed in Rossetti's soul, and he could not sleep that night. He had to return to London to give lessons in Italian to some of the highest personages in the country. Among his students was a Christian gentleman, who proposed reading the New Testament in Italian. One day the reading lesson was in the Epistle to the Ephesians. The student having read the Scripture: "by grace ye are saved," ventured to offer an opportune explanation of this saving truth. The work of grace had begun in Rossetti.

With a pure and personal faith Rossetti believed on Him that raised Jesus our Lord from the dead, who was delivered up for our trespasses, and was raised for our justification (Romans 4:25). As in the natural so in the spiritual world first impressions often remain the most vivid. The free unmerited grace of God was the first gospel truth which impressed Rossetti's heart, and it became the greatest theme of his life.

A few days after, his Christian pupil said to him: "I am going to a meeting to-night." "A meeting? What kind of meeting?" inquired Rossetti. "It is a meeting that has nothing to do with politics," replied the student, adding politely: "If you would like to come, I should take you there. It is in Orchard Street."

Rossetti went, and found a number of people met to read and meditate upon the Holy Scriptures. What a meeting that was to him! He never departed from what he learnt there. It was the old, unchangeable theology of the gospel he received, and in its rich, spiritual truths he became an established believer. Among those by whose Christian fellowship he early profited were Lord Congleton, Lord Radstock, Colonel Bell, Dr. Maclean, Mr. George Muller, Mr. R. C. Chapman, and many other eminent Christians.

Liberty had been granted in Piedmont, and the spiritual awakening there was spreading. The news of its needs reached Rossetti, while that of his conversion had reached his brethren in Italy. He had prospects of a brilliant literary career in England, but the gospel call from Italy came with such irresistible power that he went to the embassy in London and got his passport, signed by Cavour, "to preach the Gospel."

Many farewell missionary meetings have become memorable, but none more so than that held in Orchard Street, London, to bid God-speed to Rossetti, leaving England, the land of his exile, in which he had found true liberty; and now, freed, he was going to free his fellow-countrymen in Italy. Mr. Chapman's farewell address, Rossetti's touching request for the prayers of his brethren that he might be blessed to his dear Italy, the final, fervent prayer of one of the elder brethren, offered for him as on his knees he bowed, the other elders holding their hands over his head, all was worthy of the event which was to have such blessed results.

Alessandria became the first center of Rossetti's work in Italy. This Piedmontese city, which lies in a plain at the junction of the rivers Bormida and Tanaro, and possesses one of the strongest fortresses in Europe, was called after Pope Alexander III, who raised it to a bishop's see. The labors of Rossetti made it become one of the centers of evangelical testimony in Italy. He soon gathered around him a band of Christian young men, to whom he taught the Word and whom he guided in the work of God. He had a rare and valuable gift of inculcating confidence in these young native evangelists in the gospel mission, and developing the talents in them for their future service.

So widely did the gospel spread in Piedmont that even from the city of Rome there arrived monks to preach against the ardent evangelist, who had now the hearty and helpful fellowship of several able Italian brethren, a band of faithful witnesses for Christ. Some of these were men of learning and social position, and some belonged to humbler ranks: all preached the same gospel.

The enemy made a strenuous effort to get rid of the leaders of the evangelical church, and so scatter the flock. When this persecution was at its height, after one of the meetings, Rossetti put the question to the audience: "They wish to send us evangelists away. What will you do? Will you return to your idols?" Soon the reply came from one and another, assuring Rossetti and his companions that the gospel which they had preached to them would be their firm hope to the end.

Shortly after this the church in Alessandria met for the first time around the Lord's table, a testimony which for over half a century has not ceased. Rossetti had published a few of his choice hymns, which were sung by that simple, saintly company.

Meanwhile the persecution against the gospel continued. The enemy, however, changed its tactics and became more aggressive and, with the apostle, Rossetti could say, "Once was I stoned." The injury which resulted was painful and might have been very serious, but God's faithful servant preached the same evening. To the young brethren who gathered around him in sympathy, he said with a satisfied smile: "I was hoping that the stones might not wound your faith."

On another occasion Rossetti was expected to arrive at Spinetta by a certain train. Two hundred young ruffians were instigated by the priest to wait his arrival with stones and sticks! The hour arrived, the train arrived, but Rossetti did not arrive! He had missed the train. The ill-intentioned hooligans contented themselves with the hypothesis that the authorities in Alessandria had detained the evangelist, and they soon dispersed with the hope that he might never return. Those who had gathered with the good intention of hearing the gospel remained in the hall, and were discussing the situation when Rossetti appeared in their midst! He had come in a carriage rather than disappoint the people. How vain was the hope that Rossetti might never return to Spinetta may be gathered from the fact that in 1868 he convened the first annual *Agape* held there, a Christian gathering which since has proved a source of fellowship and encouragement to thousands of God's people in Italy.

But Rossetti's labors were not confined to one part of Italy. Turin, Genoa, Florence, Rome, and many other cities, as well as towns and villages enjoyed his ministry. For some time, however, symptoms of failing health had been occasionally showing themselves, but Rossetti continued in his joyful service. He reached Florence, and though weak in body he went to the morning meeting there on Sunday, June 3rd, 1883. He read Acts 7:5,6, Hebrews 13:8-15; Revelation 1:4-6; 4:1; 5:9-14; 16:13; and spoke with great feeling and power of the joy and glory reserved in Heaven for all the redeemed. Those who heard him said afterwards: "He transported us to Heaven." Having finished his happy and helpful meditation and exhortation he sat down, and was in the act of rising again to propose a hymn, when he suddenly and peacefully passed to be with the Lord whom he had so loved and served.—J.S.A.

Donald Ross
1823-1905

DONALD ROSS

D ONALD ROSS, the veteran Scottish evangelist, was born February
11th, 1823, of godly parents in Rosshire, Scotland, and was brought
up in the nurture and admonition of the Lord. Twice each day in his home
they surrounded the family altar, the Scriptures being read, and God's
help, protection, and blessing sought. He intensely disliked "family worship," feigning headache as an excuse for his absence. His description of
himself at this time is not at all flattering. He says he was "as proud as a
peacock, and as empty as a drum," and yet he "said" his prayers night and
morning, lest God would judge him. At the age of fifteen, alone among
the heather on a hillside, returning from visiting a dying brother, he was
brought to a knowledge of the soul-saving truth of the gospel through
the words of John 18:8: "If therefore ye seek me, let these go their way."

He was connected with the Established Church of Scotland, but left
it at the disruption of 1843 and identified himself with the Free Church.
On his removal to Edinburgh he attached himself to the church of which
Mr. Tasker was minister, and actively engaged in evangelistic work. From
1858 to 1860 he was missionary among the miners of Lanarkshire.

In 1860 he was appointed secretary and superintendent of the North
East Coast Mission, making the city of Aberdeen his headquarters. During the ten years that he filled this important and responsible position
he was greatly used of God in the conversion of souls. These were the
glorious "revival days" when the Holy Spirit worked so wondrously in
Scotland. Thousands of persons of all ranks and classes were aroused
from their slumber, and were earnestly inquiring what they had to do to
be saved. Multitudes were brought to know Him whom to know is life
eternal, and openly confessed Christ as their Saviour. Mr. Ross gathered
around him a band of earnest, aggressive gospellers. The "war" was carried into the enemy's camp, and citadels of Satan were attacked and cap-
tured. In country districts and in fishing villages, in towns and cities, the
heralds of the cross were busy. Brownlow North and James Turner, Hay-
M'Dowall Grant and Reginald Radcliffe, Lord Kintore and Richard

Weaver, Gordon Forlong and Harrison Ord, Duncan Matheson and
Donald Ross, gathered numerous sheaves of golden grain for the Lord of
the harvest. Duncan Matheson and Donald Ross were men of kindred
spirits, and were splendid gospel pioneers. Matheson was accustomed to
speak of his friend as "that Caledonian warrior."

Mr. Ross was a diligent student of the Scriptures. As he searched his
Bible he became exercised as to his position, and after ten years' service
in the North East Coast Mission he resigned. In 1870 he started the Northern Evangelistic Association. A number of evangelists joined him. Soon
afterwards that society was dissolved, and he ceased being connected
with any society or denomination, meeting with Christians assembling
simply in the Lord's name. He started a monthly paper, the *Northern
Evangelist and Intelligencer,* which was afterwards called the *Northern
Witness.* Since 1888 it has simply been *The Witness,* and has a world-
wide circulation of close on thirty thousand monthly.

Edinburgh was the next scene of his labors. A hall was secured and
the work was carried on amid much to discourage. In 1876 he visited the
United States of America. There he found many open doors for preaching and teaching. In 1879 he moved his family there, making Chicago,
the metropolis of the west and north-western states, his center for several years. He and three others began to remember the Lord in the breaking of bread in a tent, which was also used for evangelistic purposes.
Among the number was a gentleman who had been identified with similar meetings in England. After the breaking of bread he looked at the
tent, and remarked, "This is surely outside the camp," and never returned.
But Donald Ross kept pegging away at the gospel. In summer and winter, in rain and snow, in encouraging and discouraging circumstances,
the gospeller kept at the gospel. A number of Christians gathered around
him, were baptized, and sought to teach others what the Lord had taught
them. In this way the work in that vast and important commercial center was built up. Mr. Ross also evangelized in Boston, New York, and other
American cities, as well as in towns and country districts in Canada.

In 1887 he visited California, and spent a considerable time in San
Francisco, making the city on the "Golden Gate" his center for several
years. While in Chicago he started a tract depot in his own house, keeping a stock of tracts, Bibles, and books for Christians. For some twenty
years he issued the monthly magazine *Our Record,* and for a number of
years he edited a gospel paper. In 1894 he went to Kansas City, Missouri,

then a rising western city, and made that his headquarters, moving north and south, east and west for gospel campaigns. In 1901 he returned to Chicago, where he made his home till he was called to higher service on February 13th, 1903.

Mr. Ross was essentially a gospel preacher. He was more than a preacher and an exhorter. He was a laborer, and he toiled for the perishing at fairs and races, in tents and halls, in barns and chapels, in music halls and theatres, in cottages and in the open air, ever sounding out the wondrous story.

Near the end of his journey he said: "I will be eighty on the 11th February, and if I had other eighty before me, I would spend them in this gospel of God's grace. There is no other work of such importance in the whole world. All other investments amount to nothing compared with this."—A.M.

Thomas Ryan
_1810-1905_

THOMAS RYAN

THOMAS RYAN came of a good family stock in the south of Ireland. In earlier days he had been, like most young country gentlemen, convivial and careless, devoting his time to hunting and other rural pleasures; but being intended for "the Church," he came to Dublin to carry on his university studies. In the good providence of God he was soon brought under the influence of some of the early "Brethren," his heart was opened to the reality and power of the gospel of God, and under the teaching of the Holy Spirit the Bible became a new book to him. Conscientious difficulties respecting the Prayer Book in general, and the ordination and baptismal services in particular, soon arose, and quickly led him, much to the annoyance and disapproval of his father, to abandon his intention of becoming a clergyman, and to devote himself with increasing joy to the fellowship of spiritually-minded Christians, and to various spheres of free evangelistic work.

About this time, or very shortly afterwards, he made the acquaintance of Mr. J. N. Darby, Mr. J. G. Bellett, and many other leaders of what is known as the early "Brethren" movement. At first he threw in his lot with Mr. Darby, but retired from fellowship with Mr. Darby many years ago.

For forty years Mr. Ryan gave himself with much devotedness and catholicity of spirit to the ministry of the Word in the assemblies; and in connection with young men's Bible classes in various places did a magnificent work in opening up the Scriptures and grounding many in the foundations of the faith, specially in those truths which cluster round the person and the cross of Christ.

Being a very fair Hebrew and Greek scholar, and devoting his whole life to the prayerful and diligent study of the Word of God, he became truly "mighty in the scriptures," and, under God's blessing, large numbers received through his ministry a clear, vital hold upon the precious things of God. Many of the poor, who for years attended his gospel meetings in the Dublin City Mission and other places, rejoiced in the simplicity and affection with which he preached to them the gospel of Christ.

He was the author of "The Structure of the Acts," "Notes on the Book of Revelation," "The Birthday and After," and numberless tracts and pamphlets on doctrinal and controversial subjects, many of his volumes proving a help to a wider circle of friends than his voice could ever have reached. "The Structure" is worth securing to-day.

Those who loved Mr. Ryan best were those who knew him best. He was a warm-hearted and sincere friend, and while an uncompromising champion for the truth, was personally considerate and humble-minded. Possessed of a magnificent constitution, he carried on his labors into old age, and only within the last five years of his life did his health begin completely to fail; but up to the very last his heart was true to his Saviour and Lord, and a reference to the love of Jesus or the precious blood of Christ whispered into his ear never failed to rouse him from his weakness and stupor to respond, as he did on a recent occasion, "Everything about Him is lovely."

With marked singleness of heart he gave himself for all the latter years of his life to the fulfillment of the much-needed ministry emphasized by Paul in 2 Timothy 2:2, till on the 14th of January 1905, at the extreme old age of ninety-five this much-esteemed servant of the Lord and highly-gifted teacher passed into the presence of his Lord, where now he rests from his labors, and his works do follow him.—H.W. F.

Dr. Alfred T. Schofield
1846-1929

DR. A. T. SCHOFIELD

A LFRED SCHOFIELD, M.D., a distinguished Harley Street physician, an author of considerable repute, editor of various magazines, and one of the best known Christian workers in London, was born in Rochdale in 1846 in Schofield Hall (a building dating from Jacobean days and connected with quite a number of distinguished families in the district). Like many old families, the fortunes had varied, and when the child was four his parents moved to London. His father had some interest in the building of the Crystal Palace at Sydenham. As a youth, A. T. Schofield remembered the first great Exhibition of 1851, the *Great Eastern* visiting the Thames, the fanciful dress of Lord Dundreary, the visit of Napoleon III with the Empress Eugenie, and of Lord Palmerston to the palace.

His first school days were in the home of Arthur Pridham, a well-known author of expository volumes, in Devonshire; afterwards in various other schools and colleges.

At the age of fourteen, when entering a private academy at Ryde, I.W., he had a remarkable and sudden conversion. At fifteen he spent the early hours, from 4:00 to 8:00 a.m., of many days learning Greek, an invaluable asset to him in after days.

His first business training was under the eye of an uncle in Rochdale, where he started a Sunday school, and had many escapades. At this time he met in Ireland a young lady, who became his wife in 1871, the wedding being attended by G. V. Wigram. After a time, with his wife and family, he felt "the call of the metropolis," settling in a home at 7 Wood Street, and commenced business, we understand, in the dry goods line. At first successful, later business went down, and he was left wondering what to do. A still small voice whispered, "Be a doctor," a not-too-easy task at his age, yet he decided on a medical career, and after much study and perseverance passed the two college examinations.

After leaving the London Hospital, the doctor served as a *locum* in Yorkshire, then settled down to a practice in Westbourne Terrace. He made a bad, but long to be remembered, start in this house by throwing two crumpled £20 notes into the fire, and not having the numbers, suffered the loss. He conducted a large ambulance class in Paddington Baths, where he had audiences of one thousand at his health lectures. Hundreds of these helpful lectures were given during his lifetime.

His travels were fairly extensive. In addition to several tours of France, Switzerland, Germany, Austria, and other parts of the Continent, he attended the British Medical Association Meeting in Toronto in 1906, went to Palestine in 1904 for the World's Sunday School Convention, then made another extended tour in 1911, gathering information which forms the basis of "Where He Dwelt," "Journeys of Jesus Christ," and others of his books. This tour included Egypt, where he found a solution to the Riddle of the Sphinx. These two journeys led the doctor to engage in the preparation of "Palestine in London," or Palestine Exhibitions, several of which have now been held. The first resulted in a profit of £12,000, not for himself, but for a good cause.

From his conversion at the age of fourteen, until his home-call at the age of eighty-three, he was one of the most active leaders in various branches of Christian work. In regular fellowship with those called "Brethren" (first with "Darby," then with "Kelly," then for years with "Open") the largeness of his heart and the breadth of his sympathies reached out to all honest efforts for the extension of the kingdom of the Lord whom he loved. Even "peculiar cults" and "unorthodox workers" were of interest to him, as to what they really aimed at. Yet he never yielded one atom of loyalty to the fundamentals of the Christian faith.

When a comparatively young man he started a Sunday school in Rochdale, in one sense not a Sunday school, for then one person out of three attended these schools, which consisted of those who came as infants, grew up, married, and continued their attendance. His school numbered five hundred scholars and fifty teachers, including a good choir, for Lancashire people are musical. This school was visited more than once by Dr. Davis, "the good black doctor," of whom the Dr. Schofield wrote a most interesting story. Visiting the district forty years after, the former scholars, many of them now grandparents, packed the old schoolhouse for a happy night of remembrance.

He was one of the six founders of the "Mission to Deep Sea Fishermen" which has done such wonderful work—spiritually, morally, and physically—for these hardy sons of toil. In early days in London he took quite an interest in a West End Mission conducted by Lord Radstock, latterly held in the well-known Eccleston Hall, Victoria. He was a valued helper in the great missions of Moody and Sankey in the Albert Hall and other places; also in the missions of Torrey and Alexander. He was a member of the Prophecy Investigation Society and the Victoria Institute, as well as other societies, and a Fellow of the Royal Geographical Society.

When over eighty, he made an extended preaching tour right up through England into Scotland, then afterwards turning westward through Wales and west of England. His Bible lectures and gospel addresses on this his last tour were much blessed to all who heard them. Both in local and public halls large crowds gathered.

His closing years were spent in helping in local work in Ryde, where he had settled after his retirement, and in the south of England, with regular visits to London for special lectures or meetings. Long troubled with his heart, another trouble entirely caused his decease on April 20th, 1929, at the ripe age of eighty-three.

Austere and aristocratic in his bearing, many felt a difficulty in approaching him, yet we knew no more kindly man or sociable friend in his own home or in ours. He was indeed to all who knew him "a beloved physician," whose place in Christian work and literature will long remain unfilled.—HY.P.

John N. Scobell
1803-1883

JOHN N. SCOBELL

I N F. T. BULLEN'S charming book, "The Apostles of the South East," "setting forth the difficulties, the dangers and the triumphs of the humble class of Christians mentioned," a little assembly of Brethren, he writes of the use of a hymn book, with appendix. This small compilation was, and is, well known to many thousands of the Lord's children under the title of "Scobell's Hymn Book," the full title being, "Hymns and Spiritual Songs for the Children of God." It was published in the early days of the wonderful spiritual "Brethren" movement, and while being "the result of the communion of many Christians with a desire to promote the joy and edification of the church of God," as the compiler John Nsticke Scobell modestly states, it was without doubt largely owing to his enthusiasm, patience, and generosity that the book was published.

Dr. A. R. Short in his "History" mentions "Scobell's well-known Hymns with Appendix," and states: "It contains very many magnificent hymns to which compilers of all evangelical denominations might well pay attention."

Mr. Scobell was a B.A., a J.P. for Somerset and Cornwall, and came from a very old family in Devon. He had seats at Hallatrow Court, Somerset, and Nancealoerne Cornwall. He was born in 1803 and died at the advanced age of eighty in 1883.

Major-General Sir Charles Scott
1848-1919

MAJOR-GENERAL
SIR CHARLES SCOTT

———◦∞◦———

MAJOR-GENERAL SIR CHARLES H. SCOTT, K.C.B., R.A. was born at Portsmouth in 1848, entered the Royal Artillery in 1868 when but nineteen years of age, and was posted to a battery in India. He served in several of the campaigns on the north-west frontier of India, including the Tirah expedition of 1897-98, and filled many posts in connection with the Ordinance Service in India, including that of Director-General. In 1905 he was appointed Military Supply Member of the Viceroy's Council, which office he held for four years, when the position was abolished by Lord Morley, and Lord Kitchener became the sole representative of the military authorities in the government.

During his early years the young soldier had not felt any spiritual need. His training at Woolwich Royal Artillery Academy passed without his being conscious of definite leading; indeed, up to the time he went to India, according to his own account, he had thought little of what so soon was to be the motive power of his life. Not long after his arrival in India he awoke to his need of a Savior, became an earnest seeker and student of the Bible to find the truth, and did not seek in vain.

Soon after his conversion he came under the influence of Mr. Henry Dyer, and became associated with those known as "Brethren." He took a very decided stand for Christ, not shrinking from His reproach, and all the spare time from his official duties was given to work for his Master. A good part of his thirty years' service in India was spent at Ishapore, near Calcutta; and missionaries, work among soldiers, seamen, ships' apprentices, the Y.M.C.A., and other agencies had his untiring help.

Sir Charles retired in 1910, when the honor of Knight Commander of the Bath was conferred upon him. His wife, who was long associated with him in Christian work, predeceased him. She was the daughter of the late General J. G. Halliday, who was also a devoted servant of the Lord, for many years in the assembly at Lewisham, a south-eastern suburb of

London. The Shrubbery Road Mission, Lewisham, the Gray's Yard Mission, the Victoria Homes for Working Men, Miss Perks' Soldiers' Homes, the Soldiers' Christian Association are among the many activities with which Sir Charles Scott was closely associated in later years.

One of the last public appearances of Sir Charles Scott was to preside at a meeting of the Soldiers' Christian Association, and at the Kingsway Hall meetings. He was a devoutly spiritual speaker. Indeed, he never grudged time nor trouble to further any cause, or to cheer and help any of the very many who continually came to him for advice or assistance.

He became ill with influenza on August 30th, 1919, and after five weeks of illness, borne with most wonderful patience and sweetness, he passed, in his seventy-second year, to the rest that remaineth. The hope of Christ's coming was very real to him, and he spoke of it with longing up to the last. Miss Havergal's hymn, "Thou Art Coming, O My Saviour," was sung at the funeral, which took place at Wadhurst, October 10th, 1919.

The influence of his wonderful Christ-like spirit was felt everywhere. One who served under him writes: "I do not know another such perfect specimen of a noble-hearted gentleman in every sense of the word. He spent his life in doing good and helping others, and none who knew him ever spoke of him but in terms of the deepest affection and love."—W.H.S.

Joseph Denham Smith
1817-1889

J. DENHAM SMITH

JOSEPH DENHAM SMITH was born in July 1817. He had a happy childhood, and possessed a buoyancy of spirit which never forsook him. His widowed mother, a devoted Christian, longed for his early conversion, and abundantly were her prayers answered.

At the age of sixteen he first preached the gospel, and many were thrilled by his lifting up of Christ. Hearing of Ireland's need, he determined to settle in that land, and there for many years spent a happy and blessed life in pointing sinners to Christ. In 1841 he commenced his more recognized public ministry at Newry, where his memory is still held in affection and gratitude. Thence he removed to Kingstown in 1848, and devoted himself to the pastorate of the church that he was instrumental in planting in Northumberland Avenue, and which was destined to prove so remarkable a center of spiritual life to multitudes.

In 1859 a wave of blessing rolled over the north of Ireland, whence the work spread to other parts. In August 1859, Mr. and Mrs. John Morley, of Clapton, London, visited Ireland, to see the beauties of Wicklow and other places of interest. Mr. Denham Smith remarked: "But you will not return, will you, without seeing something of the remarkable revival?" "We had not thought of seeing it," said Mr. Morley, "but we will consider it." Accordingly, accompanied by Mr. Smith, they visited Belfast, Ballymena, and other places which formed the center of this blessed work. Mr. Denham Smith rejoiced in the wondrous movement, and received a fresh enduement of power from on high as the result of the visit. This was evidenced by a remarkable outburst of spiritual blessing on September ninth in the church at Kingstown, which continued for many months with notable blessing to thousands of souls. Services were commenced on board the express boats running between Kingstown and Holyhead, which were remarkably owned of God.

Many were brought under the saving power of the Holy Spirit. These were by no means drawn from the poorer classes only, but included people from all sections of society, many of whom are now prominent servants of God. Mr. Shuldham Henry, afterwards a well-known preacher of the gospel, was converted to God through the instrumentality of Mr. Denham Smith, whom he was induced to hear in January 1860.

From Kingstown, Mr. Smith now went forth with a yearning heart for souls, to commence services in the Irish metropolis, the Metropolitan Hall being taken, where meetings were held that will be borne in everlasting remembrance by many who shared in the blessing presented therein; the abiding fruit of these gatherings may be found in many parts of the world today. Thousands flocked together in the morning, and remained hour after hour—many without refreshments—until ten and eleven at night. Careless ones were awakened, anxious ones led into peace, and persons of all classes rejoiced in a newly-found Saviour.

As might be expected amid such scenes and services as these, Mr. Denham Smith soon felt that he could no longer be bound by denominational bonds. Accordingly he retired from the pastorate of his church at Kingstown in order to take his stand as a servant of the church at large. It was, however, the deep desire of his friends, on his leaving Kingstown, to secure the continuance of his labors among them, and, in accordance with this, it was decided to erect a suitable hall for religious services, so that Dublin might be "a center of evangelizing effort," in which building Mr. Denham Smith would have the "privilege and joy of the co-operation and fellowship of various devoted ministers and servants of Christ." In this way was erected Merrion Hall, Dublin.

Shortly afterwards Mr. Denham Smith visited Paris and Geneva, where crowded meetings were held. Then he visited London and held meetings in Freemasons' Hall, St. James's Hall, Sadler's Wells Theatre, Upper Clapton, finally settling in London, and continuing to minister regularly in St. George's Hall and Clapton Hall.

In the spring of 1886 Mr. Denham Smith's health gave way. Persistent attacks of indigestion weakened his hitherto active constitution, and caused much anxiety to his friends. He gradually weakened, till on March 5, 1889, he quietly passed Home in the presence of his wife and family.

Whilst widely known by reason of his eloquence, simplicity, power of imagery, choice of language, and force by which in pulpit and on platform he preached the gospel or expounded Scripture doctrine, Mr. Denham Smith is still more extensively known by the activity of his pen, not only in prose but in sacred verse. His literary attainments were of a high order, and in early life were exhibited in works of no mean merit.

His volumes, "The Gospel in Hosea," "The Brides of Scripture," "Green Pastures," and others are full of spiritual teaching. As a hymn-writer he will be long known by the sweet combination of poetry and doctrinal truth, as shown in such hymns as "Just As Thou Art," "Jesus, Thy Dying Love I Own," "Communion with the Lord," and others.

In the calling home of this beloved Christian the church of God on earth lost one of its brightest ornaments, and one of its most faithful servants; one who unswervingly followed his Lord, and counted it throughout his ministry of fifty years, his highest joy to spend and be spent in his Master's service. That ministry, so redolent with the savor of Christ, endeared him to many thousands in this and other lands, who never had the privilege of his personal acquaintance or of his *viva voce* exposition of the Word.

Hugh Henry Snell
1815-1891

H. H. SNELL

HUGH HENRY SNELL was born in 1815. He was converted early in life. He practised as a doctor at Lifton, on the banks of the Tamar in Devon, and also at Launceston, Cornwall. He frequently preached at the little meeting of "Brethren" at the latter place. Afterwards, on removing to Plymouth, he associated himself with J. L. Harris and Henry Bulteel—both ex-clergymen—for many years in preaching and teaching. He gave up his practice, and devoted his life entirely to the work he believed God had called him to. While at Plymouth he entertained the Lord's servants most hospitably, R. C. Chapman being a frequent guest; and John Hambleton mentions in his well-known book, "Buds, Blossoms, and Fruits," that he stayed with "Brother" Snell at Plymouth.

Later on Mr. Snell preached and taught in many of the large cities and towns of England and Ireland, besides visiting and confirming (in the true Scriptural sense, i.e., strengthening) the smaller meetings then springing up all over the country. Eternity alone will declare the value of this work. Equally gifted with his pen, he wrote largely on prophetical and other subjects. His works most known being "Streams of Refreshing," which has run through twelve editions; "Notes on the Book of Revelation," "Lectures on the Second Coming," "Inspiration of the Scriptures." He was a much valued speaker at the famous Meetings on Prophecy at the Freemasons' Hall, in 1864, and it is interesting to note that the other speakers at these meetings included such gifted "chief men" as L. Strong, J. L. Harris, H. W. Soltau, J. M. Code, Lord Cavan, P. H. Gosse, W. Lincoln, C. Hargrove, and several others. Mr. Snell fell asleep in Jesus, very happily, at Sheffield in 1891.

Henry William Soltau
1805-1875

HENRY WILLIAM SOLTAU

H ENRY WILLIAM SOLTAU, the second son of George Soltau, a merchant of Plymouth, was born on the 11th of July 1805. His father was a godly man, of great energy and foresight, and was one of the founders of the Plymouth Free School, which grew to be one of the largest schools in England. The Bible was taught daily, but no child was compelled to attend the Scripture lessons against the wishes of the parents. He opposed the building of the theater when a member of the Town Council, but without success. He died at the age of forty-four, and seemed to have a vision on his death bed of all his six children safely reaching the heavenly home. His mother was a woman of strong character and great piety, and Henry was devoted to her.

One of Henry's early recollections was being taken in a boat to row round the "Bellerophon," when Napoleon was on board her on his way to St. Helena.

When preparing to go to Cambridge, he read with a private tutor in Kent, having as companions, Samuel Wilberforce and his brother. Entering Trinity College, in 1825, he took his degree in 1827, and there proceeded to study at Lincoln's Inn, and was in due time called to the Chancery Bar. He was greatly interested in natural history and in science generally, and was widely read in many branches. He studied Hebrew in order to understand the Old Testament, and was at one time an earnest seeker after the truth, longing for rest in his soul. He said he never remembered hearing a clear gospel preached, though he listened often to Charles Simeon and to other leading evangelicals when at Cambridge; it always seemed to him that "faith in the merits of Christ and doing one's duty" were inseparably mixed. He endeavored to do what was right, observed the forms of religion, gave away to charities, and read the Bible, and other duties, but he had no peace. He settled in London, and was soon carried away by the attractions of worldly society, and was fascinated by the "innocent amusements" of the day. A great lover of music, he went often to the opera. His attractive manner, sparkling wit, keen intellect, and extensive literary acquirements made him a favorite in society, and he found life opening before him, with wealth and honors awaiting him. But God was preparing him for better things.

In January 1837, he was feeling weary of his round of pleasure, and was, as he said, like the Israelites who loathed the food they had eaten to repletion, but sever himself from his surroundings he could not. A letter from home spoke of his mother being unwell, and when a second letter came Mr. Soltau resolved to go down at once, though there was nothing alarming in what was said. As he packed his portmanteau he had the conviction that he should never see his mother alive, and when the weary coach journey was ended and he reached the last stage out of Plymouth, his uncle met him with the news that all was over. Falling down on his knees by the coffin of his beloved mother that night, he prayed his first true prayer: "Lord, if Thou dost not save me, I am lost for ever!" It was the cry of his wounded spirit, weary of the hollowness of life, and face to face with sore bereavement. Shortly after, he heard an address by Captain Hall on 2 Kings 7, and was led into the light. All things became new, and he rejoiced in the freeness of salvation, so much so that a relative said to him: "You are like the man in the third of Acts, walking and leaping and praising God."

Returning to London, he wondered how his many friends would receive him with his new experiences. He found the question soon settled, for in a very short time they let him severely alone, not relishing his "peculiar opinions." Soon after his conversion he gave up his practice at the Bar, and went to live in Plymouth with his sisters—drawn by the goodly company of the Lord's people there, gathered in so wonderful a way in Christian fellowship, learning from the fountain-head those truths they were privileged to give to the church, and which were as streams of living waters to thirsty souls.

In leaving the Church of England and casting in his lot with the Brethren movement, Mr. Soltau was cut off from most of his family. It was a step which involved much for him, but he esteemed "the reproach of Christ greater riches than the treasures in Egypt." He set himself to the study of the Scriptures and to the service of the Lord in preaching and teaching, and he was soon fully occupied in the many efforts made to take the gospel to the villages and hamlets of the west of England, too often sunk in darkness and ignorance. Great was the blessing wrought through God by the earnest men and women in those days—multitudes were saved, and gathered around the Word of God. Schools were opened, and the Word of God had free course and was glorified. Mr. Soltau and Mr. Clulow opened a tract shop in Plymouth, and by its means great quantities of literature were scattered abroad.

When the sad days of division came, Mr. and Mrs. Soltau moved to Exmouth, where they lived three years, and in 1851 went to Northam, near Bideford, where ten happy years passed, their family of three sons and six daughters growing up in the simple and wholesome atmosphere of that beautiful place. The removal to Exeter in 1861 brought Mr. Soltau more before the church, and his name became widely known through his writings, his book on "The Tabernacle, the Priesthood and Offerings," being greatly appreciated; indeed, it forms the basis for most other books, as well as most lectures, on the Tabernacle. The little book, "The Soul and Its Difficulties: a Word to the Anxious," has had a very large circulation, and been much used of God. It rejoiced the author's heart that when no longer able to minister he found that his little book was constantly being blessed. His lecture on "They Found It Written; or, Who Are the Brethren?" is one of the simplest issued, and has had an extensive sale. All three continue to be widely scattered and read in many parts of the world.

But a great affliction had overtaken him in the failure of his sight. In 1860 it seemed as if total blindness was before him, but he recovered it in measure, and was able to travel alone and to read the largest type Bible.

Mr. Soltau visited many parts, including London, where his addresses at the Freemasons' Hall meetings were so valued; Glasgow, Birmingham, Hereford, and many places in the west; also Dublin, where he was specially welcomed and his ministry valued. He seemed to take the warm-hearted Irish Christians by storm, and they never forgot his visits.

In 1867, his health, never robust, was evidently failing. He paid a short visit to London in the autumn, and on the last Sunday spoke six times. At one of these meetings in the open air, in Soho Square, he referred to the days when as a young man of fashion he lived nearby; he spoke of his conversion, and of the life of happy service for God he had been given. Shortly after he was laid low by paralysis, and he never again spoke in public. Gradually his powers failed, but he never murmured. His peace and calm were unbroken. He delighted to hear of the Lord's work in all parts of the world, especially of that in which his children were engaged.

In 1870 he moved to Barnstaple to end his days near his beloved friend, Mr. R. C. Chapman. When the end came on the first of July 1875, he had been unconscious for several weeks, but at the last he suddenly lifted his head, which had sunk on his breast, his eyes opened, and a heavenly smile lit up his face as without a sigh he breathed his last.

He had the joy of seeing all his nine children early converted, and, as they grew up, giving themselves to the Lord's service. One of them was for long a leader in the M'Call Mission in France, others occupied honored spheres. He was a wise and tender father, and the home was a center of love and happiness. What he taught in public he ever sought to practice in the home, and he was fond of dwelling upon the divine order of responsibility: "First yourself; then the home; then the church; then the world."—w.s.

Joseph Stancomb
1818-1898

JOSEPH STANCOMB

———⊶◇◦◇⊷———

JOSEPH STANCOMB was brought to the Lord in early days, and taking a decided stand as a Christian, the gift bestowed upon him was richly developed for the help and profit of those among whom he had the opportunity of ministering the Word of God. In the solemn division of 1848, Mr. Stancomb, under the firm impression that some were not as prompt as they should have been in inquiring into certain doctrines alleged to be dishonoring to Christ, took his stand with the late Mr. J. N. Darby and others, and maintained that position for about twenty years.

Having been left a widower with six children, he married in 1854, Miss Martha Murly of East Coker, near Yeovil who, after her conversion, had been much used of God for the beginning of a gracious work in that village. There he went to reside, and became the chief helper in the work that had been going on for nearly twenty years, the meeting having already been favored with the visits of various servants of the Lord for whose reception the house of the late Mr. Murly was always open. He was much used of God to the blessing of many in the neighborhood, and also moved about a good deal in a wider sphere, his ministry being much appreciated.

Mr. Stancomb was a man of singular integrity of conscience before God, and it was this that caused him to be unable to go on in the position he had taken. He was concerned, in common with some other men of discernment, by certain teachings of Mr. J. N. Darby, which they judged to be contrary to truth, and desired should be brought to the test of Scripture. Others refused even to allow a question concerning these teachings, and Mr. Stancomb very naturally asked himself: How can I stand in separation from those who are charged with sheltering unsound doctrine, through non-investigation, and yet go on with those who are allowing a similar doctrine and refusing to consider it when it is brought before them?

Careful inquiry convinced him that those from whom he had separated had really judged and cleared themselves of complicity with the evil doctrine in question, and that their aim was to be subject to the Word of God and the authority of Christ in all things. He therefore felt that there was no godly reason for remaining in separation from them, though he did feel very deeply that there was ground for much deep humiliation before God on both sides, and in this some who had occupied a different position were of one mind with him. Meetings were held, therefore, for united confession and prayer, by means of which barriers were still further broken down, and God gave much blessing.

Through the visits of dear brethren to the small conferences held at Yeovil, old links of fellowship were revived and new ones formed, and a time of deep humbling before God in one of them is remembered by some to this day. Just about this time our departed brother, Mr. W. Yapp, visited Mr. Stancomb, and sought his fellowship in the conferences proposed to be held at Leominster, the object of these conferences being that servants of Christ might be helped by spending a few days together in prayer and meditation on the Scriptures. In these he became a willing helper, with the understanding that the first day should be specially given to humiliation and prolonged waiting upon God in prayer. He was preeminently a man of meditation and prayer, and hence his prayers in public were so rich with the very language of Scripture, and so calculated to draw hearts out towards God. In larger meetings, such as those long held at Merrion Hall and Willow Park, Dublin, his ministry was much appreciated, though it was in the smaller conferences that he shone most brightly.

Through an unfortunate accident the house in which Mr. and Mrs. Stancomb and family resided at East Coker was burnt down, which led to their removing into Yeovil, where they resided until he fell asleep on the 8th of March 1893, aged seventy-five years. To the end, however, he regarded East Coker as his special place of meeting and local sphere of service—a service in which he ever had the hearty cooperation of his wife and daughters, the latter being accustomed to spend the whole of the Lord's day there, taking charge of the Sunday school and helping in other ways. While health admitted, he regularly at certain intervals ministered the Word in Yeovil with much acceptance, and monthly visits to other places were much valued, as was also his fellowship in many annual meetings and the quarterly meetings at Exeter.

While the great theme of Mr. Stancomb's ministry was the heavenly calling and hope of the church of God, he had a very firm grasp of the truth of God's electing love and what are generally known as the doctrines of grace, combined with much simplicity in preaching the gospel. Any true evangelist always found in him a ready helper, and so free was he from anything like jealousy or self-esteem that he ever made much of the ministry of others, and was even too ready to keep in the background, while giving place to men of much less ability than himself.

With all movements that grew out of a desire for more practical holiness, he had deep sympathy, though his knowledge of Scripture made him very conscious of the defects of some teachings connected with them. He increasingly feared that there was a lack of such teaching among ourselves as is calculated to lead to devotedness of heart to Christ, and that a tendency to glory in riches not actually possessed by living faith was leading to a poverty of experience as to Christ dwelling in the heart. He saw the danger of the form without the power; the shell without the kernel; a glorying in position with little regard as to condition. Those who knew Mr. Stancomb best knew how he himself thirsted for deeper experience of this reality, and how truly his one aim was to walk before God, and to be well-pleasing to Him. His public service flowed out of this, hence its value. In personal matters he was always ready to sympathize and help, and he never heard of any sorrow or cause of reproach among Christians without feeling it deeply. Anything that brought dishonor upon the name of Christ was a heavy burden to him. His spirit was very free from anything like sectarian narrowness, and he ever sought to embrace in his love and prayers the whole church of God. The divisions among the people of God were constantly mentioned in his prayers, and certain tendencies among some who seemed to be departing from the simplicity of Christ he felt very deeply. There can be little question that his own experience of former days made him dread a line of things which inexperienced brethren are ready to turn to. He felt that the siftings which God in His gracious discipline has given some, should have sufficed to keep others from following such pernicious ways, in which Christ cannot be known as both center and circumference.

While it is a joy to look back upon years of close fellowship given by God in His grace, it is still greater joy to look forward to the day for which all who are "with Christ" are waiting—the day of resurrection glory—the time of perfect fellowship, when the sorrows connected with human and divine affections, as well as service, will be all past, and without any conflict or hindrance "his servants shall serve him, and they shall see his face; and his name shall be in their foreheads."—W.H.B.

Charles Stanley
1821-1888

CHARLES STANLEY

———◦◦◦———

MANY HAVE REASON to praise God for blessing and help received through the perusal of tracts with the well-known initials, C. S., being the initials for Charles Stanley, of Rotherham. Born in a Yorkshire village, he was left an orphan at the age of four. At seven he had to earn his living in the summer by working in the fields, and in the winter months he attended the village school. When a merry little fellow of eight summers a gentleman who knew him said: "You will either be a curse or a blessing to mankind." This prediction was a true one, and by the mercy of God "C. S." became a channel of blessing to thousands of his fellow-creatures. His conversion took place when he was a boy of fourteen, and shortly afterwards he began to "tell to all around what a dear Saviour he had found."

At the age of twenty-three we find him starting on his own account in the hardware business in Sheffield. For many years he traversed England as a commercial traveller, and at the same time did "the work of an evangelist." From help he obtained through a Captain W—, the Bible became a new book to him, It was his daily study, and he "grew in grace, and in the knowledge of our Lord and Saviour Jesus Christ." Though only possessed of a small capital when he commenced business, he managed to devote a good deal of time to preaching the gospel and teaching believers in various parts of the kingdom. Speaking of those early days, forty years after, he says: "Seldom in those days did the Lord open my lips without some soul being converted. Not that this appeared at the time, but I have met them everywhere, ten, twenty, or thirty years after." Instances are given of the Lord's thoughtful and tender care when in business straits, proving the truth of the promise, "them that honour me I will honour" (1 Samuel 2:30). God marvelously blessed his labors in the salvation of the perishing, and in the edification and comfort of Christians.

"C. S." believed in the Lord's special and direct guidance of His servants. Again and again he was deeply impressed with the conviction that he ought to go to places to preach the gospel where he had never been;

and on many such occasions he found a people anxious to listen. Here is an instance. "Three of us felt led to go to Leamington. We had a little notice printed, about the size of a small envelope, asking the Christians of Leamington to come together in the Music Hall at three o'clock for prayer for the Lord's blessing on the Word to be preached in the hall that night. About two hundred came together, and oh! what a cry of united expecting prayer went up to the throne of grace. At seven the large hall was filled. That night God answered prayer. It was the birth-night of many precious souls. It was said some hundreds found deliverance and blessing that night." By the wayside and riverside, in railway carriages and steamboats, at balls and races, in halls and chapels, in kitchens and drawing-rooms, theatres and concert halls Charles Stanley nobly witnessed for his Lord and Master. "He being dead yet speaketh" by hundreds converted through his preaching, and through the scores of tracts and booklets he has written.

What Christian worker has not heard of the "C. S." tracts? He tells how he began this most blessed service for the Lord. "I had been preaching the Word at T——, and brother W—— said to me, 'Why don't you print some of those incidents of the Lord's work in the railway carriages? I am sure the Lord would use them.' I said I had never thought of it. He urged me to do so, How little did I think at that moment that the Lord would use them in so many languages" The object he had in view in writing the tracts are stated. "To look to God to give me to write just what He pleased, and to enable me to write it plainly without any adornment. To never allow me to write with a party feeling, but to write for the whole church of God, or gospel to every sinner. In every incident related to give the exact words as near as I could recollect." Speaking of his address on "Mephibosheth," he remarks: "I believe the Lord rarely ever led me to preach from Mephibosheth without souls being converted. He has been pleased to use that tract very often when repeated to the sick and the dying, and also through others preaching it. Mr. M—— told me he had preached it in almost every city and town in America and, he thought, never without souls being brought to God. It would fill a volume to tell of the great number of cases that have been brought before my own notice."

His counsel to Christian workers is most seasonable and helpful, and is worthy of prayerful and careful consideration. Invaluable is the following testimony: "I have always found blessing and results in proportion to communion with Christ in His love to the whole church, whether in writing or preaching; and no Christian can prosper in his own soul unless he is seeking the welfare of others."

Charles Stanley was called from his earthly home in Rotherham, to the heavenly home, in March 30, 1890. He has left behind him a legacy in the form of the "C. S." tracts, which will cause his name to be honored for many a day.—A.M.

Alexander Stewart
1843-1923

ALEXANDER STEWART

ALEXANDER STEWART, of Glasgow and Prestwick, was born in the year 1843, a year memorable in the history of the religious life of Scotland. It was in that year the great disruption of the Church of Scotland took place, when many of its members seceded and formed the Free Church of Scotland. Mr. Stewart's parents were respected members of the Church of Scotland.

For the first nineteen years of his life he lived without God. One day, walking along a street in Glasgow, he took a giddy turn, and immediately the thought occurred to him that if he had expired on the street he would have gone to a lost eternity. Deep conviction of sin took possession of his soul, and for nine long months he endeavored without success to find peace. He commenced to attend church, which for a long time he had neglected. He even called upon his minister, but, as he himself said, he got little real spiritual help. He took a class in the Sunday school, and all the time was in the dark as to how peace with God could be found.

Mr. Stewart tells his experience and conversion thus: "I was lying on my bed one day in sore anxiety of soul when that Scripture came to me, 'It is finished,' and immediately I entered into peace. I saw for the first time I was eighteen hundred years on the other side of a finished work. I had been looking forward to something to be done by me, whereas I now saw that the work had been finished by another, the Lord Jesus Christ, on the cross of Calvary."

Having found peace, Mr. Stewart joined the church, but after his first communion he became so miserable that he left, and for two years he did not identify himself with any religious body. Like Noah's dove, he went about trying to find a resting-place for his soul.

One Sunday morning during this period he went to an assembly of Exclusive Brethren (so-called) in Sauchiehall Street, Glasgow, and they welcomed him to the Lord's table. He met there Dr. W. T. P. Wolston,

Andrew Miller (author of "Church History"), and others, whose fellowship he valued; but his sympathies were too broad to permit of him identifying himself with any party which prevented him having fellowship with all true Christians.

Possessed with a love for the perishing, he commenced to preach in the open air at Phoenix Corner, Cowcaddens, Glasgow. In this open-air work he was associated for a time with a young man named Murray M'Neil Caird, the son of the Procurator-Fiscal of Wigtownshire, who was at that time studying law in the city.

Mr. Stewart never had any difficulty in finding a congregation. His rich, commanding voice, gentlemanly bearing, marked ability joined with deep spirituality, secured for him at all times, either outside or inside, a respectful and attentive hearing.

As a result of his gospel efforts in open air, in kitchens, and halls, converts multiplied, and the question arose what was to be done with them. Some of them commenced to remember the Lord in the breaking of bread on Sunday mornings, which continued in various buildings until eventually they secured a suitable place called Clarendon Hall. Later they removed to Union Hall, where Mr. Stewart ministered the Word of life for many years to large and appreciative audiences.

Later he removed his home from Glasgow to Prestwick, on the Ayrshire coast, and threw in his lot with the little assembly there, which under his godly care and rich spiritual ministry largely increased.

In addition to being an able speaker, he had the pen of a ready writer, and throughout his life many helpful articles from his pen appeared in the pages of *The Witness*. He also wrote some beautiful hymns, two of the richest of them "Lord Jesus Christ, We Seek Thy face," and "O Lamb of God, We Lift Our Eyes," appear in the Believers' Hymn Book.

He was never robust physically, and when only twenty-seven years of age, through overstrain in preaching and working, he had to take a voyage to Australia. He was only absent eight months, returning again to the old country and to his loved work for his worthy Master. For some time he was rather feeble and was confined to bed. As in health, so in sickness, his conversation ever was about the Lord, His Word and His work. Parting with a friend who had visited him he said: "If we never meet again, remember it has been mercy from first to last." To another he remarked: "I'm only a sinner, saved by grace."

He passed peacefully home on April 27th, 1923, and thus ended a useful and fruitful life, filled with service to the Lord and rich in blessing to man.—J.G.

William James Stokes
1807-1881

WILLIAM JAMES STOKES

W ILLIAM JAMES STOKES was one of the first seven to meet as Brethren at Aungier Street, Dublin, in company with J. G. Bellett, Francis Hutchinson, John Parnell (afterwards Lord Congleton), J. N. Darby, A. N. Groves, and E. Cronin, he being the youngest of the party—about twenty years of age. He was born in 1807.

Aungier Street was the first public room hired by Lord Congleton for their use on Lord's day. His idea was that the Lord's table should be a public witness of their position. There they commenced breaking bread. It was a large auction room, and in order to clear the place for the meeting on Lord's day morning three or four of the brothers were in the habit of moving the furniture aside on Saturday evening.

One of these active brothers, referring to their Saturday night's work, after a lapse of nearly fifty years, said: "These were blessed seasons to my soul—J. Parnell, W. Stokes, and others moving the furniture and laying the simple table with the bread and wine—and never to be forgotten; for surely we had the Master's presence, smile, and sanction in a movement such as this was."

Mrs. E. Trotter, in her most interesting book "Undertones of the Nineteenth Century," says: "The inspiration came to them at first alone, and not under the influence of large multitudes; neither did it die out, but energized and sustained them in lives of unusual toil and unusual length."

This may be truly said of W. J. Stokes. Greatly loving all Christians, and beloved by many, he was very helpful in large Bible readings, in private houses, and elsewhere, attended by godly clergymen and Christians of all denominations. He held a sizable Bible class for men in connection with the Y.M.C.A. at Sackville Street, Dublin, the attendance numbering between one and two hundred. He was much used in ministry amongst Assemblies. By his gentle, tactful, and Christlike sympathy he was enabled to heal many breaches and minor difficulties in them. Some of his addresses at the Dublin believers' meetings have been published; also a book, "Truth in Season," containing notes of addresses by R. C. Chapman,

H. Dyer, and himself. He frequently visited England, and in the late "six-ties" addressed Christian young women in Devon with J. L. Harris, Capt. T. H. Hall, H. W. Soltau, and others.

Mr. Stokes' courageous initiative with Mr. Robert Keane (solicitor), of Dublin, resulted in the formation of what is now known as the Harold's Cross Protestant Orphanage, Dublin, and also a Rescue Home at 31 Marlborough Street, Dublin, still in existence at the time of this writing. He was in ill health for many years before the end, but always cheerful, happy, and praising God for all His mercies. Had he lived until the 11th of March 1881, he would have been seventy-four, but he fell asleep on the third. Surely "the memory of the just is blessed."—C.E.F.

James Butler Stoney
1814-1897

J. B. STONEY

———— ⟫⟫∘∘∘∘⟪⟪ ————

JAMES BUTLER STONEY was born at Portland, County Tipperary, on May 13th, 1814. His father was a strict Puritan and his mother (see Butler) equally strict from a different point of view. Her four sons remarkably answered to her culture in mind, in address, and in manner of life. They had private tutors, and lived in a country home, with only country pursuits and pleasures.

J. B. S. entered Trinity College, Dublin, at fifteen, placing seventy out of ninety-two. At nineteen he was senior freshman and well up in classics and law. His first religious impression was as a boy, when the Reverend Baker Stoney, rector of Castlebar, the friend and fellow worker with Mr. Nagle of Achill, came to Portland. At family prayers he read Acts 9, and dwelt on the fact that God's salvation was so great that He could send a "light from heaven" to arrest one soul, and in that light was seen a Saviour in the glory of God for a man on earth who was stamping out His name from the earth. He saw that just One and heard the voice of His mouth (Acts 22 and 26).

The youthful mind is "wax to receive and marble to retain," and he never lost the sense of the revelation in Christ of the "kindness and love of God our Saviour toward man" (Titus 3:4). But the ambitions and joys of youth left little room for serious thought. He was eagerly following his studies for the Bar; all his prospects in life depended on his success at the Bar.

In 1831 men were dying of cholera all around in Dublin. He was suddenly taken ill, and his first thought was, "How can I meet a holy God?" The agony of his soul was worse than that of the body. He rang for his servant to go for the doctor. "Thomas, I am afraid I am dying." "Surely you are, sir," said Thomas. Alone he threw himself on his face, and cried to the God he had heard of as a boy, who could receive the chief of sinners because the "Crucified One" was at His right hand. When the doctor came he was exhausted and appeared dying, but quite calmly said: "Jesus will have me. Lord Jesus, receive my spirit." A long sleep restored him, and he was soon able to return to his studies. But he had been "born again," born for a new world, new hopes, new life. "No more law for me," he said. "I'll be a witness to grace," the grace that could only be revealed from glory for sinners.

He joined the Divinity Class at Trinity College, Dublin, where there were really good men at that time, but he had to wait nearly four years. He could not be ordained until he was twenty-four years of age. His family were very angry; his uncle would have nothing more to do with him; as his fine talents and opportunities were being thrown away for a curate's pay.

But during those four years he was studying the Scriptures with all the earnestness of a soul that had learned that unseen things are for eternity, the seen things of this life passing away. As he studied the Epistles he found that the "gifts" for ministry in the church of God were given directly from the ascended Man to each one, so that by Christ's own appointment one became an evangelist or a teacher, etc. (Ephesians 4). He would not wait for a curacy; he would go out at once into the highways and hedges and invite sinners to come to God's great salvation: "Come; for all things are now ready."

He wrote a little book called "Discipline in the School of God," dealing with the Old Testament characters, and contributed to several periodicals. He spoke somewhere every day and travelled much. A fervent, impressive speaker, he anxiously avoided anything like eloquence, feeling that the Spirit of God was the only power for holy things.

J.B.S. died on May 1st, 1897, just before his eighty-second birthday. God was his exceeding joy to the end—while telling of Him he gently fell asleep. He rejoiced to say: —C.E.F.

> Tis the treasure I found in His love
> That has made me a pilgrim below.

Leonard Strong
1797-1874

LEONARD STRONG

L EONARD STRONG was born in 1797. His father was rector of Brampton Abbots, in Herefordshire. He entered the navy at the age of twelve, served as a midshipman in the French and American wars, and was many times in action.

Once, when on duty in the West Indies, he was all but drowned owing to his shore-going boat upsetting in a squall. This brought his sins before him, and he cried to God for mercy. Being saved, he left the navy, went to Oxford, where he was converted, and desired to be a missionary. He was ordained in the Church of England as curate of Ross-on-Wye.

But the West Indies called him and he went out to British Guiana in 1826 as rector of a parish there. His preaching and ministry were greatly blessed, and he devoted himself to work among the slaves, braving the wrath of the planters, who threatened to shoot him and eventually got him removed.

He went to Peter's Hall and Georgetown and began his work again. Meanwhile his diligent and independent study of the Scriptures was teaching him some practical truths as to worship and service that he found impossible to reconcile with his position in the Church of England. Years before, Anthony Norris Groves and his friend, Leonard Strong, read the same Bible and found the same principles. So he gave up his living, worth £800 a year, and his manse, and met simply for worship among his converts, many hundreds of whom followed him. The first meeting was held in a large shed used for drying coffee, about two thousand being present.

Another start was made in Georgetown, and the assemblies continue to the present day. They were "breaking bread" in Georgetown earlier than in Dublin or Plymouth.

Mr. Strong left Demerara for good in 1848 or '49. He settled at Torquay, where his ministry was much valued. He wrote several beautiful tracts and books, including some on prophetical subjects, notably one on "Daniel." He was always a welcome speaker at the meetings held in London and elsewhere on prophecy.

He was one of the first writers to the well-known missionary periodical of "Brethren," the *Echoes of Service in Many Lands*. The claims of perishing souls in the regions beyond ever had a warm place in his heart. A man of rich gifts and rare grace, he was greatly beloved. He died in London in 1874, aged seventy-seven, but was buried in Torquay, where he had lived and labored so faithfully since leaving the West Indies.

Clarence Esme Stuart
1823-1903

C. E. STUART, M. A.

$\Longrightarrow \infty \infty$

CLARENCE ESME STUART was the youngest son of Mr. William Stuart, of Tempsford Hall, Sandy, and grandson of Hon. William Stuart, Archbishop of Armagh, who enjoyed the special confidence of King George III. The Earl of Bute was direct ancestor, likewise of the present Marquis of Bute. The family descends collaterally from the old royal house of Stuart, and C. E. Stuart was by some regarded as bearing a likeness to Charles I. His mother was a maid-of-honor to Queen Adelaide as Duchess of Clarence, who was his godmother; hence the name Clarence. The name Esme is one familiar to students of Scottish history.

Clarence Stuart was born in 1828 and was educated at Eton, from which he proceeded to St. John's College, Cambridge, in accordance with the custom of his family. Here he took his degree of M.A., after gaining one of the earliest of the Tyrwhitt University scholarships in Hebrew. For sacred study he had early conceived a special taste; the more so as, under the fostering care of a Christian mother, C. E. Stuart in his youth experienced the spiritual change by which we pass "from death unto life" (John 5:24). He would, doubtless, in due course have taken orders in the Church of England to which his family belonged, but a defect in his speech seems to have occasioned his remaining what is termed a layman.

Mr. Stuart, marrying a daughter of Colonel Cunninghame, of Ayrshire, settled in Reading, where for several years he interested himself in church work of the evangelical type, that with which his family was traditionally identified. Among other forms of activity, Mr. Stuart at this period of his life promoted the operations of the British and Foreign Bible Society.

About the year 1860 Mr. Stuart's attention was called to the position taken by those Christians commonly called "Plymouth Brethren" (though they have consistently rejected any such title), represented in Reading by a large "gathering," amid which ministered the late William Henry Dorman, a former Congregational minister, whose connection with the "Brethren" dated from about the year 1840. In the years 1845-1848 Mr. Dorman figured as a trusted ally of the late John Nelson Darby in the formation of what has since been denominated the "Exclusive" section of Brethren, the continued unhappy effect of which his eldest son, Mr. W. H. Dorman, of Stafford, endeavored to some extent to remedy. Mr. Stuart became convinced, under the late Mr. Dorman's influence, of the untenable character of his own churchmanship, and without more ado took his place, as the expression was, in the Reading fellowship, which for years was identified especially with his own name

During the years 1864-1866, Mr. Stuart's fidelity to "J.N.D.," like that of others, was tested by Mr. Dorman's uncompromising opposition to Mr. Darby's teaching with reference to a class of sufferings of our Lord, discriminated as "non-atoning," as derived from His association with Israel. This doctrine "W. H. D." put on the same plane as that of B. W. Newton, which brought about the split in 1848. The close acquaintance, however, of C. E. Stuart with the usage of Hebrew words which came into play for any Biblical scholar having to consider such a question, aided him in determining the direction of his own sympathies in the matter. He did not follow the example of his Reading associate, who then seceded from the Darby fellowship.

In 1881, when "J. N. D." lent himself to another unsettlement among Brethren, Mr. Stuart again stood with him; and in the next year, when that remarkable man passed away, the hearty voice of "C.E.S." was one raised over his interment. For three years longer Mr. Stuart remained in the company of those who had owned the special leadership of "J. N. D."

In 1885 a storm arose over some of his own views which then acquired prominence. These were deemed by many inconsistent with the traditional teaching of Brethren, especially as regards the standing of the children of God. In a further cleavage, which searched many hearts, some rallied to "C. E. S.," and accepted his view as a distinct advance in truth, while others, not prepared to commit themselves definitely to it, held that the difference of judgment manifested from this time afforded no sufficient reason for severance from "C. E. S."

The eighteen years from then till his death proved full of activity for his pen. In addition to independent books and papers issued by him, Mr. Stuart was a constant contributor to a periodical entitled *Words in Season*.

His earlier writings comprised a book on the Sacrifices, "Simple Papers on the Church of God," an article on "The Atonement, as Set Forth in the Old Testament," his "Textual Criticism of the New Testament, for English Readers," and a "Review of Robertson Smith's Lectures on the

Old Testament in the Jewish Church," a paper the value of which was acknowledged by many English clergymen. In textual criticism Mr. Stuart was an adherent of the school of Tregelles rather than that of Scrivener.

Publications belonging to the two last decades of his career commenced with a pamphlet on "Christian Standing and Condition," which called forth much acrimonious discussion, culminating in a division. This, and cognate pamphlets were followed by a series of papers on Propitiation. From long familiarity with the scheme of Old Testament types, Mr. Stuart insisted upon the detailed fulfillment of the presentation of the blood of the Antitype after death, as the propitiation *par excellence,* against the view that the cross covers the whole ground of the atoning work. The line thus taken by him tended to accentuate the difference existing between him and his old associates, who held that the Old Testament should bend to the New, and not *vice versa.* Then came a series of devotional expositions of the Gospels of Mark, Luke, and John, the Acts of the Apostles, the Epistles to the Romans and Hebrews, and the Book of Psalms, the spiritual value of the latter being acknowledged by Professor Cheyne.

Among the latest of his writings was a pamphlet entitled "The Critics: Shall We Follow Them?" In this case "C. E. S." did battle for traditional views of the Old Testament against the Higher Critics. Nevertheless, he kept abreast of the most recent scholarship valuing, for example, Professor Driver's "Treatise on the Hebrew Tenses." His library contained all the standard works used by Biblical scholars, with some rare specimens from the past, including a valuable copy of the Complutensian Polyglot, which in his old age he presented to the library of his college.

As an interpreter, Mr. Stuart must be ranked with those who adhere closely to the wording of the text of Scripture, and to belief in verbal inspiration. He little heeded extraneous sources, such as Patristic interpretation; least of all the suggestions of "modern thought." With independent judgment he held firmly the general body of "recovered" truth, ecclesiastical and prophetic, characteristic of "Brethren."

Simple in his demeanor, with much charm of manner, he endeared himself to the poor of the flock, to whom he was "good." He delighted to share with them the light which he enjoyed. C. E. Stuart must be reckoned with those of whom it may be said that, although dead, they yet speak.—E.E.W.

Herbert Wilbraham Taylor
1847-1899

HERBERT W. TAYLOR

H ERBERT WILBRAHAM TAYLOR was born on May 27th, 1847. He was the son of Mr. Wilbraham Taylor, who was Gentleman Usher to Queen Victoria. Herbert was endowed with gifts of no ordinary power, and he used them freely and exclusively for the great Giver.

It is not often that the gifts of preacher and teacher combine in one man, but Mr. Taylor was an exception, inasmuch as he was highly appreciated both as teacher and preacher. His name is to be found as a speaker at various conferences, notably Dublin, and he frequently spoke at the Iron Room, Upper Clapton.

Possessing a heart for the gospel and a love for perishing souls, He visited many of the large towns preaching the gospel with great power, and numbers were brought to a saving knowledge of the truth through his ministry. By his knowledge of the Word he was also able to lead the young converts on in "the ways that be in Christ."

He was courageous in declaring God's truth, and ready at all times to take advantage of every opportunity to speak a word on behalf of his Lord and Master. He did not confine his service to halls, but loved to tell out the old, old story in the open air.

In and around his native town of Barnet he specially loved to work. One writes, "He was a great open-air preacher, and used to drive with his coachman to the market place in Enfield town on Saturday evenings and preach the gospel from his buggy to a large crowd. It was also his great joy to visit in the same way other centers or market places in the Lord's service. He was indeed a faithful steward, who did not shun to declare the whole counsel of God.

Herbert Taylor wrote a large number of tracts for the "Clapton and Iron Rooms Series," many small gospel books, and a larger work, "Abraham," all with suggestive thoughts for young Christians.

In addition, he was a poet of no mean order, some of his compositions appearing from time to time in the *Latter Rain*, and other papers. Mr. Taylor married in 1872 Miss Rebekah Hope Morley, daughter of Mr. Samuel Morley, and departed to be with Christ on June 14th, 1899, at the comparatively early age of fifty-two.—C.E.F.

George Frederick Trench
1841-1915

GEORGE F. TRENCH

———— ✦ ————

GEORGE FREDERICK TRENCH, B.A. was the son of Frederick Fitz-John Trench, formerly a cavalry officer in India, latter rector of Staplestown, Ireland. Born in 1841, he was aroused as to the state of his soul while being prepared for confirmation. He was deeply convicted through an address of Grattan Guinness on John 3:7, and soon afterwards found deliverance. When at college, where he obtained his B.A., a friendship sprung up between himself and a student, who afterwards became Sir Robert Anderson, K.C.B., LL.D., and continued without interruption for fifty years.

Following on the wonderful Irish Revival of 1859, the early 60's were "days of unleavened bread" in the south and west, as well as in the north of Ireland. The two student friends united in various evangelistic efforts in many parts of Ireland, and had considerable fruit in some of the districts visited. F. C. Bland, J. Denham Smith, R. J. Mahony, T. Shuldham Henry, Lord Congleton, and many other veteran workers were active at this time. Visits which left an impression behind were made by Richard Weaver, Harry Moorhouse, Reginald Radcliffe, John Hambleton, and many others.

Mr. Trench married Miss Talbot-Crosbie (a name honored in the southwest of Ireland), and made his home at Abbeylands, Ardfert, County Kerry. For many years his influence for Christ and His gospel was great in these parts. He regularly held meetings in the Granary at Ardfert, and many were led into the light or helped on in the ways of Christ. During the troublesome times in Ireland, Mr. Trench was held in high esteem and little molested, although once the horse on which he was riding was stabbed under him.

When the well-known American workers, Moody and Sankey, visited Ireland Mr. Trench threw himself heart and soul into the work as a work after his own heart. Having received clear light on the evil of sectarianism in his younger days, he was clear in heart and ways to the end. No man was more loyal to the truths dear to those who seek to gather in the worthy name alone.

An ardent worker, a diligent student, an able minister of the Word, ever a friend of the young, he was also interested in ministry to policemen, soldiers, and other special branches of work. His influence was most widely extended by his pen. For over forty years articles bearing the initials G. F. T. appeared in *The Witness, The Christian*, and various other magazines, invariably to the profit and edification of the readers. His large volumes are: "After the Thousand Years," which was much read, but has not generally been accepted; "The Life that is Life Indeed," a sane, helpful work on life more abundant, and "Walking with God," his latest and one of his most helpful volumes.

After suffering for some time, his closing days were very peaceful. The home-call came on November 11th, 1915 and his remains were laid to rest in Mount Jerome Cemetery, Dublin, there to await the time when the changed saints shall cry, "O death, where is thy sting?" the raised saints cry, "O grave, where is thy victory?" and the united shout be heard, "Thanks be to God, which giveth us the victory through our Lord Jesus Christ."—HY.P.

William Trotter
1818-1865

WILLIAM TROTTER

WILLIAM TROTTER was born in 1818 and died in 1865, at the early age of forty-seven, having done the work of three lives. He was converted at twelve years of age and found peace through the ministry of William Dawson, the Methodist preacher famous in the north as "Billy Dawson." At fourteen he began to preach, and at nineteen was an ordained minister of the Methodist New Connexion, and was much used of God in a revival at Halifax. He was also a minister at York, where his work was greatly owned of God in the conversion of sinners, and many souls were saved. It was while being so signally used that the conference, or some such body, conceived the idea that it would be a very good thing to transfer him to London, to a chapel which had gone down in popularity and whose members were dwindling, with the result that his mouth was virtually closed in his ministry, and he shortly afterwards resigned.

He saw what a terrible thing it was for a man, or number of men to come between his work and God, and the thoroughly unscripturalness of it, and henceforth associated with Brethren, where his ministry was much owned of God. He was a very kind, loving, and affectionate man, and W. B. Neatby, in his "History of the Brethren," speaks of him as being "more highly spoken of by every one who knew him than almost any other Plymouth Brother," and his untimely death, while he was yet under fifty, was felt to be a heavy loss, of the kind that Christians can least afford.

He wrote with great vigor at the time of the sad troubles in 1848 about Plymouth and Bethesda, but is best remembered for his excellent works, "Eight Lectures on Prophecy" and "Plain Papers on Prophetic Subjects." He also edited for a few years a little paper, *The Christian Brethren's Journal and Investigator*, giving an account of the activities of the "little companies of earnest men who began to meet in the early part of the nineteenth century in various parts of the country, unknown to each other, and under no human leadership,...the inception of this movement arising from a new illumination of the personality of Jesus Christ, and of the essential unity of all who believe in Him, under whatever name they were differentiated" ("Undertones of the Nineteenth Century").

John Victor
1820-1894

JOHN VICTOR

JOHN VICTOR, pastor, teacher, preacher, was born at Marazion, in Cornwall, in 1820. He was brought up among the Methodists, and being converted at the early age of seventeen, and showing an aptitude for preaching, he was placed on the plan as a local preacher. It is stated as a proof of his earnestness that he studied and learned the French language in order to preach to the French sailors visiting the little Cornish port.

In the course of a few years he went to Bristol, where he soon came into contact with the two devoted servants of God—George Muller and Henry Craik—and connected himself with the company of believers meeting at "Bethesda" in that city. He frequently preached in the open air, especially in the slums, and began a work which subsequently grew to large proportions. Removing to Clevedon in 1852, his exceptional gifts as pastor, teacher, and preacher led to his assuming the oversight of the small company of believers meeting in that town, which had been under the care of Honorable Mr. Methuen, formerly rector of Corsham, Wilts.

One writes: "The blessing of God rested manifestly on the labors of His servant, so that the premises used for the meetings became inadequate and a chapel was erected....As time advanced, and the blessing of the Lord continued to rest on Mr. Victor's labors, his ministry ripened and attracted such numbers that two more enlargements of the building took place....The appreciation of Mr. Victor's ministry was by no means confined to his regular church and congregation. Clevedon grew in public favor as a holiday resort, and many of the visitors delighted to listen to the eloquent pastor. Indeed his ministry powerfully influenced the choice of many, and took them year by year to the same spot that they might gain in spiritual blessing as well as in bodily health. The extent of his usefulness in this way it is impossible to trace....Preaching stations were established in several surrounding villages, and for the supply of these Mr. Victor made himself responsible. He frequently visited the various stations, and it was a great delight to him to get among the village folk, many of whom were brought to the saving knowledge of the Lord through his labors.

In a remarkable way Mr. Victor combined the gifts of pastor, teacher, and evangelist. As pastor, he was full of sympathy and continually alive to the needs of the people. He lived among them and was ever ready with sympathy and help. He was emphatically a teacher, and his ministry was eminently calculated to edify believers. At the same time the elementary truths of the gospel ever had a prominent place in his preaching, and made his discourses second to none for evangelistic tone and quality. He had learned the true secret of a staying power in his ministry—the inexhaustible nature of the Word of God. He was a diligent student of the Bible, and was enabled continually to 'bring out of his treasury things new and old.'"

John Wood, secretary of the Evangelization Society, once said: "There are not ten men in England who know their Bible better than John Victor."

Mr. Victor was laid aside from active work for about three years before his departure, during which period he had to endure intense suffering. The end came peacefully on March 22, 1894, at the age of seventy-four.—C.E.F.

Captain Honorable William H. G. Wellesley
1806-1875

WILLIAM H. G.
WELLESLEY

CAPTAIN HONORABLE WILLIAM HENRY GEORGE WELLESLEY, the second son of the first Baron Cowley, was born in 1806 and died 1875. He was a nephew of the great Duke of Wellington, the Iron Duke.

Mrs. E. Trotter writes: "Weary with the strife of sect and party, and inspired with a profound longing to conform in life and practice to the apostolic ideal, little companies of earnest men began to meet in the early part of the nineteenth century, in various parts of the country, unknown to each other, and under no human leadership....The inception of this movement arose from a new illumination of the personality of Jesus Christ. Here was a vision; this was the burning secret at the core of life, transforming it from within and without.

> I have seen the face of Jesus—
> Tell me not of aught beside,
> I have heard the voice of Jesus—
> All my soul is satisfied.

In this light all other lights paled. Among the men who were affected by it were men of brain, born leaders, men of birth, of large means, scholars, and students, who would have made their mark at any time and in any walk of life; lawyers of acute critical judgment, officers of promise in both services, and large landowners.

The inspiration came to them at first alone, and not under the influence of great multitudes, neither did it die out, but energized and sustained them in lives of unusual toil and unusual length."

Among the men of birth was Captain Wellesley, who suffered a great deal for the Master's sake by taking up the cross, forsaking all, and following the Lord.

In the early days of the movement his name is frequently met with at conferences and special gatherings of Brethren, where his weighty words of ministry or earnest, loving gospel addresses always made an appeal to all who were privileged to hear him.

John Hambleton says of him: "One great feature in this revival is, that God has raised up men of affluence and influence to receive those poor laborers into their dwellings who have, in this world, neither one nor the other to recommend them. One honorable gentleman, Captain Wellesley, who had forsaken this world's wisdom and greatness that he might become wise in Christ, received me into his house....He was well taught in the Word, and saw death and resurrection to be the key of the whole Scriptures."

Death and resurrection culminate in Him. And this is the gospel that Christ died for our sins, and was buried; the third day He rose again, according to the Scriptures; and the redeemed creation will yet rise with Him from its groans and cries into the bloom and beauty of immortal life.—C.E.F.

George V. Wigram
1805-1879

G. V. WIGRAM

G EORGE VICESIMUS WIGRAM, the twentieth child of Sir Robert
Wigram—hence his middle name —was born in 1805. Two of his
brothers distinguished themselves in their respective careers: James, who
became vice-chancellor in the Old Court of Chancery; and Joseph Cotton, who became bishop of Rochester.

George V. Wigram was converted while a subaltern officer in the army,
and in 1826 entered Queen's College, Oxford, with the view of taking orders. As an undergraduate he came into contact with Mr. Jarratt of the
same college and with Messrs. James L. Harris and Benjamin Wills Newton, both of Exeter College, who were all destined to take part in the ecclesiastical movement with which Wigram's name is also prominently connected. This connection was strengthened from about the year 1830,
when these friends, all Devonians, were associated in the formation of a
company of Christians at Plymouth, who separated from the organized
churches and were gathered to the name alone of Jesus, in view of bearing a testimony to the unity of the church, and to its direction by the
Holy Spirit alone, while awaiting the second coming of the Lord.

Wigram was active in the initiation of a like testimony in London,
where by the year 1838 a considerable number of gatherings were formed
on the model of that at Plymouth, and he began to feel that some kind of
organization was needed whereby these neighboring companies should
act in concert; hence his letter to J. N. Darby, which will be found in W. B.
Neatby's "History." The formation of a London Saturday-evening administrative "central meeting" dates from that year.

Several years before this, Wigram's interest had been engaged in the
preparation of concordances which should aid especially Bible students
with no, or little, knowledge of the original languages. The plan of these
was determined on after conference with Mr. De Burgh, who found the
workers, while there can be no doubt Wigram himself provided the
money, although he humbly speaks of this only as "passing through my
hands." The first to appear, in 1839, was the "Englishman's Greek and

English Concordance to the New Testament". It was followed in 1843 by the "Englishman's Hebrew and Chaldee Concordance to the Old Testament". These volumes have largely aided intelligent, if not scholarly, acquaintance with the background of the Bible in both its parts, so that their issue by Wigram was a signal service of his rendered to the church of God, which after the lapse of years still makes itself felt. Compilers of later works on similar lines have more or less been indebted to his scheme (cf. Scrivener's Reference Paragraph Bible).

In the years 1845-1850 Wigram was prominently concerned in the upheaval, with its melancholy result, which originated at Plymouth and affected Bristol in particular. His sincerity was never questioned, his motives always recognized by the late George Muller, much to the credit of this venerated brother.

A magazine known as the *Christian Witness* had for several years served as chief organ of the movement in its beginning. This had now lapsed, and a new periodical entitled, *The Present Testimony*, took its place under the editorship of Wigram. Among the papers it contained are his own on the Psalms, in which the divine names are distinguished in the text.

In 1856 he produced a new hymn book, "Hymns for the Poor of the Flock," which for some twenty-five years remained the staple of praise in the meetings with which he was associated, and in altered form is still used by most companies known as "Exclusives."

Ten years after the first appearance of the hymn book edited by him, he stood by J. N. Darby once again at a critical juncture, when the question of the doctrine maintained by the latter on the sufferings of Christ introduced some further dissension. During the rest of his life he paid visits to the West Indies, New Zealand, etc., where his ministry seems to have been much appreciated. He passed away in 1879.

He was one accounted familiar with the spiritual, who cared little to counsel others in their difficulties, referring them to the same resource, God's Word. It is only upon the excellencies of such a man that one cares to dwell. Let all else, for those immediately concerned, sink into oblivion.—E.E.W.

Dr. Walter T. P. Wolston
1840-1917

DR. W. T. P. WOLSTON

WALTER THOMAS PRIDEAUX WOLSTON was born at Brixham, Devon, on September 6th, 1840. He says himself that before he was converted he was a most thoroughgoing young worldling, deeply immersed in its pleasures and its sin. On leaving school he entered a lawyer's office in his native town intending to follow the legal profession.

On December 4th, 1860, he left his country home in Devonshire for the great city of London to further pursue his legal studies there, intending to return home for a visit at Christmas, as he had to fulfil a number of worldly engagements in connection with the Glee Band, of which he was a prominent member. Before Christmas came round, however, the Lord had met and saved him. The first Sunday after reaching London it was suggested by a fellow-lodger that they should both go and hear Richard Weaver, the collier preacher, in Surrey Theatre, whose earnest and rousing preaching of the gospel was attracting thousands. He was convicted of his sin that night, but it was not until the following Sunday evening, after hearing Charles Stanley preach the gospel, that the light dawned in his soul, and Walter Wolston entered into peace. He immediately came right out for God.

Recognizing that a promise is a debt, and that every Christian should honorably pay his debts, he immediately wrote to the conductor of the Glee Band, informing him that since leaving home he had been converted, that the Lord had put a new song into his mouth, and although he was willing to fulfill his legitimate engagements, he could only now sing of the Saviour who had done so much for him. Needless to say he was relieved of his obligation.

He dearly loved the gospel, and it mattered not what subject he discoursed upon to Christians, he never finished without preaching God's salvation.

In 1864, under the distinct impression that the Lord called him to work in Scotland, even with the offer of considerable advancement, he left London and came to Edinburgh where, after training for the medical profession, he was appointed House Surgeon to the Old Infirmary. Later he established himself as a physician in the Scottish capital, where by his skill he acquired a large practice. In Dr. Wolston were combined personality, ability, and grace, so that he was universally acknowledged to be a skillful and kindly Christian doctor. He always found time in the midst of his busy practice to tell out the old, old story, and he used to rent halls and theatres for this purpose; few business men in Scotland were privileged to preach the gospel to so many and for so long a period. He had a wonderful influence over young men, and frequently lectured to students in Edinburgh on spiritual subjects.

He was the editor of the magazine entitled *God's Glad Tidings*, afterwards altered to *The Gospel Messenger*, for forty-five years, and many clearly written gospel booklets have come from his pen. He also produced a number of volumes on spiritual subjects, which have been helpful to many. Among them are: "Simon Peter: His Life and Letters;" "Young Men of Scripture," "Another Comforter," "Night Scenes of Scripture," "Behold the Bridegroom," "Forty Days of Scripture," "Seekers for Light," and "The Church." So that by means of the printed page Dr. Wolston has been, through the grace of God, a means of blessing to thousands of both saints and sinners.

He gave up his medical practice in 1909, and thereupon fulfilled a long-standing wish to visit Australia and New Zealand. He afterwards paid two visits to Norway. During the second visit to Norway, in February 1915, he was stricken with paralysis, and was brought home to Weston-su-per-Mare, where he lay helpless for two years. During all this period of physical helplessness he was happy in the Saviour's love, and never was he heard to murmur or complain. A few weeks before the end he had another seizure, which rendered him unconscious to everything of earth, but it was quite evident to his devoted wife he was in constant and uninterrupted communion with the Lord he had loved so long and served so faithfully. On March 11th, 1917, at the age of seventy-six, this devoted worker passed into the presence of the King.—J.G.

James Wright
1826-1905

JAMES WRIGHT

JAMES WRIGHT was born in Bristol in the year 1826. His parents were God-fearing members of the Society of Friends, who brought their children up in "the nurture and admonition of the Lord." The children being "Friends" by birth, regularly attended the Meeting-house, and early in life had instilled into them those principles of integrity which characterize that body.

At the age of fourteen the Spirit of the Lord wrought in his heart and showed him that, although born a "Friend," he was a sinner by nature and practice, and needed to be "born again." He yielded, and became "a new creature in Christ Jesus." The new life soon showed itself in love for the Word of God. He confessed to the writer that the very long pauses in the meetings of "Friends" were turned to account by reading chapter after chapter in his New Testament.

The Lord further opened his eyes to the truth of believers' baptism, and also that it is the privilege and duty of all true believers to remember the Lord's death in His own appointed way by the "breaking of bread." He manifested that obedience to the teaching of God's Word which was ever afterwards a marked feature in His Christian character. He severed his connection with the Society of Friends, and was baptized in Tottenham. In 1840 he returned to Bristol and joined the church at Bethesda, in which, at that time, Messrs. Muller and Craik were the leading brethren.

On leaving school he went into business. In 1851 he married Miss Ann Willington Hitchins. In 1856 business again took him to London, and he lived in Hackney for several years.

Mr. Wright's earliest form of Christian work was Sunday school teaching. His success in this work was such that in 1856, when he was thirty years old, he became superintendent of the Sunday school at Paragon Road, Hackney.

In 1859 Mr. Muller, who had known him from boyhood, wrote asking if he would become one of his helpers in the work at Ashley Down.

He accepted the invitation, joined Mr. Muller, and remained in the work until his death—a period of nearly forty-five years. During the eleven years from 1859 to 1870 he was, to use Mr. Muller's words, "one of the most valuable helpers in the work." After he had been there one year it was impressed upon Mr. Muller's mind that this was the one whom the Lord was preparing to become his successor. For ten years he and Mr. Muller brought the matter before the Lord, and both of them became, to use Muller's own words, "more and more assured that in Mr. Wright God had given to us what we desired."

In February 1870, Mr. Muller, shortly after the death of his first wife, opened his mind to Mr. Wright, telling him that he considered it to be the will of God that he should, at that time, become his successor. Mr. Muller wrote: "His great humility, however, found a number of reasons why he considered himself unfit for it, none of which I could allow to stand in the way as a hindrance, as I knew him so well with regard to his fitness. A second difficulty was that his excellent Christian wife considered that he would be greatly burdened by accepting my proposal. After some weeks, however, she yielded her objections if he saw it to be the will of God. Mr. Wright then, after long hesitation, came to the conclusion that it would not be his duty any longer to refuse." Very shortly after this Mr. Wright's wife died; thus within a few months both Mr. Muller and Mr. Wright sustained a similar bereavement.

In August 1871, Mr. Muller wrote: "Today Mr. Wright asked for the hand of my beloved daughter. This request was as unlooked for on my part as anything could have been while at the same time I knew no one to whom I could so willingly entrust my choicest earthly treasure. My beloved daughter had the greatest conflict in her mind for about two weeks before she accepted this offer, her only and great difficulty being because of having to leave me." Mr. Muller told her it would be a joy to him to see her married to such a man, so she accepted the offer, and they were married three months later. In May 1872, Mr. Wright became associated with Mr. Muller as director.

Between the years 1875 and 1892, during which Mr. Muller went on preaching tours all over the world, Mr. Wright was left in sole charge of the work at Ashley Down for many months together.

In 1890 Mrs. Wright fell asleep after a short illness. Their eighteen years of married life Mr. Wright described as a time of "unbroken felicity." Being an intensely affectionate man, he felt her removal keenly; yet he bowed to and worshipped, with childlike submission, the God who in wisdom had taken his loved one from him.

From the autumn of that year he lived with his nieces, the Misses Withy. On March 6th, 1898, the sudden home-call of Mr. Muller left him in the position of sole director. After he had published his first report, Dr. Pierson wrote of him: "He shows himself God's chosen successor in the work evidently like-minded with the departed director." After some weeks of waiting on God, Mr. Wright asked G. Frederick Bergin, whom he had known intimately for twenty-five years, to become associate director. He consented, and for seven years they had intense mutual joy in working together.

Mr. Wright was a man of no ordinary graces and gifts, all of which were willingly laid at the Master's feet. His beautiful face and radiant smile showed, better than any words possibly could, that peace and joy ruled in his heart. His dignified yet gracious demeanor at once won the respect of all. Of his faith and love his works bear witness, but it may be added that his humility was equally apparent to an observing mind.

As a teacher, he was widely known and deeply appreciated; his good memory, originality, versatility, wonderful command of language, and profound knowledge of Scripture impressed and riveted his hearers. Many sinners have been wooed to Christ by his loving appeals, and thousands of Christians have had their faith strengthened, and their love for the Lord and His Word greatly deepened by listening to his helpful exposition of the truth.

He was very fond of music, having a beautiful bass voice, and for many years he led the singing in Bethesda. It was a great pleasure to him to join with others round a piano or organ, and sing hymn after hymn from the Bristol Tune Book.

Mr. Wright continued in full vigor of body and mind until the beginning of 1905, when he was laid aside with a carbuncle, which led after a time to blood poisoning. The illness lasted a month and was accompanied by much suffering, which was borne with patience and beautiful submission to the will of God. Just before the end came, Mr. Bergin said to him, "Nearing home, beloved brother!" to which he seemed to assent by a grip of his hand. Shortly after that, at four o'clock on Sunday afternoon, January 29th, 1905, he quietly fell asleep at the advanced age of seventy-eight.—W.M.B.

WILLIAM YAPP

1800(?)-1874

BROUGHT TO THE LORD in his youth William Yapp immediately yielded his body a living sacrifice to God, and the sacrifice once laid on the altar seems never to have been withdrawn. To the church of God his whole life proclaimed him "your servant for Jesus' sake."

Mr. Yapp loved the people of God because they were precious to Him, and he cared not how he toiled, or journeyed, or suffered if he could but cheer a child of God, or help him to follow the Lord more fully. Of him it may be said, perhaps more than of any other whom it has been our privilege to know, that his love never failed. His heart might break, but his love never gave in, even though he had often to say with Paul, "the more abundantly I love you, the less I be loved," and with Paul he could add, "But be it so." By him all saints were recognized as having a claim on him; the sorrowing and the erring drew out his sympathy and his help, and many a bereaved heart has been made to sing for joy. Nor were the children forgotten; they had a large share of his tender love and care, and a sight of Mr. Yapp's kindly face coming along the road would cause their eyes to sparkle and their feet to go faster till they met him, and they went on their way with lighter hearts for his cheery word and loving smile, still fragrant a memory after over a quarter of a century!

It was not alone his ministry, varied and precious as it was, that drew hearts everywhere to him, and caused them to look beyond the servant to the Master; it was "the love of God...shed abroad" by word and deed that drew and held fellow-saints in a manner those who did not personally know him can have little conception of. "Gaius, mine host" and "the well-beloved Gaius" were names he was often called by; and no one better deserved the title of honor, for his heart and home were ever open to receive, and to seek to lead on in the truth of God, any of His children.

For many years in Hereford, and subsequently in London and

Leominster, Mr. Yapp took a large share in gospel work. Well-sustained gospel testimony was carried on in the villages around, extending to neighboring towns; Worcester, Malvern, Ross, Ledbury, Leominster, and Ludlow were reached from Hereford by horses and traps. At one time Mr. Yapp kept five horses in his own stables for this purpose. Regular meetings were begun in a large room at the back of Mr. Yapp's house. Breaking of bread was instituted every Lord's day morning, and the room becoming too small was enlarged to seat three to four hundred persons. Brethren and sisters sold their silver-plate and superfluous furniture to defray cost. It was Acts 2:44-47 on a smaller scale.

Many of the believers connected with this movement, in which Mr. Yapp had a prominent share, had been connected with the Church of England, some of them being professional men of high standing in Hereford, many first class tradesmen, and a number of others. Gifts which their church position had hitherto repressed were now exercised, and they became evangelists, pastors, teachers, etc. Grace, love, and power prevailed; God was glorified in them, and many from the world were thoroughly converted. In those days the house and its furniture, dress and its fashions, amusements, occupations, business, and customs, all were tested by the Word of God. Among these men of God it was said that "Mr. William Yapp was head and shoulders above every one else in his love and self-sacrifice, ever willing to give up time, comfort, and purse for the welfare and spiritual good of others." He married the sister of Mrs. Maclean, long of Bath.

Lest it may be thought that Mr. Yapp was rich (through his generous distribution to saints and large hospitality), it may be well to state that he began life as a chemist's assistant without a penny, but by his cordial geniality, faithfulness, and intrinsic worth he made his way and was offered three partnerships, accepting the one with his employer—and he soon made it the best business in the county. He continued in business till health failed, always conducting it on godly principles, putting the Lord first in everything. Thus he was prospered in every transaction he put his hand to, and was a prince among his brethren.

In 1853 Mr. Yapp removed from Hereford to London where for ten years he faithfully served his heavenly Lord and Master. He commenced publishing in Baker Street, and issued many pamphlets and books, being afterwards joined by James E. Hawkins, the firm being Yapp & Hawkins. The Bibles with flap edges were suggested by Mr. Yapp, and for long were named in trade lists as "Yapp" Bibles. The Welbeck Street meeting owed much to his ministry of love during these years. One whose hair has grown white with age remarked lately that he "would never forget his first meeting with dear Mr. Yapp". When leaving his home in Scotland with a letter of commendation to the Welbeck Street meeting, he was on the first Lord's day introduced to Mr. Yapp, who promptly said in his own genial way, "You will dine with me to-day." After the meeting he introduced him to Lord Congleton, who also said, "You will dine with me to-day, brother T." Such hospitality was new to this young brother, who thought he had come among strangers, and the genuine brotherly love manifested to him quite overcame him, leaving an impression that forty years has not effaced.

Failing health compelled Mr. Yapp to leave London in 1863, and he returned to end his days on earth in Leominster where his school days and early youth had been spent. His genial character drew other able brethren to the town, among them Dr. Maclean and Colonel Colbeck, the result being increased fellowship, full attendances at meetings, and a large Sunday school, with conversions. The first Sunday Mr. Yapp said, "This room is too small," and within a week arrangements were made to take the large room in Waterloo House. One of the last acts of this noble-hearted brother was to rent and furnish the other parts of Waterloo House, Leominster, for the purpose of accommodating brethren whom he hoped to assemble together in the Lord's name for mutual prayer, counsel, and conference on matters concerning the welfare of the church of God. The four who signed the first circular of invitation to these conferences were W. Yapp, W. Lincoln, H. Groves, and Dr. J. L Maclean. Mr. Yapp had the joy of seeing four conferences held in the Waterloo that year (1874), and many, at the time of writing, still remember some of those first ministering brethren. Three of the chief were Messrs. Henry Groves, Henry Dyer, and Henry Heath.

Mr. Yapp edited *The Golden Lamp* for five years till his home-call on November 28th, 1874. When conscious that he was about to depart he cried out, "Loose me and let me go, Lord Jesus! Take me to Thyself, Lord Jesus!" So ended a noble, consecrated, and devoted life, having one purpose, and that CHRIST.—M.M.D.